全国商务英语本科专业规划教材

国际商法

International Business Law

■ 主　编　陈建平　邹日强

■ 副主编　王鉴棋　高现伟　李　静　党磊磊
张利敏　赵　丽　许志珊　孟献策
黄晓翔　宋　强　钱家骏

■ 策　划　汤定军

苏州大学出版社

图书在版编目(CIP)数据

国际商法/陈建平,邹日强主编. —苏州:苏州大学出版社,2012.1
全国商务英语本科专业规划教材
ISBN 978-7-81137-963-1

Ⅰ.①国… Ⅱ.①陈…②邹… Ⅲ.①国际商法—高等学校—教材 Ⅳ.①D996.1

中国版本图书馆 CIP 数据核字(2012)第 008138 号

用书单位或个人如需本书的课件等资料,请致电 0512-65222096 或发 e-mail 给汤定军先生(tangdingjun@suda.edu.cn),我们将为您提供热忱的服务。

书　　名:国际商法
International Business Law

作　　者:陈建平　邹日强　主编
责任编辑:汤定军
策划编辑:汤定军
封面设计:刘　俊

出版发行:苏州大学出版社(Soochow University Press)
社　　址:苏州市十梓街 1 号　**邮编**:215006
印　　刷:丹阳市兴华印刷厂
网　　址:www.sudapress.com
E-mail　:tangdingjun@suda.edu.cn
邮购热线:0512-67480030
销售热线:0512-65225020

开　　本:787 mm×960 mm　1/16　**印张**:20.25　**字数**:400 千
版　　次:2012 年 1 月第 1 版
印　　次:2012 年 1 月第 1 次印刷
书　　号:ISBN 978-7-81137-963-1
定　　价:48.00 元

前言

商务英语教学在我国已有近50年的历史。20世纪五六十年代初期由于国家外贸人才稀缺，商务英语首先是针对外贸业务人员的语言培训而发展起来的。自20世纪80年代改革开放以来，商务英语教学取得了快速发展，并由最初的一两门课程发展至现在相对独立的专业教学体系。目前我国有近700所院校开设商务英语类课程或专业方向。2007年，经教育部批准，对外经济贸易大学率先设立商务英语本科专业；2008年，上海对外贸易学院和广东外语外贸大学也经教育部批准设立了该专业。至2010年，国内已有15所高校获批开设了商务英语本科专业。

商务英语快速发展的同时，编写特色鲜明且具有较强科学性、先进性和适用性的商务英语本科专业教材已是当务之急。我们认为，商务英语专业主要培养英语语言与国际商务密切结合的应用型、复合型人才，其知识结构体系应包括英语专业知识、英语专业技能、商务专业知识、商务专业技能、人文素养及跨文化交际能力等几个部分。其中，商务专业知识主要包括国际贸易、国际投资、国际金融、国际营销、商务法律、商务管理等方面的专业知识。在充分调研国内商务英语教材编写和使用现状的基础上，结合在商务英语领域多年的教学和实践经历，本教材编写组以《国际商法》双语教材为试点，期望编写和出版一套适合商务英语本科教学的高质量的系列教材。

《国际商法》教材旨在使读者在英语语境中较为系统地学习国际商务法律知识，熟悉和掌握英文商务法律术语、基本概念及基础理论，在此基础上深刻领会法律英语在语义、语用、语篇等方面的特殊性及其变化规律，提高专业英语技能。本书分9个部分，共23个单元，重点介绍国际货物买卖法、合同法、商事组织法、代理法、产品责任法、国际投资法、知识产权法、国际商务中的争端解决等内容。

本书在编写上具有以下特点：

1. 在结构编排上，呈现立体式趋势。各个章节首先明确了重要概念和学习目标，课后配有参考文献、阅读书目、课文注释、问题讨论、案例分析等栏目，便于教师有效地组织课堂教学及学生自主学习。

2. 在内容体系上，注重国际商务法律与我国商务法律、专业知识与英语知识的有机统一，使学生能在专业英语语境中较为系统地学习国际和国内商务法律知识，强化专业英语技能。

3. 课文注释注重背景知识和专业术语介绍。各个单元较为详细地介绍了相关专业背景知识，并对专有名称、专业词汇等进行中文翻译和解释，以帮助学生更好地理解课文内容，拓展知识面。

邹日强副研究员编写了本书的第9、14、15、16、18、19、20、21章。本书的多数章节已作为内部教材在编者学校中使用三年，效果较好。

本书主要用作高等院校商务英语本科专业国际商法和法律英语教材，也可作为英语专业、法律专业及经济、管理类专业的国际商法双语、法律英语教材或教学参考用书，此外，还可作涉外经济部门的法律英语和国际商法的培训教材或自学参考书。

本书配有教学课件，如有需要请与我们联系(chenjianping@ nbu. edu. cn, tangdingjun@ suda. edu. cn)。

在编写、出版过程中，苏州大学出版社汤定军先生给予了大力支持和帮助，在此谨表衷心的谢意。

由于编者水平有限，书中错误或不当之处在所难免，敬请学界同仁及读者批评指正。

编　者

2011年9月

Contents

Chapter 1

Introduction to International Business Law

Key Concepts

International law	private international law	public international law
conflicts of law	international business law	international economic law
common law	civil law adversarial procedure	inquisitorial procedure

Learning Objectives

1. Understand the relevant concepts of internal law and international business law.
2. Understand the differences between international business law and international economic law.
3. Understand the sources of international business law.
4. Be familiar with the differences between civil law system and common law system.

International Law

The body of legal rules and norms that regulates activities carried on beyond the legal boundaries of a single state. In particular, it regulates three international relationships: (1) those between states and states, (2) those between states and persons, and (3) those between persons and persons.

International law falls into public international law[1] and private international law[2]. Public international law deals primarily with the rights and duties of the states and intergovernmental organizations as between themselves, while private international law deals primarily with the rights and duties of individuals and nongovernmental organizations in their international affairs.

Public international law should not be confused with "private international law", which is concerned with the resolution of conflict of laws. In its most general sense, international law "consists of rules and principles of general application dealing with the conduct of states and of intergovernmental organizations and with their relations inter se, as well as with some of their relations with persons, whether natural or juridical".

Conflict of laws (or private international law) is a set of procedural rules which determine which legal system, and the law of which jurisdiction, applies to a given dispute. The rules typically apply when a legal dispute has a "foreign" element such as a contract agreed by parties located in different countries, although the "foreign" element also exists in multi-jurisdictional countries such as the United Kingdom and the United States.

The term "conflict of laws" itself originates from situations where the ultimate outcome of a legal dispute depended upon which law applied, and the common law courts manner of resolving the conflict between those laws. In civil law lawyers and legal scholars refer to conflict of laws as private international law. Private international law has no real connection with public international law, and is instead a feature of municipal law which varies from country to country.

The three branches of conflict of laws are:

- Jurisdiction—whether the forum court has the power to resolve the dispute at hand;
- Choice of law—the law which is being applied to resolve the dispute;
- Foreign judgments—the ability to recognize and enforce a judgment from an external forum within the jurisdiction of the adjudicating forum.

Comity is the practice, or courtesy, between states of treating each other with goodwill and civility.

The subject matter of international law has changed dramatically in recent years. Traditionally, this area of law dealt only with conduct between states and was called public international law.

International Business Law

International business law refers to the body of rules and norms regulating international business transactions and the relationships between business organizations across national boundaries. It focuses on the business activities conducted between individuals and enterprises from different countries. By contrast, international economic law[3] is thought to be in the scope of public international law, it deals primarily with the rights and duties of states and intergovernmental organizations in their international business (economic) affairs, and does not regulate the international business relationship between individuals and business entities. Nevertheless, in a broad sense, international economic law encompasses both the conduct of sovereign states in international economic relations, and the conduct of private parties involved in cross-border economic and business transactions as well.

Lex Mercatoria[4]

Lex mercatoria refers to that part of international commercial law which is unwritten, including customary commercial law, customary rules of evidence and procedure, and general principles of commercial law. Lex mercatoria is the Latin expression for a body of trading principles used by merchants throughout Europe in the medieval period. Meaning literally "merchant law", it evolved as a system of custom and best practice, which was enforced through a system of merchant courts along the main trade routes. It functioned as the international law of commerce. It emphasised contractual freedom, alienability of property, while shunning legal technicalities and deciding cases *ex aequo et bono*.

A distinct feature was the reliance by merchants on a legal system developed and administered by them. States or local authorities seldom interfered, and surrendered some of the control over trade within their territory to the merchants. In return, trade flourished under the lex mercatoria (or business law), increasing tax revenues.

The lex mercatoria was originally a body of rules and principles laid down by merchants themselves to regulate their dealings. It consisted of usages and customs common to merchants and traders in Europe, with slightly local differences. It originated from the problem that civil law was not responsive enough to the growing demands of commerce: there was a need for quick and effective jurisdiction, administered by specialized courts. The guiding spirit of the merchant law was that it ought to evolve from commercial practice, respond to the needs of the merchants, and be comprehensible and acceptable to the merchants who submitted to it. International commercial law today owes some of its fundamental principles to the lex mercatoria as it was developed in the medieval ages. This includes choice of arbitration institutions, procedures, applicable law and arbitrators, and the goal to reflect customs, usage and good practice among the parties.

Sources of International Business Law

(1) International business conventions and treaties[5] (establishing rules expressly recognized by contesting states); treaties are legally binding agreements between two or more states; conventions are legally binding agreements between states sponsored by international organizations, such as the United Nations.

(2) International business customs[6] (as evidence of a general practice accepted as law): A custom is a long established tradition or usage that becomes customary law if its consistently and regularly observed, and recognized by those observing it as a practice that they must obligatorily follow. For instance, UCP, INCOTERMS which are made out by the International Chamber of Commerce shall be important international trade customs.

(3) International business cases.

(4) Business laws of nations.

Main Contents of International Business Law

International business law may involve international trade law, contract law, agency law, product liability law, corporate law, partnership law, international investment law, intellectual property law, etc.

Two Major Legal Systems

Civil Law[7]

The civil law system is the oldest and most influential of the legal families. It is derived from Roman and Germanic practice. As distinguished from public law, the body of the law deals with rights of private citizens. It is also called Romano-Germanic Family or Continental System. The French Civil Code of 1804 and the German Civil Code of 1896 are now regarded as the very basis of the modern civil law.

Civil law is a legal system inspired by Roman law[8], the primary feature of which is that laws are written into a collection, codified, and not (as in common law) interpreted by judges.

Conceptually, it is the group of legal ideas and systems ultimately derived from the *Code of Justinian*[9], but heavily overlaid by Germanic, ecclesiastical, feudal, and local practices, as well as doctrinal strains such as natural law[10], codification, and legislative positivism.

Materially, civil law proceeds from abstractions, formulates general principles, and distinguishes substantive rules from procedural rules. It holds legislation as the primary source of law, and the court system is usually inquisitorial, unbound by precedent, and composed of specially trained judicial officers with a limited authority to interpret law. Juries separate from the judges are not used, although in some cases, volunteer lay judges participate along with legally trained career judges.

The principle of civil law is to provide all citizens with an accessible and written collection of the laws which apply to them and which judges must follow. It is the most widespread type of legal system in the world, applied in various forms in approximately 150 countries and oldest surviving legal system in the world. Colonial expansion spread the civil law system and European civil law has been adopted in much of Latin America as well as in parts of Asia and Africa.

The civil law system takes as its major inspiration Roman law, and in particular the Corpus Juris Civilis of Emperor Justinian, and subsequent expounding and developments in medieval roman law. Roman law was received differently in different countries. In some it went into force wholesale by legislative act, i. e., it became positive law, whereas in others it was diffused into society by increasingly influential legal experts and scholars.

Roman law was in place in the Byzantine Empire until its final fall in the 15th century. However, subject as it was to multiple incursions and occupations in the latter Middle Ages, its laws became widely available in Western Europe. It was first received into the Holy Roman Empire partly because it was considered imperial law, and it spread in Europe mainly because its students were the only trained lawyers. It became the basis of Scots law, though partly rivaled by feudal common law. In England, it was taught academically at Oxford and Cambridge, but underlay only probate and matrimonial law, inherited by canon law when secularized, and maritime law, adapted from the law merchant through the Bordeaux trade.

Consequently, neither of the two waves of Romanism completely dominated in Europe. Roman law was a secondary source that was applied only when local customs and laws were found lacking on a certain subject. However, after a time, even local law came to be interpreted and evaluated primarily on the basis of Roman law (it being a common European legal tradition of sorts), thereby in turn influencing the main source of law. Eventually, the works of Civilian glossators and commentators led to the development of a common body of law and writing about law, a common legal language, and a common method of teaching and scholarship, all termed *jus commune*, or law common to Europe, which consolidated canon law and Roman law, and to some extent, feudal law.

An important characteristic, beyond Roman law foundations, is the extended codification of the adopted Roman law, i. e., its inclusion into civil codes. The system of codification has its origins in the Code of Hammurabi, written in ancient Babylon during the 18th century BC.

The concept of codification was further developed during the 17th and 18th centuries AD, as an expression of both Natural Law and the ideas of the Enlightenment. The political ideal of that era was expressed by the concepts of democracy, protection of property and the rule of law. That ideal required the creation of certainty of law, through the recording of law and through its uniformity. So, the aforementioned mix of Roman law and customary and local law ceased to exist, and the road opened for law codification, which could contribute to the aims of the above mentioned political ideal.

Another reason that contributed to codification was that the notion of the nation state required the recording of the law that would be applicable to that state.

Certainly, there was also reaction to the aim of law codification. The proponents of codification regarded it as conducive to certainty, unity and systematic recording of the law; whereas its opponents claimed that codification would result in the ossification of the law.

In the end, despite whatever resistance to codification, the codification of European private laws moved forward. Codifications were completed by Denmark (1687), Sweden (1734), Prussia (1794), France (1804), and Austria (1811). The French codes were imported into areas conquered by Emperor Napoleon and later adopted with modifications in the Netherlands (1838), Italy and Romania (1865), Portugal (1867), Spain (1888), Germany (1900), and Switzerland (1912). These codifications were in turn imported into colonies at one time or another by most of these countries. The Swiss version was adopted in Brazil (1916) and Turkey (1926).

Because Germany was a rising power in the late 19th century and its legal system was well organized, when many Asian nations were developing, the German Civil Code became the basis for the legal systems of Japan and South Korea. In China, the German Civil Code was introduced in the later years of the Qing Dynasty and formed the basis of the law of the Republic of China.

Several legal institutions in civil law are similar to institutions in Islamic law and jurisprudence during the Middle Ages, and some have suggested a borrowing. For example, the Islamic *Hawala* institution is the basis of the *Avallo* in Italian civil law and the *Aval* in French civil law.

Common Law[11]

Common law system is also called Anglo-American law system (British-American law system). It is the legal system of England and countries that were once English colonies. It is based on court-made rules and precedents. An import aspect of the common law is its basis in the customary practice of the courts, and the term itself is often used to describe that part of English law that is not based on statutory law or legislation.

Common law (also known as case law or precedent) is law developed by judges through decisions of courts and similar tribunals rather than through legislative statutes or executive branch action. A "common law system" is a legal system that gives great precedential weight to common law, on the principle that it is unfair to treat similar facts differently on different occasions. The body of precedent is called "common law" and it binds future decisions. In cases where the parties disagree on what the law is, an idealized common law court looks to past precedential decisions of relevant courts. If a similar dispute has been resolved in the past, the court is bound to follow the reasoning used in the prior decision (this principle is known as *stare decisis*). If, however, the court finds that the current dispute is fundamentally distinct from all previous cases (called a "matter of first impression"), judges have the authority and duty to make law by creating precedent. Thereafter, the new decision becomes precedent, and will bind future courts.

In practice, common law systems are considerably more complicated than the idealized system described above. The decisions of a court are binding only in a particular jurisdiction, and even within a given jurisdiction, some courts have more power than others. For example, in most jurisdictions, decisions by appellate courts are binding on lower courts in the same jurisdiction and on future decisions of the same appellate court, but decisions of lower courts are only non-binding persuasive authority. Interactions between common law, constitutional law, statutory law and regulatory law also give rise to considerable complexity. However *stare decisis*, the principle that similar cases should be decided according to consistent principled rules so that they will reach similar results, lies at the heart of all common law systems.

Common law legal systems are in widespread use, particularly in England where it originated in the Middle Ages, and in nations or regions that trace their legal heritage to England as former colonies of the British Empire, including the United States, Malaysia, Singapore, Bangladesh, Pakistan, Sri Lanka, India, Ghana, Cameroon, Canada, Ireland, New Zealand, South Africa, Zimbabwe, Hong Kong, and Australia.

Main Differences between the Two Legal Systems

The common law is based on court decision or precedents whereas the civil law's grounds for deciding cases are found in codes, statues, and prescribed texts. The way in which the common law spread around the world is different from how the civil law was distributed. Those nation in which the common law developed are Australia, Canada, India, Ireland, New Zealand, and the United States. Most European continental nations and Latin American nations are civil law nations.

Common law is a matrix of case law and statutes; it uses the jury system and the doctrine of supremacy to limit the actions of the government. The common law adopts adversarial procedure[12] while the civil law uses inquisitorial procedure[13]. The adversarial system (or adversary system) of law is the system of law that relies on the contest between each advocate representing his or her party's positions and involves an impartial person or group of people, usually a jury or judge, trying to determine the truth of the case. As opposed to that, the inquisitorial system has a judge (or a group of judges who work together) whose task is to investigate the case. The adversary procedure requires the opposing sides to bring out pertinent information and to present and cross-examine witnesses. This procedure is observed primarily in countries in which the Anglo-American legal system of common law predominates.

Under the adversary system, each side is responsible for conducting its own investigation. In criminal proceedings, the prosecution represents the people at large and has at its disposal the police department with its investigators and laboratories, while the defense must find its own investigative resources and finances. Both sides may command the attendance of witnesses by subpoena. If the defendant is indigent, his attorney's opportunities for a broader investigation are limited by the provisions of the jurisdiction in which the trial is conducted. In criminal law under the adversary system, the accused need not be present in grand jury indictment proceedings (no longer conducted in Great Britain and recommended by some authorities for eventual abolition in the United States). If an indictment is handed down by the grand jury, its proceedings are available to the defendant. Under civil law the adversary system works similarly, except that both plaintiff and respondent must prepare their own cases, usually through privately engaged attorneys.

In any adversary trial, the opposing sides present evidence, examine witnesses, and conduct cross-examinations[14], each in an effort to produce information beneficial to its side of the case. Skillful questioning can often produce testimony that can be made to take on various meanings. What seemed absolute in direct testimony can raise doubts under cross-examination. The skills of the attorneys are also displayed at the time of summation, especially in a jury trial, when their versions of what the jury has heard may persuade the jury to interpret the facts to the benefit of the side that is most persuasive.

In adversary proceedings before juries the judge functions as moderator and referee on points of law, rarely taking part in the questioning unless he or she feels that important points of law or fact must be made clearer. In a bench trial (without a jury) the judge makes findings of fact as well as of law. Since a witness called by the opposing party is presumed to be hostile, cross-examination does permit leading questions. A witness called by the direct examiner, on the other hand, may only be treated as hostile by that examiner after being permitted to do so by the judge, at the request of that examiner and as a result of the witness being openly antagonistic and/or prejudiced against the opposing party.

The main purposes of cross-examination are to elicit favorable facts from the witness, or to impeach the credibility of the testifying witness to lessen the weight of unfavourable testimony. Cross-examination frequently produces critical evidence in trials, especially if a witness contradicts previous testimony. The advocate Edward Marshall-Hall built his career on cross-examination which often involved histrionic outbursts designed to sway jurors. Most experienced and skilled cross-examiners, however, refrain from caustic or abrasive cross-examination so as to avoid alienating jurors.

Cross-examination is, arguably, the main purpose of a trial. Though the closing argument is often considered the deciding moment of a trial, effective cross-examination wins trials.

An inquisitorial system is a legal system where the court or a part of the court is actively involved in investigating the facts of the case, as opposed to an adversarial system where the role of the court is primarily that of an impartial referee between the prosecution and the defense. Inquisitorial systems are used in some countries with civil legal systems as opposed to case law systems. Also countries using case law, including the United States, may use an inquisitorial system for summary hearings in the case of misdemeanors such as minor traffic violations. In fact, the distinction between an adversarial and inquisitorial system is theoretically unrelated to the distinction between a civil legal and case law system. Some legal scholars consider "inquisitorial" misleading, and prefer the word "nonadversarial".

The inquisitorial system applies to questions of criminal procedure as opposed to questions of substantive law; that is, it determines how criminal enquiries and trials are conducted, not the kind of crimes for which one can be prosecuted, nor the sentences that they carry. It is most readily used in some civil legal systems.

However, some jurists do not recognize this dichotomy and see procedure and substantive legal relationships as being interconnected and part of a theory of justice as applied differently in various legal cultures.

In some jurisdictions, the trial judge may participate in the fact-finding inquiry by questioning witnesses even in adversarial proceedings. The rules of admissibility of evidence may also allow the judge to act more like an inquisitor than an arbiter of justice.

Although international tribunals intended to try crimes against humanity, such as the Nuremberg Trials and the International Criminal Court, have generally used a version of the adversarial system, they have also incorporated some key features of the inquisitorial system, such as the use of professional career judges, and in the case of the International Criminal Court, the use of a pre-trial examining or investigative division.

Notes

1. public international law　国际公法

国际公法是国家之间的法律,具体来说就是指处理各个国家及政府组织之间各种关系的规则和各项基本原则的总和,但有时也包括代表一定国家意志的法人、自然人等特殊主体。

2. private international law　国际私法

调整涉外民商事法律关系的法律部门,在大陆法系中习惯称为“国际私法”,而英美普通法系则更多地称其为“冲突法”。国内立法是国际私法的主要渊源。

3. international economic law　国际经济法

国际经济法是调整国家之间、国际组织之间、国家与国际组织之间的相互经济关系的法律规范的总称。狭义的国际经济法是国际公法的一个特殊部门。

4. Lex Mercatoria　商人习惯法

从历史上看,它是中世纪时期逐渐形成的“商业惯例”,主要特点有:(1)它超越国界,普遍适用于各国商人;(2)它不是由专业法官来掌管,而是由商人自己选出的法官来掌管的;(3)它的程序比较简单,而且不拘泥于形式;(4)它强调按公平、合理的原则来处理案件。与中世纪的商人习惯法相比,“新的商人习惯法是由制法机构精心制定的,表现为国际公约、示范法、国际商会等组织公布的文件。”也就是说,现代商人习惯法是在各主权国家的同意或认可的基础上发展起来的,它与主权国家是协调一致的。正因为如此,人们又很难给它下一个准确的定义,一般只能把它界定为“从事国际商事交易的人们普遍遵守的原则和规则”。

5. conventions and treaties　公约和条约

国际公约是指国际间有关政治、经济、文化、技术等方面的多边条约。公约通常为开放性的,非缔约国可以在公约生效前或生效后的任何时候加入。国际条约是国际法主体之间以国际法为准则而为确立其相互权利和义务而缔结的书面协议。

6. international business customs　国际商务惯例

国际商务惯例是指在长期的国际商务实践中逐渐形成的、为大家所普遍接受和经常遵守的任意性行为规范。国际商务惯例是国际商法的重要的渊源。国际贸易中通行的主要惯例大都由国际商会制定,如《国际贸易术语解释通则》、《跟单信用证统一惯例》、《托收统一规则》等。

7. civil law　民法,民法法系

民法法系又称罗马法系、法典法系、大陆法系、罗马-日尔曼法系,是与英美普通法系并列的当今世界两大重要法系之一,覆盖了当今世界的广大区域,德国、法国、中国、日本等均为大陆民法法系地区。民法法系,是指以古罗马,特别是以19世纪初《法国民法典》和《德国民法典》为传统产生和发展起来的法律的总称。以古罗马法为发端,并以罗马法在中世纪意大利的复兴和神圣罗马帝国中的继承为源流,在近代法国民法和德国民法的基础之上发展形成。始终与罗马法有密切关系,以法典为主要渊源。由于该法系的影响范围主要是在欧洲大陆国家,特别是法国和德国,且主要法律的表现形式均为法典,所以又称为大陆法系、罗马-德意志法系、法典法系。属于这一法系的除了欧洲大陆国家外,还有曾是法国、德国、葡萄牙、荷兰等国殖民地的国家及因其他原因受其影响的国家。

8. Roman law　罗马法

罗马法一般泛指罗马奴隶制国家法律的总称,存在于罗马奴隶制国家的整个历史时期。它既包括自罗马国家产生至西罗马帝国灭亡时期的法律以及皇帝的命令、元老院的告示、成文法和一些习惯法,也包括公元7世纪中叶以前东罗马帝国的法律。

9. Code of Justinian　《查士丁尼法典》

《查士丁尼法典》是东罗马帝国皇帝查士丁尼一世下令编纂的一部汇编式法典,是罗马法的集大成者。法典内容为东罗马帝国时期的皇帝敕令以及权威的法学家对于法律的解释。《查士丁尼法典》颁布后,又陆续颁布了《查士丁尼法学总论》、《查士丁尼学说汇编》和《查士丁尼新律》3个部分,作为《查士丁尼法典》的续编,最后完成于公元530年左右。

10. natural law　自然法

在法学中,自然法的学说指在自然状态中固有的正义法则以及(或者)在解决冲突的自然过程中显现的规律(具体化为习惯法)。

11. common law　普通法,普通法系

普通法系又称英美法系,是指以英国普通法为基础发展起来的法律的总称。它首先产生于英国,后扩大到曾经是英国殖民地、附属国的许多国家和地区,包括美国、加拿大、印度、巴基斯坦、孟加拉、马来西亚、新加坡以及非洲的个别国家和地区。到18世纪至19世纪时,随着英国殖民地的扩张,英国法传入这些国家和地区,英美法系终于发展成为世界主要法系之一。英美法系的主要特点是以判例法为主要形式。

12. adversarial procedure　抗辩程序

英美法系的诉讼程序以原告、被告及其辩护人和代理人为重心,法官只是双方争论的

"仲裁人"而不能参与争论。与这种抗辩式程序同时存在的是陪审团制度,陪审团主要负责作出事实上的结论和法律上的基本结论(如有罪或无罪),法官负责作出法律上的具体结论,即判决。

13. inquisitorial procedure 讯问程序

大陆法系的诉讼程序以法官为重心,突出法官职能,具有讯问程序的特点,而且多由法官和陪审员共同组成法庭来审判案件。

14. cross-examinations 交叉询问

文叉询问是由一方当事人向另一方当事人所提供的证人提出的诘问,一般是在提供证人的一方首先向自己的证人提问后进行的。交叉询问是意图使证人改变、限定、修正或撤回提出的证据。在交叉询问中允许进行诱导性提问,询问证人的当事人通常比对方当事人有更大的自由。在任何情节上不对证人进行询问,一般就暗示接受证人对该情节的举证。一项证据已经或将要被给予的效力不同于证人所陈述的效力,那么在交叉询问中必须就此证据的效力同证人见面,以使他能够作出承认、否认或解释。英美法系关于证人质证几乎就是交叉询问的同义词。大部分证据,包括证人证言、被害人陈述、被告人供述、当事人陈述以及书证、物证,均可以交叉询问来进行质证。交叉询问被一些英美法学者视为专业性很强的法庭技术,要求律师有高明的技巧和丰富的经验。

Study Questions

1. What are international law, public international law, private international law, international business law and international economic law?
2. What are the sources of international business law?
3. What are the differences between two legal systems?
4. What are the main contents involved in international business law?

Sources of Information and Further Readings

1. http://en.wikipedia.org/wiki/International_law
2. http://en.wikipedia.org/wiki/Conflict_of_laws
3. http://en.wikipedia.org/wiki/International_commercial_law
4. http://en.wikipedia.org/wiki/Civil_law
5. http://en.wikipedia.org/wiki/Common_law

Chapter 2

INCOTERMS[1]

Key Concepts

FOB CFR CIF INCOTERMS symbolic delivery of the goods
physical delivery of the goods the charter party

Learning Objectives

1. Understand the essentials of 13 trade terms in Incoterms 2000.
2. Understand the differences between symbolic delivery of the goods and physical delivery of the goods.
3. Understand the differences between Incoterms 2000 and Incoterms 2010.
4. Be familiar with ICC.

Incoterms or International Commercial terms are a series of pre-defined commercial terms published by the International Chamber of Commerce (ICC) widely used in international commercial transactions. A series of three-letter trade terms related to common sales practices, Incoterms are intended primarily to clearly communicate the tasks, costs and risks associated with the transportation and delivery of goods. Incoterms are accepted by governments, legal authorities and practitioners worldwide for the interpretation of most commonly used terms in international trade.

They are intended to reduce or remove altogether uncertainties arising from different interpretation of such terms in different countries. In 1936, the first set of Incoterms was published. The first set remained in use for almost 20 years before the second publication in 1953. Additional amendments and expansions followed in 1967, 1976, 1980, 1990 and 2000. The eighth and current version of Incoterms—Incoterms 2010—was published on January 1, 2011.

Incoterms 2000

E Term

E Term has only one term—EXW. EXW means that the seller fulfills his obligations to deliver when he has made the goods available at his premises (i. e., works, factory, warehouse, etc) to the buyer. Under this term, unless the contract stipulates otherwise, the seller is not bound to load the goods on board the vehicle provided by the buyer, or to clear the goods for export. The buyer bears all costs and risks involved in taking the goods from the seller's premises to the desired destination. Hence, this term represents the minimum obligation for the seller.

F Terms

F Terms involves three terms—FAS, FOB and FCA.

FAS (Free Alongside Ship) means that the seller fulfills his obligation to deliver when the goods have been placed alongside the vessel on the quay or in the lighters at the name port of shipment. From that moment the buyer has to bear all costs and risks of the loss or damage to the goods. Under this term, the seller is bound to clear the goods for export.

FOB (Free on Board) means that the seller fulfills his obligations to deliver when the goods, cleared for export, have passed over the rail of the vessel at the named port of shipment. This means that the buyer shall, from that point, be responsible for all costs and risks of the loss or damage to the goods. Under this term, it is the buyer who arranges the ship for the shipment of the goods. So, the parties must try to ensure that the goods and the ship arrive at the same loading port concurrently. The loss caused by the untimely arrival or delay of the ship shall be compensated by the buyer while the loss arising from the untimely arrival or delay of the goods will be covered by the seller. At the request of the buyer, the seller may make the charter party[2] or book shipping space on behalf of the buyer, but the cost as well as the risk shall be covered by the buyer.

FCA (Free from Carrier) means that the seller fulfills his obligations to deliver when he has handed over the goods, cleared for export, into the charge of the carrier named by the buyer at the appointed place or point. If the seller hands over the goods to the carrier at his own premises, the seller is bound to load the goods on board the vehicle, while the seller is not bound to unload the goods from the vehicle if the goods are handed over to the carrier at the place appointed by the buyer. This term may be used for any mode of transport, including the carriages by air, road, rail, sea, inland waterway, or by a combination of such modes.

C Terms

C Terms includes CFR, CIF, CPT, CIP.

CFR (Cost and Freight) means that the seller covers the cost of carriage but does not bear the risk arising from the carriage of the goods. That is to say, the seller must pay the cost and freight necessary to bring the goods to the named port of destination but the risk of the loss or damage to the goods, as well as any additional cost due to the events occurring after the goods have been delivered on board the vessel, is transferred from the seller to the buyer when the goods pass over the rail of the vessel in the port of shipment. This term is only used for sea and inland waterway transport. Under this term, the buyer shall effect the insurance.

CIF (Cost, Insurance and Freight) means that the seller shall not only have the same obligations as under CFR, but also procure marine insurance against the buyer's risk of loss of or damage to the goods during the carriage.

CPT (Carriage Paid To) means that the seller pays the freight for the carriage of the goods to the named destination. The risk of the loss of or damage to the goods, as well as any additional costs due to the event occurring after the time the goods have been delivered to the carrier, shall be transferred from the seller to the buyer when the goods have been handed over into the custody of the carrier. This term may be used for any mode of transport.

CIP (Carriage Insurance Paid To) means that the seller shall have the same obligations as under CPT, in addition, the seller shall procure the insurance against the buyer's risk of loss of or damages to the goods during the carriage.

Under C and F terms, the symbolic delivery of the goods[3] is applied, that is, once the seller has delivered the goods and acquired the necessary documents, he is entitled to the payments of the goods even if the carriages are lost during the transit. If the goods are lost during the transit, the buyer, instead of the seller, is to ask the insurance company to cover the losses. So such delivery also means to transfer the necessary documents at the stipulated time.

D Terms

This group contains five terms: DAF, DES, DEQ, DDU and DDP.

DAF (Delivered at Frontier) means that the seller fulfills his obligation to deliver when the goods have been made available, cleared for export, at the named point or place at the frontier, but before the customs border of the adjoining country. This term is primarily intended to be used when the goods are to be carried by rail or road, but it may also be used for any other mode of transport.

DES (Delivered Ex Ship) means that the seller fulfills his obligation to deliver when the goods have been made available to the buyer on board the ship at the named port of destination. The seller has to bear all costs and risks involved in bring the goods to the named port of destination. The buyer shall clear the goods for import. This term can only be used for sea or inland waterway transport.

DEQ (Delivered Ex Quay) means that the seller fulfills his obligation to deliver when the goods have been made available to the buyer on the quay at the name port of destination. The seller shall bear all risks and costs of delivering the goods thereto. But the buyer shall clear the goods for import.

DDU (Delivered Duty Unpaid) means that the seller fulfills his obligation to deliver when the goods have been made available to the buyer at the named place in the country of importation. The seller shall bear the risks and costs involved in bring the goods thereto. The buyer shall clear the goods for import and pay customs duties.

DDP (Delivered Duty Paid) means that the seller fulfills his obligation to deliver when the goods have been made available at the named place in the country of importation. Under this term, the seller shall not only bear costs and risks involved in bringing the goods thereto, but also clear the goods for import and pay customs duties. This term represents maximum obligations for the seller.

E Terms and D Terms may be called physical delivery of the good[4], that is, the seller shall deliver the contracted goods at agreed time, place and in the agreed manners to the buyer. Before the goods have been made available for the buyer's disposal, the seller shall be responsible for all costs and risks.

Incoterms 2010[5]

The eighth published set of pre-defined terms, Incoterms 2010 defines 11 rules, reducing the 13 used in Incoterms 2000 by introducing two new rules ("Delivered at Terminal", DAT; "Delivered at Place", DAP) that replace four rules of the prior version ("Delivered at Frontier", DAF; "Delivered Ex Ship", DES; "Delivered Ex Quay", DEQ; "Delivered Duty Unpaid", DDU). In the prior version, the rules were divided into four categories, but the 11 pre-defined terms of Incoterms 2010 are subdivided into two categories based only on method of delivery. The larger group of seven rules applies regardless of the method of transport, with the smaller group of four being applicable only to sales that solely involve transportation over water.

General Mode of Transportation

The seven rules defined by Incoterms 2010 for general modes of transportation are:

EXW—Ex Works (named place)

The seller makes the goods available at his premises. The buyer is responsible for all charges. This trade term places the greatest responsibility on the buyer and minimum obligations on the seller. The Ex Works term is often used when making an initial quotation for the sale of goods without any costs included. EXW means that a seller has the goods ready for collection at his premises (works, factory, warehouse, plant) on the date agreed upon. The buyer pays all transportation costs and also bears the risks for bringing the goods to their final destination. The seller delivers the good at seller's premises or named place (works, factory and warehouse, etc), but not loaded on collecting vehicles and not cleared for export. The seller has no obligation to load the goods, even though in practice he may be in a better position to do so. If the seller does load the good, he does so at buyer's risk and cost. If parties wish seller to be responsible for the loading of the goods on departure and to bear the risk and all costs of such loading, this must be made clear by adding explicit wording to this effect in the Contract of sale.

FCA— Free Carrier (named places)

The seller hands over the goods, cleared for export, into the custody of the first carrier (named by the buyer) at the named place. This term is suitable for all modes of transport, including carriage by air, rail, road, and containerized/multimodal sea transport. This is the correct "freight collect" term to use for sea shipments in containers, whether LCL (less than container load) or FCL (full container load).

CPT— Carriage Paid To (named place of destination)

The general/containerized/multimodal equivalent of CFR. The seller pays for carriage to the named point of destination, but risk passes when the goods are handed over to the first carrier.

CIP— Carriage and Insurance Paid (To) (named place of destination)

The containerized transport/multimodal equivalent of CIF. Seller pays for carriage and insurance to the named destination point, but risk passes when the goods are handed over to the first carrier.

DAT—Delivered at Terminal

Seller pays for carriage to the terminal, except for costs related to import clearance, and assumes all risks up to the point that the goods are unloaded at the terminal.

DAP—Delivered at Place (named place of destination)

Seller pays for carriage to the named place, except for costs related to import clearance, and assumes all risks prior to the point that the goods are ready for unloading by the buyer.

DDP—Delivered Duty Paid (destination place).

Water Transportation

The four rules defined by Incoterms 2010 for sales where transportation is entirely conducted by water are:

FAS—Free Alongside Ship (named loading port)

The seller must place the goods alongside the ship at the named port. The seller must clear the goods for export. Suitable only for maritime transport but NOT for multimodal sea transport in containers (see Incoterms 2010, ICC publication 715).

This term is typically used for heavy-lift or bulk cargo.

FOB—Free on board (named loading port)

The seller must load the goods on board the ship nominated by the buyer, cost and risk being divided at ship's rail. The seller must clear the goods for export. Maritime transport only but NOT for multimodal sea transport in containers (see Incoterms 2010, ICC publication 715). The buyer must instruct the seller the details of the vessel and port where the goods are to be loaded, and there is no reference to, or provision for, the use of a carrier or forwarder. It does not include Air transport. This term has been greatly misused over the last three decades ever since Incoterms 1980 explained that FCA should be used for container shipments.

CFR—Cost and Freight (named destination port)

Seller must pay the costs and freight to bring the goods to the port of destination. However, risk is transferred to the buyer once the goods are loaded on the ship (this rule is new since 2010). Maritime transport only and Insurance for the goods is NOT included. Insurance is at the Cost of the Buyer.

CIF—Cost, Insurance and Freight (named destination port)

Exactly the same as CFR except that the seller must in addition procure and pay for insurance for the buyer. Maritime transport only.

Notes

1. INCOETERMS 《国际贸易术语解释通则》

INCOETERMS 这一缩略词源于 International Commercial Terms 三词。该套术语由国际商会 ICC (International Chamber of Commerce)于 1936 年制定。为了适应国际贸易的不断发展,国际商会于 1953 年、1967 年、1976 年、1980 年、1990 年、2000 年、2010 年先后对 INCOTERMS 作了修订和补充。该套贸易术语在国际上得到广泛的承认和采用,为国际货物买卖最为重要的贸易惯例。此外,有关贸易术语的国际贸易惯例还有《1932 年华沙-牛津规则》(Warsaw-Oxford Rules 1932)及《1941 年美国对外贸易定义修订本》(Revised American Foreign Trade Definitions 1941)。

2. charter party 租船合同

在 FOB 合同中,应有买方负责安排运输,办理租船或订舱手续,并支付运费。在实务中,对于大宗货物(包括散装货)需作整船装运时,买方通常自行租船,而货物只需部分舱位时则常委托卖方向班轮公司订舱。

3. symbolic delivery of the goods 象征性交货

2000 年版《国际贸易术语解释通则》的 F 组、C 组项下,卖方是通过向买方提交货运单据(主要有提单、商业发票、装箱单、保险单等)来完成其交货义务的。卖方所提交的单据等同于交付货物。由于这两组术语下都具有在装运港(装运地)交货的性质,因此其性质属于装运合同。

4. physical delivery of the goods　实际交货

依照 2000 年版《国际贸易术语解释通则》,D 组术语成交时,卖方应承担货物运至目的地的所有费用及风险,即在目的地履行其交货义务,因此其性质上属于到达合同。

5. Incoterms 2010　《2010 年国际贸易术语解释通则》

《2010 年国际贸易术语解释通则》(International Rules for the Interpretation of Trade Terms 2010,缩写 Incoterms 2010)是国际商会根据国际货物贸易的发展对《2000 年国际贸易术语解释通则》的修订,2010 年 9 月 27 日公布,于 2011 年 1 月 1 日实施。《2010 年国际贸易术语解释通则》删去了《2000 年国际贸易术语解释通则》4 个术语:DAF (Delivered at Frontier)边境交货、DES (Delivered Ex Ship) 目的港船上交货、DEQ (Delivered Ex Quay)目的港码头交货、DDU (Delivered Duty Unpaid) 未完税交货,新增了两个术语: DAT (Delivered at Terminal)在指定目的地或目的港的集散站交货、DAP (Delivered at Place)在指定目的地交货。即用 DAP 取代了 DAF,DES 和 DDU 3 个术语,DAT 取代了 DEQ,且扩展至适用于一切运输方式。

修订后的《2010 年国际贸易术语解释通则》取消了"船舷"的概念,卖方承担货物装上船为止的一切风险,买方承担货物自装运港装上船后的一切风险。在 FAS,FOB,CFR,CIF 等术语中加入了货物在运输期间被多次买卖(连环贸易)的责任义务的划分。考虑到对于一些大的区域贸易集团内部贸易的特点,Incoterms 2010 不仅适用于国际销售合同,也适用于国内销售合同。

尽管 Incoterms 2010 于 2011 年 1 月 1 日正式生效,但并非 Incoterms 2000 就自动作废。国际贸易惯例本身不是法律,对国际贸易当事人不产生必然的强制性约束力。国际贸易惯例在适用的时间效力上并不存在"新法取代旧法"的说法,即 Incoterms 2010 实施之后并非 Incoterms 2000 就自动废止,当事人在订立贸易合同时仍然可以选择适用 Incoterms 2000 甚至 Incoterms 1990。

Study Questions

1. What are the essentials of 13 trade terms in Incoterms 2000?
2. What are the differences between symbolic delivery of the goods and physical delivery of the goods?
3. What are the differences between Incoterms 1990 and Incoterms 2000?
4. What are the differences between Incoterms 2000 and Incoterms 2010?
5. What do you think of Incoterms 2010?

Sources of Information and Further Readings

1. http://en.wikipedia.org/wiki/Incoterms
2. http://www.icc.org/
3. http://en.wikipedia.org/wiki/International_Chamber_of_Commerce

Chapter 3

The Law of International Marine Cargo Transport[1]

Key Concepts

liner transport	charter transport	B/L
order B/L	Hague Rules	Hamburg Rules

Learning Objectives

1. Understand the differences between liner transport and charter transport.
2. Understand the varieties of Bill of Lading.
3. Understand the carrier's responsibilities in marine transport.
4. Understand the differences between Hague-Visby Rules and Hamburg Rules.

There are different ways to carry the goods to their destination, such as marine transport, land transport, air transport and multi-mode transport, etc. In choosing one mode of transport, one shall consider such elements as the availability of the transport vehicles, the time of transport, the quantity of the goods and the safety of the goods, etc.

Modes of Marine Transport

Marine transport falls into two groups: liner transport and charter transport[2]. Liners operate on a scheduled service between a group of ports. Liners sail on the scheduled dates and times irrespective of whether the ships are full or not. The respective obligations and liabilities of the consignors and the carriers are listed in the bill of lading issued by the liner companies.

The freight of liners comprises basic charges and additional charges. There are several ways to be used to calculate the basic charges. The cargoes are usually charged by W/T, M/T, A/V[3], the numbers of the goods, or as arranged by the consignor and carrier. The additional charges may contain long length surcharge, over weight surcharge, currency adjustment factor, optional charge, port congestion surcharge, transshipment surcharge, bunker adjustment factor, alternation surcharge, and port surcharge, etc.

The goods are usually classified into 20 grades which are listed in the liner's freight tariff. The basic freight rates are charged according to their respective grades. One may acquire such information in the liner's freight tariff of the shipping company.

Charter transport, also called tramp transport, unlike the liner transport, does not operate on a fixed route and a fixed schedule. The tramps go all over the world in search of the goods, primarily bulk shipments, like coal, grain, timber, mineral ores, fertilizers, etc. They are usually carried in complete shiploads. Tramp vessels are engaged under charter on a time, voyage or demise basis. Voyage charter might be determined by one single or consecutive single voyages or one return or consecutive return voyages, while time charter is on time basis. It might be several months, a year, or even many years. Under demise, or bareboat charter, the charterer has to supply by himself the crew, and the vessel is completely under his control.

Marine Transport Bill of Lading

Marine Transport Bill of Lading, shortened as B/L, is issued by the captain or the shipping company or its agent. It is a document to testify that the goods have been received or shipped on board, and will be delivered to a certain place of destination by the carrier. In legal sense, it is a receipt issued by the carrier to have received the goods. It is also a document of title, with which the seller may come to the bank for negotiation of payment, and the bearer can get the goods at the port of destination from the carrier. Furthermore, B/L is the evidence of the carriage contract between the consignor and the carrier.

In general, B/L may contains the following information:

- Carrier
- Shipper
- Consignee (This column shall be filled in with great care, if L/C is involved, with instructions of L/C.)
- Notified party
- B/L No.
- Name of vessel and V/N
- Port of discharge
- Port of delivery
- Shipping marks
- Description of the goods
- G/W, N/W, Measurement
- Freight prepaid or to collect
- Signature of the master or his agent and the date

While an air waybill (AWB) must have the name and address of the consignee, a BL may be consigned to the order of the shipper. Where the word order appears in the consignee box, the shipper may endorse it in blank or to a named transferee. A BL endorsed in blank is transferable by delivery. Once the goods arrive at the destination they will be released to the bearer or the endorsee of the original bill of lading. The carrier's duty is to deliver goods to the first person who presents any one of the original BL. The carrier need not require all originals to be submitted before delivery. It is therefore essential that the exporter retains control over the full set of the originals until payment is effected or a bill of exchange is accepted or some other assurance for payment has been made to him. In general, the importer's name is not shown as consignee. The bill of lading has also provision for incorporating notify party. This is the person whom the shipping company will notify on arrival of the goods at destination. The BL also contains other details such as the name of the carrying vessel and its flag of nationality, the marks and numbers on the packages in which the goods are packed, a brief description of the goods, the number of packages, their weight and measurement, whether freight costs have been paid or whether payment of freight is due on arrival at the destination. The particulars of the container in which goods are stuffed are also mentioned in case of containerized cargo. The document is dated and signed by the carrier or its agent. The date of the BL is deemed to be the date of shipment. If the date on which the goods are loaded on board is different from the date of the bill of lading then the actual date of loading on board will be evidenced by a notation the BL. In certain cases a carrier may issue a separate on board certificate to the shipper.

B/L may fall into the following varieties:

- On board B/L and Received for shipment B/L
- Straight B/L, Order B/L and Open B/L
- Clean B/L and Unclean B/L
- Direct B/L, Transshipment B/L and Through B/L

Straight Bill of Lading

In this importer/consignee/agent is named in the bill of lading, it is called straight bill of lading. It is a document, in which a seller agrees to use a certain transportation to ship a good to a certain location, where the bill assigned to a certain party. It details to the quality and quantity of goods.

Order Bill of Lading

This bill uses express words to make the bill negotiable, e. g. , it states that delivery is to be made to the further order of the consignee using words such as "delivery to A Ltd. or to order or assigns". Consequently, it can be indorsed (legal spelling of endorse, maintained in all statute, including Bills of Exchange Act 1909 (CTH)) by A Ltd. or the right to take delivery can be transferred by physical delivery of the bill accompanied by adequate evidence of A Ltd. 's intention to transfer.

Clean Bill of Lading

A clean bill of lading states that the cargo has been loaded on board the ship in apparent good order and condition. Such a B/L will not bear a clause or notation which expressively declares a defective condition of goods and/or the packaging. Thus, a B/L that reflects the fact that the carrier received the goods in good condition. The opposite term is a soiled bill of lading, which reflects that the goods are received by the carrier in anything but good condition.

A straight bill of lading by land or sea, or sea/air waybill are not documents that can convey title to the goods they represent. They do no more than require delivery of the goods to the named consignee and (subject to the shipper's ability to redirect the goods) to no other. This differs from an "order" bill of lading which are possessory title documents and negotiable, i. e., they can be endorsed and so transfer the right to take delivery to the last endorsee. Nevertheless, bills of lading are "documents of title", whether negotiable or not, under the terms of the Uniform Commercial Code.

Multi-Modal Transport Documents

The advent of unitization in air and sea transportation brought about many innovations in international transportation of goods. Multimodal or combined transport is one such innovation. Cargo today can be moved from an inland freight station in the exporting country to an inland destination in the importing country. Goods may be picked up and transported using different modes of transport. For example a consignment of garments may be containerized at a factory in Mysore, customs cleared at ICD Bangalore, moved by rail to Cochin, by sea to Dubai, by air to Frankfurt and road to Düsseldorf, all under a single transport document. In such an operation, involving one or more land legs and/or air or sea legs, one carrier makes itself responsible for the entire transport operation. The contracting carrier is referred to as a multimodal or a combined transport operator (MTO). He is liable in contract to the shipper if the goods are damaged at any stage of the carriage. The multimodal transportation document may be issued either in non-negotiable or negotiable form. The multimodal transportation document (MTD), whether negotiable or non-negotiable, is prima facie evidence of the MTO taking charge of the goods for transportation. MTDs are of two types, the COMBIDOC evolved by the Baltic International Maritime Council (BIMCO) and FBL or FIATA MT Bill of Lading evolved by the International Federation of Freight Forwarders' Associations

(FIATA). This document (FBL) has been approved by the International Chamber of Commerce (ICC) for the purpose of documentary credit. FIATA has evolved specific norms for the use of FBLs. Having seen what is covered by sea, air and multimodal transport let us look at other modes including courier and charter movements. The ICC has a publication called the Uniform Customs and Practices, UCP 600 (UCP 500 and UCP 400 were the earlier editions) which among other things deals with various transport documents, including those we have already looked at. Articles 20 to 24 of the UCP 600 deal with these documents.

Carrier's Responsibilities

According to the maritime law of china, the responsibilities of the carrier with regard to the goods carried in containers cover the entire period during which the carrier is in charge of the goods, starting from the time the carrier has taken over the goods at the port of loading, until the goods have been delivered at the port of discharge. The responsibilities of the carrier with respect to non-containerized goods cover the period during which the carrier is in charge of the goods, starting from the time of loading of the goods onto the ship until the time the goods are discharged therefrom. During the period the carrier is in charge of the goods, the carrier shall be liable for the loss of or damage to the goods, except as otherwise provided for in the law. The carrier may enter into any agreement concerning carrier's responsibilities with regard to non-containerized goods prior to loading onto and after discharging from the ship.

The carrier shall, before and at the beginning of the voyage, exercise due diligence to make the ship seaworthy, properly man, equip and supply the ship and to make the holds, refrigerating and cool chambers and all other parts of the ship in which goods are carried, fit and safe for their reception, carriage and preservation. The carrier shall properly and carefully load, handle, stow, carry, keep, care for and discharge the goods carried. The carrier shall carry the goods to the port of discharge on the agreed or customary or geographically direct route.

The carrier shall be liable for the loss of or damage to the goods caused by delay in delivery due to the fault of the carrier, except those arising or resulting from causes for which the carrier is not liable.

The carrier shall be liable for the economic losses caused by delay in delivery of the goods due to the fault of the carrier, even if no loss of or damage to the goods had actually occurred, unless such economic losses had occurred from causes for which the carrier is not liable.

The carrier shall not be liable for the loss of or damage to the goods occurred during the period of carrier's responsibility arising or resulting from any of the following causes:

- Fault of the master, crew, pilot or servant of the carrier in the navigation or management of the ship;
- Fire, unless caused by the actual fault of the carrier;
- Force majeure and perils, dangers and accidents of the sea or other navigable waters;
- War or armed conflict;
- Act of the government or competent authorities, quarantine restrictions or seizure under legal process;
- Strikes, stoppages or restraint of labor;
- Saving or attempting to save life or property at sea;
- Act of the shipper, owner of the goods or their agents;
- Nature or inherent vice of the goods;
- Inadequacy of packing or insufficiency of illegibility of marks;
- Latent defect of the ship not discoverable by due diligence;
- Any other causes arising without the fault of the carrier or his servant or agent.

The carrier who is entitled to exonerate from the liability for compensation under the abovementioned causes, shall, with the exception of the fir cause, bear the burden of proof.

The carrier shall not be liable for the loss of or damage to the live animals arising or resulting from the special risks inherent in the carriage thereof. However, the carrier shall be bound to prove that he has fulfilled the special requirements of the shipper with regard to the carriage of the live animals and that under the circumstances of the sea carriage, the loss or damage has occurred due to the special risks inherent therein.

The amount of indemnity for the loss of the goods shall be calculated on the basis of the actual value of the goods so lost, while that for the damage to the goods shall be calculated on the basis of the difference between the values of the goods before and after the damage, or on the basis of the expenses for the repair. The actual value shall be the value of the goods at the time of shipment plus insurance and freight.

Where the performance of the carriage or part of the carriage thereof has been entrusted to an actual carrier, the carrier shall nevertheless remain responsible for the entire carriage. The carrier shall be responsible, in relation to the carriage performed by the actual carrier, for the act or omission of the actual carrier and of his servant or agent acting within the scope of his employment or agency. Where a contract of carriage by sea provides explicitly that a specified part of the carriage covered by the said contract is to be performed by a named actual carrier other than the carrier, the contract may nevertheless provide that the carrier shall not be liable for the loss, damage or delay in delivery arising from an occurrence which takes place while the goods are in the charge of the actual carrier during such part of the carriage.

Where both the carrier and the actual carrier are liable for compensation, they shall be jointly liable within the scope of such liability.

International Conventions on Marine Transport[4]

Hague-Visby Rules

The Hague-Visby Rules are a set of international rules for the international carriage of goods by sea. The official title is "International Convention for the Unification of Certain Rules of Law relating to Bills of Lading" and was drafted in Brussels in 1924. After being amended by the Brussels Amendments (officially the "Protocol to Amend the International Convention for the Unification of Certain Rules of Law Relating to Bills of Lading") in 1968, the Rules became known as the Hague-Visby Rules. The premise of the Hague-Visby Rules (and of the earlier English Common Law) is that a carrier has far greater bargaining power than the shipper; and that to protect the interests of the shipper/cargo-owner, the law should impose minimum obligations upon the carrier. Key provisions are as follows:

- Basis of liability: imperfect liability with fault
- Period of responsibility: tackle to tackle
- Amount of limitation of liability: 100 pounds/unit
- Limitation of actions: 1 year

Hamburg Rules

The Hamburg Rules are a set of rules governing the international shipment of goods, resulting from the United Nations International Convention on the Carriage of Goods by Sea adopted in Hamburg on 31 March 1978. The Convention was an attempt to form a uniform legal base for the transportation of goods on oceangoing ships. A driving force behind the convention was the attempt of developing countries' to level the playing field. It came into force on 1 November 1992. As of May 2011, the convention had been ratified by 34 countries. Key provisions are as follows:

- Basis of liability: presumed liability with fault
- Period of responsibility: reception to delivery
- Amount of limitation of liability: 835SDR/unit
- Limitation of actions: 2 years

Rotterdam Rules

The Rotterdam Rules, formally the United Nations Convention on Contracts for the International Carriage of Goods Wholly or Partly by Sea, is a treaty comprising international rules that revises the legal and political framework for maritime carriage of goods. The convention establishes a more modern, uniform legal regime governing the rights and obligations of shippers, carriers and consignees under a contract for door-to-door shipments that involve international sea transport. The aim of the convention is to extend and modernize international rules already in existence and achieve uniformity of admiralty law in the field of maritime carriage, updating and/or replacing many provisions in the Hague Rules, Hague-Visby Rules and Hamburg Rules.

The final draft of the Rotterdam Rules, which was assembled by the United Nations Commission on International Trade Law, was adopted by the United Nations on December 11, 2008 and a signing ceremony commenced in Rotterdam, Netherlands (the convention's informal namesake) on September 23, 2009. Signers included United States, France, Greece, Denmark, Switzerland and the Netherlands; in all, signatures were obtained from countries which are said to make up 25 percent of world trade by volume. The World Shipping Council is a prominent supporter of the Rotterdam Rules.

The following are critical provisions and law changes found in the Rotterdam Rules.

- It extends the period of time that carriers are responsible for goods to cover the time between the point where the goods are received to the point where the goods are delivered. (Note: This applies only if there is a sea leg involved in the transport. Thus, the Rotterdam Rules are not completely multimodal since all multimodal carriage excluding a sea leg is outside of the scope of application.)

- It allows for more e-commerce and approves more forms of electronic documentation.
- It obligates carriers to have ships that are seaworthy and properly crewed throughout the voyage. The level of care is set to due diligence, which is the same as in the Hague Rules.
- It increases the limit liability of carriers to 875 units of account per shipping unit or three units of account per kilogram of gross weight.
- It eliminates the "nautical fault defence" which had prevented carriers and crewmen from being held liable for negligent ship management and navigation.
- It extends the time that legal claims can be filed to two years following the day the goods were delivered or should have been delivered.
- It allows parties to certain "volume" contracts to opt-out of some liability rules set in the convention.

Notes

1. International Marine Cargo Transport　国际海上货物运输

国际货物运输是指采用一种或多种运输方式将货物从一国或地区运至另一国或地区的某一地点。国际货物运输涉及多种运输方式，包括海运（marine transport）、空运（air transport）、铁路运输（rail transport）、公路运输（road transport）、邮政运输（parcel post transport）、内陆水道运输（如江河运输、湖泊运输）（inland waterway transport）、管道运输（pipe transport）、国际多式联运（international multimodal transport）等。其中，海上运输为最重要的运输方式，它具有货运量大、成本低等优点，国际贸易业务中约有 2/3 的货物采用海运。此外，现在的运输规则也大都是从海运发展起来的。因此，本单元重点讨论国际海运方面的实务和法律知识。

2. liner transport and charter transport　班轮运输和租船运输

班轮运输是指货轮按固定的航线、固定的停靠港口、固定的航运时间表及相对固定的费率进行航行。租船运输又称不定期船（tramp）运输，它没有班轮运输中的"4 个固定"，而需经过租船人（charterer）与船东（ship owner）在租船契约（charter party）中进行约定。租船运输主要有定程租船、定期租船、光船租船 3 种形式。

3. W/T, M/T, A/V　重量吨、尺码吨、从价

W/T, M/T, A/V 分别为 weight ton, measurement ton, Ad Valorem 的缩略词，可理解为：货物的运费按货物毛重、货物体积、货物价值计收。

4. international conventions on marine transport　国际海运公约

国际货物海上运输规则主要包括 1924 年的《海牙规则》（Hague Rules）、1968 年的《维斯比规则》(Visby Rules)及1978年的《汉堡规则》(Hamburg Rules)。我国未参加上述3个公约,但我国的海商法在有关班轮运输方面的法律规定借鉴了这3个规则的相关内容。

Study Questions

1. Which methods are often used in calculation of the basic freight charges in liner transport?
2. Can a straight B/L be negotiable? Why?
3. What are the differences between clean B/L and unclean B/L?
4. What are the legal functions of B/L?
5. What are the differences between imperfect liability with fault and presumed liability with fault?

Sources of Information and Further Readings

1. http://en.wikipedia.org/wiki/Bill_of_lading
2. http://en.wikipedia.org/wiki/Chartering_(shipping)
3. http://en.wikipedia.org/wiki/Admiralty_law
4. http://en.wikipedia.org/wiki/Hague-Visby_Rules
5. http://www.jus.uio.no/lm/un.sea.carriage.hamburg.rules.1978/

Chapter 4

The Law of Insurance in International Cargo Transport[1]

Key Concepts

insurance policy	right of subrogation	General Average	franchise
abandonment	F. P. A.	W. A.	All Risks

Learning Objectives

1. Understand the basic principles of insurance.
2. Be familiar with right of subrogation.
3. Appreciate the differences between insurance policy and insurance certificate.
4. Be familiar with F. P. A., W. A., and All Risks.

Insurance is a form of risk management in which the insured transfers the cost of potential loss to another entity in exchange for monetary compensation known as the premium. Insurance allows individuals, businesses and other entities to protect themselves against significant potential losses and financial hardship at a reasonably affordable rate. Insurance works by pooling risk. What does this mean? It simply means that a large group of people who want to insure against a particular loss pay their premiums into what we will call the insurance bucket or pool. Because the number of insured individuals is so large, insurance companies can use statistical analysis to project what their actual losses will be within the given class. They know that not all insured individuals will suffer losses at the same time or at all. This allows the insurance companies to operate profitably and at the same time pay for claims that may arise. For instance, most people have auto insurance but only a few actually get into an accident. You pay for the probability of the loss and for the protection that you will be paid for losses in the event they occur.

Insurance against perils is an important aspect of international commercial transactions. In the event of loss or damage to cargo due to hazards during voyage, an insured party will be able to recover losses from the insurer. The type of insurance required depends on the mode of transport agreed between parties to transport the cargo. Such insurance forms include marine, aviation and land.

The type of insurance contract depends on the Incoterms adopted by the parties in a sale contract. A CIF sale contract requires the seller to obtain insurance cover for the voyage. An FOB contract however places no obligation on the buyer or seller to obtain insurance, although it is prudent for the buyer to protect against potential losses. It is not uncommon for the buyer in a FOB contract to request the seller to arrange insurance on an understanding that they will reimburse the insurance costs incurred.

Incoterms 2000

(1) Indemnity—the insurance company indemnifies, or compensates, the insured in the case of certain losses only up to the insured's interest.

(2) Insurable interest—the insured typically must directly suffer from the loss. Insurable interest must exist whether property insurance or insurance on a person is involved. The concept requires that the insured have a "stake" in the loss or damage to the life or property insured. What that "stake" is will be determined by the kind of insurance involved and the nature of the property ownership or relationship between the persons.

(3) Utmost good faith—the insured and the insurer are bound by a good faith bond of honesty and fairness. Material facts must be disclosed.

(4) Subrogation—the insurance company acquires legal rights to pursue recoveries on behalf of the insured; for example, the insurer may sue those liable for insured's loss.

(5) Proximate cause—the cause of loss (the peril) must be covered under the

insuring agreement of the policy, and the dominant cause must not be excluded.

(6) Principle of loss minimization—in case of any loss or casualty, the asset owner must attempt to keep the loss to a minimum, as if the asset was not insured.

Insurance Policy

A contract of marine insurance is a contract whereby the insurer undertakes, as agreed, to indemnify the loss to the subject matter insured and the liability of the insured caused by perils covered by the insurance against the payment of an insurance premium by the insured. A contract of marine insurance comes into being after the insured puts forth a proposal for insurance and the insurer agrees to accept the proposal and the insurer and the insured agree on the terms and conditions of the insurance. The insurer shall issue to the insured an insurance policy or other certificate of insurance in time, and the contents of the contract shall be contained therein. Insurance policy is an evidence for conclusion of the insurance contract. It is issued by the insurer and has legal effect and shall be binding upon the insurer and the insured. The insurance policy may involve the following contents on its front page:

- the insurer and the insured
- invoice No. and insurance policy No.
- description of the goods and packing, quantity and marks
- the insured amount and the currency
- premium
- date and place of shipment and place of destination
- risks to be covered
- inspection agent and place where claim may be made
- date of issuance
- signature and seal by the insurer

In addition, on the back of the insurance policy, standard clauses have been made, which may involve the obligations and rights between the insurer and the insured. But in respect to the insurance certificate, it is just the simplified insurance policy, and has no such clauses on its back.

Upon failure of the insured to truthfully inform the insurer of the material circumstances[2] due to his intentional act, the insurer has the right to terminate the contract without refunding the premium. The insurer shall not be liable for any loss arising from the peril insured against before the contract is terminated.

Unless otherwise agreed in the contract, neither the insurer nor the insured may terminate the contract after the commencement of the insurance liability.

Right of Subrogation[3]

To prevent the insured from recovering twice from the same loss, the insurer is entitled to be subrogated to all the rights and claims the insured has against the third party which has caused the damages of the goods provided he has duly indemnified the insured. This is called the right of subrogation. In practice, the insured usually will sign a letter of subrogation for the insurer after he has received the indemnity. Then the insurer, with the right of subrogation and the required documents, such as the bill of lading, will claim against the third party.

Franchise[4]

For the goods which are easy to be breakable and lose weight, franchise is usually claimed by the insurer. Franchise falls into nondeductible franchise and deductible franchise[5]. If the loss does not exceed the franchise, the insurer does not cover the loss. If the loss has exceeded the franchise, the insurer who claims nondeductible franchise will cover the losses including that with the franchise while the insurer who claims deductible franchise will only cover the losses in excess of the franchise.

Actual Total Loss and constructive Total Loss

It means the whole lot of the consignment has been lost or damaged or found valueless upon the arrival at the port of destination.

Constructive total loss takes place in case the actual loss of the insured goods is unavoidable, or the ship or the consignment has to be abandoned because the cost of the salvage or recovery would exceed the value the ship and the consignment in sound condition upon the arrival at the port of destination.

Abandonment[6]

In case of occurrence of constructive total loss, the insured may ask the insurer to cover the actual loss or total loss of the insured goods. Under the latter case, the insured must present to the insurer a notice of abandonment by which he means to transfer all his interest and obligations to the insurer so that he might cover his total loss. The abandonment is effective only after it is accepted by the insurer.

General Average[7]

Partial loss means the loss of or damage to the goods is only partial. Partial loss can either be general average or particular average. Particular average means a particular consignment is only partially damaged.

When both the ship and the consignments on board are endangered and the captain, for the safety of the ship and the consignments on board, intentionally and reasonably does some sacrifices or makes some expenses. The losses or expenses arising to that effect, shall be borne by both the carrier and consignors in proportion to the value of their interest thus saved. It is called general average contribution. In practice, the typical example is when the ship goes aground and both the ship and consignments on board are in peril, the captain, after all his efforts to refloat the ship have failed, may decide to jettison part of consignments on board to lighten the ship. Thus the losses shall be borne by both the carrier and the consignors.

Perils of the sea

A. Natural Calamity

Natural calamity refers to the perils under force majeure such as vile weather, thunder storm and lightning, tsunami, earthquake, flood, etc. The ordinary action of the winds and waves is not taken as natural calamities.

B. Fortuitous Accidents

Fortuitous accidents are such risks as ship stranding, ship collision, ship sinking, ship missing, striking upon the rocks, colliding with icebergs or other objects, fire and explosion and the like.

C. Extraneous Risks

Extraneous risks can further be general extraneous risks and special extraneous risks. Risks caused by theft, rain and fresh water, leakage, shortage, breakage, dampness, mildewing, heating, taint of odor, hooking and rusting are called general extraneous risks. Risks caused by on deck, war, strikes, failure of delivery and rejection, etc. are called special extraneous risks.

Ocean Marine Insurance Under China Insurance Clause

F.P.A (Free from Particular Average)

It covers the following losses:

(1) Actual total loss or constructive total loss of the consignment caused by natural calamities.
(2) Total loss or partial loss caused by fortuitous accidents.
(3) Partial loss of the insured goods attributable to vile weather, where the ship has been in peril of fortuitous accidents, irrespective of whether the event took after or before such accidents.
(4) Partial or total loss consequent on falling of an entire package or packages into the sea during loading, unloading and transshipment.
(5) Reasonable expenses the insured makes for salvages of the goods insured, and for averting or minimizing the losses, provided the expenses do not exceed the insured amount.
(6) Expenses incurred by discharge of the insured cargo at the port of distress following a sea peril as well as special charges arising from loading, warehousing and forwarding of the goods at an intermediate port of call or refuge.
(7) Sacrifice in and contribution to general average and salvage charges.
(8) Such proportion of losses sustained by the ship owners as is to be reimbursed by the insured under the contract of carriage "both to blame collision".

W.A (With Average)

Aside from the risks covered under F. P. A., W. A. also covers partial losses of the insured goods caused by natural calamities.

All Risks

Aside from the risks under F. P. A. and W. A., all risks also cover partial or total loss of the insured goods arising from general extraneous risks during transit.

Institute Cargo Clauses (ICC)

Institute Cargo Clauses are made out by the Institute of London Underwriters. This set of clauses has played a vital role in the development of international insurance. Most countries in the world have referred more or less in making their own insurance clauses. The ocean marine cargo clauses of the People's Insurance Company of China are basically the same as the old clauses of ICC. ICC has undergone revisions for many times. The latest revision came into effect on January 1, 1982.

Clause A

Clause A does cover all risks except for the exclusions under its coverage. Its exclusions fall into five groups:

(1) General exclusions. The insurer does not cover the losses or expenses caused by deliberate or illegal activities of the insured, the loss or expenses caused by natural leakage, ordinary wear or tear, or inappropriate or insufficient packing, or by the innate defects of the goods, or by delay, or by bankruptcy of the owner or manager or the ship charterer, or by atomic or nuclear bombs.

(2) Exclusions of unseaworthiness or uncargoworthiness[8].

(3) Exclusion of war (antagonistic activities, capture, detention, underwater mines or torpedoes, except those by pirates).

(4) Exclusion of strikes.

(5) Exclusion of malicious damages (caused by terrorists or people with outer political motives).

Clause B

Clause B covers all of the risks listed under its coverage.

(1) Fire, explosion.

(2) Striking upon rocks, sinking or capsizing of the cargo-carrying ship or barge.

(3) Overturn or derail of the overland transport vehicles.

(4) Striking of the carrying ship, barge, or transportation vehicle upon other objects.

(5) Unloading of the goods at the port of distress.

(6) Earthquake, eruption of volcano, lightning.

(7) General average contribution.

(8) Jettison either because of general average or some other reasons.

(9) Loss overboard.

(10) Entering of sea water, lake water, river water into the cargo carrying ship, barge, vehicle, container, or storehouse.

(11) The total loss caused by cargo dropping into sea or on the ground while loading or unloading.

(12) Such proportion of losses sustained by the ship owners as is to be reimbursed by the consignors under "both to blame collision" clause.

Clause C

Clause C covers the losses due to the perils listed under Clauses B except for (6), (9), (10) and (11) as shown above.

Notes

1. Insurance in International Cargo Transport 国际货物运输保险

国际货物运输保险是国际货物贸易的重要组成部分,而保险人和被保险人在保险活动中应遵循保险利益原则(the principle of insurable interest)、最大诚信原则(the principle of utmost good faith)、损失补偿原则(the principle of indemnity)及近因原则(the principle of proximate cause)。由中国人民保险公司制定的《中国保险条款》(China Insurance Clause)(包括海洋、陆地、航空和邮政运输保险条款)在我国对外贸易中被广泛采用。此外,伦敦保险业协会所制定的《协会货物条款》(Institute Cargo Clauses)对国际货物运输保险的影响也很大,实际上,我国的保险条款制定就是以此为基础的。

2. material circumstances 重要情况

在订立保险合同前,被保险人应将其知道的或应知道的有关影响保险人据以确定保险费率或确定是否承保的"重要情况"如实告知保险人,这也是最大诚信原则的体现。

3. right of subrogation 代位权

代位权或代位求偿权也是保险业务中的一个重要概念,它体现了保险补偿性原则。

4. Franchise 免赔率

免赔率通常为那些易碎和易短量的货物而设定的。

5. nondeductible franchise and deductible franchise 相对免赔率和绝对免赔率

两者区别在于,如果损失数额超过免赔率,前者不扣除免赔率,予以全部赔偿,而后者则要扣除免赔率,只赔超过部分。

6. Abandonment 委付

委付仅适用于推定全损的场合,被保险人将保险标的转让给保险人,而向保险人请求赔付全部保险金额。这种转让保险标的的权利称之为“委付”。而对于保险人而言，可以接受委付，也可拒绝之。

7. General Average 共同海损

共同海损构成要件：危险必须是确实存在或难以避免的；所采取的措施是有意识且合理的；作出的牺牲和支出的费用最终是有效的（即避免了危险）。

8. unseaworthiness or uncargoworthiness 不适航或不宜载货

不适航或不宜载货，即船舶不能经受航程中的一般风险，或者船舶不适宜接收、保管和运输货物。

Study Questions

1. What are the principles of insurance?
2. What is an insurance policy?
3. What are the differences between insurance policy and insurance contract?
4. What are the marine perils?
5. What are the basic risks for ocean transportation to be covered under CIC?

Sources of Information and Further Readings

1. Chen, Jianping. *Legal English in International Business.* Zhejiang University Press, 2004.
2. http://en.wikipedia.org/wiki/Insurance
3. http://www.investopedia.com/university/insurance/insurance2.asp
4. http://en.wikipedia.org/wiki/Insurance_law
5. http://en.wikipedia.org/wiki/International_commercial_law

Chapter 5

The Law of International Settlement of Payment[1]

Key Concepts

draft	promissory note	D/A	endorsement	L/C
check	acceptance	D/P	right of recourse	

Learning Objectives

1. Understand negotiable instruments, remittance and collection.
2. Understand the differences between D/A and D/P.
3. Be familiar with the procedures of the L/C.
4. Understand the changes of UCP600.

Draft

A draft or a bill of exchange is an instrument signed by the issuer, authorizing the payer to pay unconditionally a certain sum of money to the payee or the bearer when the bill is presented at a specified time. A draft shall specify the following information: the word of "draft", authorization of unconditional payment, a fixed sum, the name of the payer, the payee, the issuing date, signature of the drawer. A draft may become null and void if any of the above-mentioned items is not specified therein.

Types of Draft

Banker's Draft and Commercial Draft

Banker's draft or bill is drawn by the bank, which is chiefly used in remittance, while commercial draft or bill is issued by a commercial firm.

Sight Draft and Usance Draft

Under a sight draft, the draft is payable on demand or at sight, that is, the drawee is required to pay immediately when the draft is presented to him. In case of the usance or time draft, the draft will be payable within a fixed period after the date of the draft, e. g. "pay three months after date". A draft may be expressed as being payable within a fixed period after sight; here sight means the presentation of the draft to the drawee for acceptance.

Clean Draft and Documentary Draft

In the transfer of the draft, if the draft is accompanied by the shipping documents it is a documentary draft; if not, it is a clean bill. In international trade, the documentary draft is frequently employed for the settlement of payment, while the clean draft is occasionally used to collect the small amount of payment or sundry charges.

Endorsement[2]

Endorsement refers to the act of putting relevant items in writing and making signature or seal on the back of the bill or on an allonge[3]. The bearer must endorse the draft where he intends to transfer his rights to the draft to other persons. When the issuer writes the term "non-transferable" on the draft, then it cannot be transferred. If the draft is transferred by means of endorsement, there shall be an uninterrupted series of endorsement in a draft. Here "an uninterrupted series of endorsement" denotes that, in the course of transfer of an instrument, the endorsement of the person endorsing the transfer of the draft shall be made by immediate prior endorsee to acquire the draft. A person to whom a draft is transferred by means other than endorsement or who acquires a draft by other legitimate means shall provide evidence in accordance with the law showing his rights to it.

No conditions can be attached to the endorsement, any conditions attached to endorsements shall have no effect on the bill. After the draft has been endorsed and transferred, the endorser shall be liable for guaranteeing the acceptance and payment of the draft held by the subsequent party. In cases of non-acceptance or non-payment of the draft, the endorser shall compensate the bearer with the sum of the unpaid draft, interest and other relevant expenses. When the endorser writes the term "non-transferable" on the draft and his subsequent party reendorses and transfers it, the original endorser shall not bear any responsibility for any guarantees made to the subsequent party's endorsee.

Acceptance[4]

Acceptance denotes the act whereby the payer of the draft promises to pay the sum of the money in the draft at its maturity. Where a draft is payable on a fixed date or within a fixed period after the date of issue, the bearer shall present the draft to the payer for acceptance before the date of maturity. When accepting a bill, the payer shall write the word "accepted" and the date of acceptance on the draft and sign it. In addition, the payer shall accept it unconditionally; if conditions have been added, this is deemed to be a refusal. When the payer has accepted the draft, he shall bear the liability of paying it at maturity.

Guaranty

The responsibility of guaranteeing the payment of the draft shall be borne by the guarantor. The guarantor shall be someone other than the debtor of the draft. Where the draft is guaranteed, the guarantor and the person to whom the guaranty is given shall undertake joint liability to the bearer. In case the guaranteed draft has not been paid at its maturity, the bearer is entitled to demand payment from the guarantor who shall pay the draft in full. If there two or more guarantors, they shall undertake joint liability. After the guarantor has paid the debt in the draft, the guarantor may exercise his right of recourse against the person to whom the guaranty is given and his prior parties.

Payment

The bearer shall present the draft for payment or acceptance within the prescribed period as stipulated in the relevant laws and regulations. According to the negotiable instruments law of PRC, a draft payable on sight should be presented to the payer within one month of the date of issue; while a draft payable on a fixed date, within a fixed period after the date of issue or within a fixed period after sight shall be presented for acceptance within 10 days of the date of maturity. Presentation for payment made to the payer by an authorized bank or by means of exchanging system for the instruments shall be deemed as that by the bearer. When paying a draft, the payer or his agent shall check the continuity of the series of endorsement, as well as the legitimacy of the identification of the person presenting the draft and other valid certificates. In case the payer or his agent makes payment out of malice or with gross negligence, they shall bear liability accordingly. Once the draft has been paid in full, all debtors shall be discharged from liability.

Right of Recourse

When the payer dishonors the draft or refuses to accept it, the bearer may exercise the right of recourse against the endorsers, the issuer and other debtors of the draft. If the acceptor dies or flees, or has been declared bankrupt according to the law or has been ordered to cease business activities due to the violations of the law, the bearer may also exercise the right of recourse. In exercising the right of recourse, the bearer shall provide sufficient evidences such as the protest or a statement noting reasons for non-acceptance, or relevant judicial documents, etc.

The issuer, endorser, acceptor and guarantor of the draft are jointly liable to the bearer. The bearer may exercise the right of recourse against any one or all of the persons hereto without being required to observe the order in which the debtors have become bound.

Promissory Note

A promissory note is an instrument issued and signed by the issuer promising to pay unconditionally the payee or bearer a certain sum of money when the note is presented or at a specified time. Under a promissory note, there are only two parties concerned, that is, the issuer and the payee. A promissory note can be sight promissory note or time promissory note. As a promissory note is a promise by the issuer to pay to the payee, it is not necessary for the bearer to present a time note for acceptance by the payer. A promissory note can also be made by a commercial firm or a banker. If it is issued by the banker, it is also called cashier's check or cashier's order, and shall be a sight one.

According to the negotiable instruments law of PRC, a promissory note denotes a banker's promissory note.

Check

A check is an instrument issued and signed by the issuer authorizing any bank or any other financial institution handling business of depositing checks to unconditionally pay a certain sum of money to the payee or to the bearer at sight. Checks may be payable in cash or payable into an account. If a check is payable only into an account, this shall be specified on the face of the check. A cash check can only be used for payment in cash, while a crossed check can not be used for payment in cash but only for settlement into an account. A check shall specify the following information such as the word of check, authorization of unconditional payment, a certain sum, the name of the payer, the date of issue and the signature of the issuer. The sum specified on a check by the issuer shall not exceed the issuer's balance in the bank paying it, otherwise the check is a rubber one, and it will be dishonored by the paying bank. The issuer is prohibited to issue a rubber check. If the paying bank marked "certified" with signature on the check, then it is a certified check which will not be dishonored.

Remittance

Remittance means the remitter remits a certain sum of money to the beneficiary by the bank transfer. It is also called favorable exchange. In remittance, there are four parties involved: the remitter, the beneficiary, the remitting bank, and the receiving bank. In international trade, remittance is chiefly used in those sales under the terms of payment in advance, cash on delivery or open account.

Remittance falls into Mail Transfer (M/T), Telegraphic Transfer (T/T), Demand Draft (D/D).

Mail Transfer

By mail transfer, on receipt of the customer's instruction, the remitting bank will advise the overseas bank which is usually its branch or correspondent bank in the beneficiary's country to pay a specific amount to the beneficiary. The payment instruction is made by ordinary or airmail, and must be signed by the authorized signatories.

Telegraphic Transfer

If T/T is used, the same procedure as for mail transfer is adopted. However, the payment instruction to the overseas bank is sent by telegraphic means, such as cable, telex or SWIFT. In case of telex, the overseas bank will require a special authenticating code word, which is called "test key", before it will act.

Demand Draft

D/D is in effect a bill of exchange drawn by one bank on another payable on demand. The customer will forward the draft to the beneficiary who will obtain the money from the paying bank on presenting it.

Collection[5]

Collection is also called adverse exchange, under it, the exporter takes initiative to collect the payment from the importer. The exporter draws a bill of exchange on the importer for the sum due, with or without relevant shipping documents attached, and authorizes his bank to effect the collection of the payment through its branch or correspondent bank in the importer's country. Collection falls into clean collection and documentary collection. In case of collection on clean draft, only a draft is needed, no shipping documents are attached to it. This type of collection is occasionally used in the payment of the balance, sundry charges, and the like.

Documentary collection is frequently used in international settlement. The operation of documentary credit is as follows:

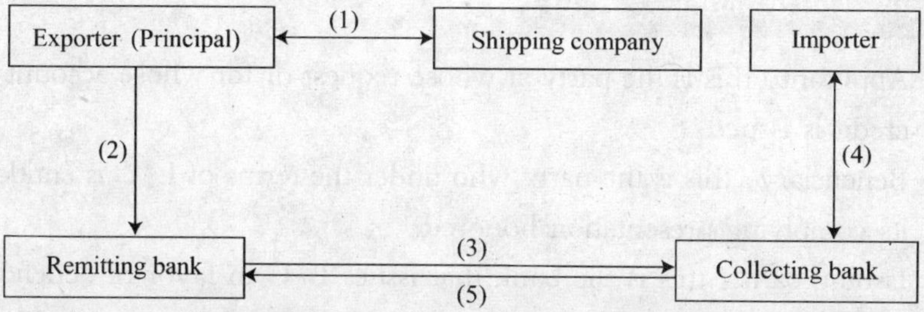

- The exporter ships the goods and obtains documents of title from the shipping company.
- The exporter who is known as the principal, hands over the shipping documents and the draft to his bank (the remitting bank) for collection.
- The remitting bank sends collection instruction and documents to the importer's bank (the collection bank).
- The collection bank will release the documents to the importer against payment under D/P, or against acceptance under D/A.
- If and when the draft is paid, the collection bank sends funds to the remitting bank for credit to the principal's account.

Documentary collection falls into D/P (Documents Against Payment) and D/A (Documents Against Acceptance). Under D/P, the shipping documents will be released to the importer only when he effects the full payment of the goods. In case of D/A, the shipping documents will be released to the buyer when he duly accepts the draft.

Documentary Credit[6]

Definition

According to UCP500, a documentary credit is an arrangement, however named or described, whereby a bank (the issuing bank) acting at the request and on the instructions of a customer (the applicant) or on his behalf

- is to make a payment to or to the order of a third party (the beneficiary), or is to accept and pay draft drawn by the beneficiary, or
- authorizes another bank to effect such payment, or to accept and pay such draft, or
- authorizes another bank to negotiate, against stipulated documents, provided that the terms

and conditions of the credit are complied with.

Parties to a Documentary Credit

(1) Applicant, this is the party at whose request or for whose account a letter of credit is issued.

(2) Beneficiary, this is the party who under the terms of L/C is entitled to have its complying presentation honored.

(3) Issuing bank, this is the bank that issues L/C in favor of beneficiary.

(4) Advising bank, this is the bank which, at the request of an issuing bank, a confirming bank, or another advising bank, notifies the beneficiary that L/C has been issued, confirmed, or amended.

(5) Confirming bank, this is a nominated bank which undertakes, at the request or with the consent of the issuing bank, to honor a presentation directly under L/C issued by another.

(6) Nominated bank, this is a bank which the issuing bank designates or authorizes to pay, accept, negotiate, or otherwise give value under L/C or undertakes by agreement or custom and practice to reimburse.

How a Documentary Credit Operates

Assume that an importer and exporter have agreed that the payment terms will be by way of an irrevocable, confirmed documentary credit. The procedures are as follows:

- The importer asks his bank (issuing bank) to issue an irrevocable credit and to request confirmation by another bank (confirming bank).
- The issuing bank requests a bank (advising bank) to advising the beneficiary (the exporter) of the details.
- After consignment, the beneficiary obtains the shipping documents and presents the documents to the confirming bank. The confirming bank pays the beneficiary provided that the documents are in full compliance with the terms and conditions of the credit.
- The confirming bank sends the documents to the issuing bank and gets reimbursement from it.
- The issuing bank settles the payment with the importer, and then the importer is given the documents for delivery of the goods.

Types of Documentary Credit

Payment Credit

The meaning of the term "payment" is self-evident. The nominated bank will pay the beneficiary on receipt of the specified documents and on fulfillment of all terms of the credit.

Sometimes the issuing bank nominates itself as paying bank, in which case payment will be made on receipt of the correct documents at their counters abroad. On other occasions, usually with confirmed credits, the issuing bank will nominate the advising to pay. The term "payment" only applies to the sight drafts, and sometimes, deferred payment.

Negotiation Credit

Sometimes the issuing bank will nominate the advising bank to negotiate a credit, or it may even make the credit freely negotiable, in which case any bank is a nominated bank. If a bank negotiates a credit, it will advance the money to the beneficiary on presentation of the required documents and will charge interest on the advance from the date of the advance until such time as it receives reimbursement from the issuing bank. Under such negotiation, the negotiating bank enjoys the right of recourse. If payment is not ultimately forthcoming from the issuing bank, the negotiating bank will be able to claim repayment from the beneficiary of the advance, plus interest.

Acceptance Credit

The acceptance credit is also referred to as usance credit, which means that the seller draws a draft on the nominated bank, and demand payment at some determinable future date, e. g. , at 60 days' sight instead of at sight.

The term "acceptance" can only apply when the credit calls for usance bills, i. e. , bills of exchange payable at a specified time after acceptance by the drawee. And bills should be drawn on a bank.

In practice, this means that instead of receiving immediate payment on presentation of the documents, the seller's draft is returned to him accepted on face by the nominated bank.

Deferred Payment Credit

In deferred payment credits, there is no need for the exporter to draw a draft. The issuing bank simply promises that the payment will be made on a fixed or determinable future time date, provided that the other conditions have been fulfilled.

One benefit of deferred credits is that they avoid the need for payment of stamp duty on drafts.

Transferable Credit

A transferable credit is defined in Article 48 of UCP500. Under UCP, a credit is only transferable if it is expressly indicated as being transferable by the issuing bank. The transferable credit may be used when the supplier of the goods sells them through a middleman and does deal with the ultimate buyer. In such case, the supplier is in effect the second beneficiary while the middleman is the first beneficiary.

A transferable credit can be transferred only once. Under it, L/C can be transferred to several suppliers at the same time, provided that the total amount transferred does not exceed that of the original L/C.

Back-to-Back Credit

Back-to-back credit consists of two entirely separately documentary credits, but one credit may act as security for the other. They apply in transactions when original suppliers and ultimate buyers deal through a middleman. Under such case, the middleman will first receive a L/C from the buyer, then on hypothecation of the original credit (master or prime credit), he will ask his bank to open another credit in favor of the supplier. In fact, back to back credit are used in the same situations as transferable credits, but the rights and obligations of the parties differ between the two types of credit. In addition, under transferable credits, the ultimate buyer is aware that he is dealing with a middleman while under back to back credits, he is not.

Revocable Credits and Irrevocable Credits

A revocable credit involves risks to the beneficiary, since it can be amended, revoked or cancelled without the beneficiary's consent and even without prior notice to the beneficiary. The revocable credit is normally accepted as usage between affiliated parties or subsidiary companies, or as a substitute for a promise to pay.

An irrevocable credit gives the beneficiary greater assurance of payment. It can not be cancelled or modified without the express consent of the issuing bank, the confirming bank (if any) and the beneficiary. It constitutes a definite undertaking of the issuing bank, provided that the stipulated documents are presented to the nominated bank or to the issuing bank and that the terms and conditions of the credit are complied with, to pay, accept the draft and or documents presented under the documentary credit.

Confirmed Credit

A confirmation of an irrevocable documentary credit by a bank (the confirming bank) upon the authorization or request of the issuing bank constitutes a definite undertaking of payment by the confirming bank, in addition to that of the issuing bank, provided that the stipulated documents are presented to the confirming bank or to any other nominated bank on or before the expiry date and the terms and conditions of the documentary credit are complied with.

Revolving Credit

A revolving credit is one by which, under the terms and conditions thereof, the amounts is renewed or reinstated without specific amendments to the documentary credit being required. A documentary credit in this nature can be cumulative or non-cumulative. If it is stated to be "cumulative", any sum not utilized during the first period carries over and may be utilized during the subsequent period. If it is "non-cumulative", any sum not utilized in a period ceases to be available, i. e., it is not carried over to a subsequent period.

Anticipatory Credit

Under anticipatory credit or prepaid credit, the issuing bank authorizes the paying bank to effect the payment in advance to the exporter. The payment can be made in full or partial amount. In such case, the beneficiary is usually required to draw a draft upon the paying bank, and present a statement declaring the required documents will be produced in due time.

Reciprocal Credit

Under reciprocal credits, the beneficiary of the first credit is the applicant of the second credit. The credits can take effect either simultaneously or at different times. Under the former case, the first credit does not take effect upon its arrival until the advising bank has received the notice that the returned credit has been received. Under the latter case, the credit takes effect when it reaches the beneficiary.

Stand-by Credit

Like a commercial credit, stand-by credit is a promise by the issuer to honor the beneficiary's presentation of the document(s) specified in the credit. In a stand-by credit, the parties do not normally expect that the presentation of documents will occur. The issuer is merely "stand-by", just in case the obligation in the underlying transaction is not performed by the obligor. A stand-by credit anticipates the possibility that something will go wrong or a negative event will occur while a commercial credit, by contrast, is a method of payment that anticipates a positive event, the consummation of the underlying transaction.

UCP500

The Uniform Customs and Practice for Documentary Credits is a set of internationally accepted rules and definitions which involve the liabilities and obligations of all parties to documentary credits. All bank authorities and advices of documentary credits shall state the credit is subject to UCP500. UCP was first published by ICC in 1933. Revised versions were issued in 1951, 1962, 1974 and 1983. UCP500 was adopted by the ICC Executive Board in April 1993, and first published as ICC Publication No. 500 in May 1993.

Some Main Provisions of UCP500

Article 3: Banks are concerned only with the documents presented under the credit. Even when the underlying sales contract is mentioned in the credit, the bank's decision to pay depends solely on whether the documents presented conform to the credit.

Article 4: Banks are only concerned with documents, not goods nor the performance of the underlying contract.

Article 6: Credits should clearly indicate whether they are revocable or irrevocable. In the absence of any such indication, the credits are deemed irrevocable.

Article 7: The advising bank must take reasonable care to check that the credit is genuine, if it elects to advise the credit. If the advising bank cannot establish authenticity, it must inform the bank from which the instructions appear to have been received without delay. The advising bank may advise an unauthenticated credit but if it does so it must inform the beneficiary that authenticity has not been established. In all cases, there is no obligation on the part of the advising bank to advise a credit, but if it elects not to do so, it must inform the issuing bank without delay.

Article 13: Banks must examine all documents with reasonable care to ensure that on the face of it they appear to be in order. Documents with on the face of it appears to be inconsistent with one another will be considered as not appearing to comply with credit terms. Any documents which are not called for by the credit will not be examined by the banks.

Article 15: Banks shall have a reasonable time, not to exceed seven banking days following the day of receipt of documents, to examine the documents and determine whether to take up or refuse the documents and to inform the party from which the documents were received of the decision.

If the credit contains terms and conditions without stating the document(s) to be presented in compliance with such conditions, then banks will disregard the conditions.

Banks assume no liability for the genuineness of documents.

Article 17: Banks assume no liability or liability or responsibility for the consequences arising out of the interruption of their business by Acts of God, riots, civil commotions, insurrections, wars or any other causes beyond their control, or by any strikes or lockouts. Unless specifically authorized, banks will not, upon resumption of their business, pay, incur a deferred payment undertaking, accept draft(s) or negotiate under credits which expired during such interruption of their business.

Article 32: A clean transport document is one which bears no clause or other indication which declares that the goods or the packing are defective. Where such clauses exist, banks must reject the documents, unless the credit specifically authorizes such clauses or notations.

Article 39: The word "circa" or "about" or "approximately" indicate that a difference of 10% either way can be allowed. Where the goods are described by volume or weight, a 5% tolerance in the amounts actually shipped is allowed, provided the monetary amount claimed is adjusted accordingly.

Article 40: Partial shipments are allowed, unless the credit states otherwise.

Article 44: When the expiry date of a credit falls on a non-business day, banks will accept presentation on the following business day.

UCP600[7]

The latest revision of UCP is the sixth revision of the rules which was made in July 2007. It is the fruit of more than three years of work by the ICC's Commission on Banking Technique and Practice.

Main Changes of UCP600

A major theme in the revision was to ensure clarity and consistency in approach. This was achieved by means of changes to the overall structure of the rules and more fundamental changes in content of certain key rules. UCP600 both clarifies how certain pre-existing rules should be interpreted and also adds new conditions and parameters for documentary credit practice. ICC Position Papers and a number of the ICC Banking Decisions will no longer be used to interpret the rules. The restructuring condenses the provisions from 49 to 39 articles and streamlines the procedure and should, in theory at least, leave less room for inconsistent application. It is clear that the rules have been carefully considered both individually and as a whole. There are a number of provisions or amendments to provisions which should aid clear interpretation and consistent application:

Fuller definitions are provided, including full definitions of "advising" and "confirming" banks, "issuing" bank and also the concept of "honour" (i. e., "honour" means to pay immediately or, alternatively, to pay at maturity having either incurred a deferred payment undertaking or accepted a "draft"/bill of exchange).

The term "negotiation", which was previously unclear, has now been defined properly. It means the purchase of drafts or documents under a complying presentation by advancing or agreeing to advance funds to the beneficiary on or before the banking day on which reimbursement is due to the nominated bank. This appears to apply to silent confirmations as well.

Defining "honour" and "negotiation" should create an improvement in practice since these terms have been the subject of disputes in the past.

A "banking day" is defined and can be distinguished from a business day since the drafters wanted to exclude days on which a bank would be open for business but not for checking documents presented under credits. Unfortunately, the wording arguably does not achieve this aim since it provides that a "banking day means a day on which a bank is regularly open at the place at which an act subject to these rules is to be performed".

An entirely new section containing interpretations aims to ensure clarity and consistency in application of the rules.

Some of the interpretations are not new. For instance, the requirement to disregard terms such as "prompt", "immediately" and "as soon as possible" appear under UCP500 but only towards the end of the rules, like an afterthought. The new interpretations section in UCP600 is given prominence as the third article under the rules. Here a note of caution is given in relation to calculating time in the context of a shipment period. In particular, the new rules provide that calculation of the number of days "from" a certain date in the context of a shipment period must include the date mentioned. This is not the way most people would approach such a calculation.

Further quite simple changes provide clarity and remove previous problem areas. For instance, the phrases "without delay" and "reasonable time which must not exceed seven banking days", being the period in which banks previous had to accept or reject documents under UCP500, have now been replaced with a defined period of five days without any qualification.

Similarly, banks cannot now impose a time limit for rejection of amendments to the credit. This effectively puts a halt on some banks' previous practice under the UCP500 of setting down a time limit within which an amendment had to be accepted or rejected and, if the deadline was not complied with by the due date, the amendment would, somewhat unfairly, be deemed accepted.

Standard for Examination of Documents

The conflict between the doctrine of strict compliance in documentary credit practice and the need to ensure commercial workability was raised in the introduction to this article. One of factors driving the need for revision of the UCP was the high level of rejections of documents on first presentation. Indeed, the introduction to UCP600 specifically refers to concerns that documentary credits will be undermined as international payment mechanisms if certain issues are left unaddressed. A major concern was banks being able to continue rejecting documents on purely technical grounds when, in fact, there is no real or actual discrepancy.

One key change under UCP600 which goes to the root of the problem is the fact that documents presented under a credit are now not required to be an exact replica or mirror image of each other. Rather, the data in documents must not be inconsistent or, as set out in Article 14, must "not conflict" with other data. This alters the previous requirement under the UCP500 that such data had to be consistent. This is sensible in that data in two documents which is not "consistent" might at the same time not actually conflict. It is a matter of degree, and by changing the requirement to a lack of conflict, the drafters have lowered the threshold slightly.

Typographical errors have in the past been a sticky area when it comes to technical as opposed to real discrepancies. There are numerous examples of typographical errors in documents causing problems and particularly common are typing errors in addresses. In this situation, the document checker might not be aware whether he is considering two entirely different addresses or whether the discrepancy is merely a typographical error. Under UCP600, with the exception of addresses in transport documents, the addresses of the beneficiary and the applicant need not be identical provided that they are in the same country as the addresses provided in the credit. Moreover, contact details such as telex, telephone, fax and the like will be disregarded. This change will go some way towards ensuring that documents presented under a credit cannot be rejected on purely technical grounds.

In the same vein, Article 14 requires that non-documentary conditions are disregarded. A non-documentary condition would be a condition in the credit which does not stipulate a corresponding document to indicate compliance with the condition. For instance, a credit may specify that goods are carried on a first class vessel but not require a class certificate to be tendered establishing the vessel's classification. Similarly, the credit may state that the goods be of a certain origin but not call for presentation of a certificate of origin for those goods.

The aim of these changes is to reduce the number of rejections of documents tendered under documentary credits. It is still early days but the outlook is favorable in that it is easier for a document to be compliant under UCP600 and there is less room for rejecting documents presented under a credit on purely technical grounds. If this is wrong and the figure of 70% of documents rejected on first presentation is not reduced, there are likely to be further changes by the ICC.

URC522

For many years, this practical set of rules help banks, buyers and sellers in the collections process. The first revision was issued in 1971 and the latest revision became effective as of January 1st, 1996. It describes the rules governing collections, including those for the presentation, payment and acceptance terms. The articles also specify the responsibilities of the banks and the principals.

Some Main Provisions

Article 4: The principal should insert the complete address of the drawee in the collection order. If the complete address is not shown, the collecting bank may try and ascertain the information, but it is under no obligation to do so. Any loss or delay caused by an incomplete drawee's address will rest with the principal. In practice the remitting bank should check that the full address appears on the collection order.

Article 7: The collection order should indicate D/A or D/P. In the absence of such a statement, documents can only be released on payment.

Articles 9 and 10: These two articles state that bank will act in good faith and exercise reasonable care. Banks must check that they appear to have received the documents which are specified in the collection order, but they have no obligation to examine the documents any further.

Article 11: Where the principal specifies a collecting bank, the remitting bank will use that bank. Where no collecting bank is specified, the remitting bank will choose a collecting bank. In practice, it is better for the choice to be left to the remitting bank. Not all overseas banks can be relied upon, and it is much safer for the remitting bank to select one of the collecting overseas banks, which it knows will carry out instructions properly.

Articles 12 and 14: Banks have no liability for any delay or loss caused by postal or telecommunication failure.

Article 21: A collection order must state whether charges and interest can be waived if refused.

Article 24: The collection order should give specific instructions about whether or not to protest in the event of non-payment or non-acceptance. In the absence of such instructions no protest need be made. Any legal fees incurred by the presenting bank in a protest will be charged to the remitting bank who will debit the principal's account.

Article 25: Where the collection order indicates a case of need, an agent of the exporter who is resident in the importer's country, his powers must be clearly stated. In the absence of such indication banks will not accept any instruction from the case of need.

Notes

1. The Law of International Settlement of Payment 《国际结算法》

与国内货款结算相比,国际货款结算要复杂得多,它不仅涉及不同的货币和结算工具,而且还涉及不同国家的法律和国际惯例。票据(negotiable instruments)是国际结算的重要支付工具,票据包括汇票、本票和支票3种,而流通性、无因性、文义性和要式性为票据的4个特性。国际贸易中的常见支付方式主要有3种,即汇付、托收和信用证。本单元重点介绍有关国际结算中的支付工具及支付方式的实务及相关法律知识。

2. Endorsement 背书

背书是一种以转让票据权利为目的的票据行为。票据的流通就是通过票据转让来实现的,例如,持票人转让汇票应当背书并交付汇票。背书可分为记名背书(special endorsement)和空白背书(blank endorsement)。

3. allonge 粘单

票据凭证如果不能满足背书人记载事项的需要,可以加附粘单,粘附于票据凭证上。

4. Acceptance 承兑

承兑是指汇票付款人承诺在汇票到期日支付汇票金额的票据行为。

5. Collection 托收

托收与汇付不同,它是由出口商委托银行向进口商收款的一种方式,因此又称之"逆汇"(adverse exchange)。

6. Documentary Credit 跟单信用证

目前,信用证已成为国际贸易中使用最广、最为重要的一种结算方式。信用证是指银行按进口商的请求,向出口商开具的凭符合规定的单据进行付款的一项书面保证。信用证项下,银行负首要付款责任(primary liability for payment)。信用证是一项自足文件(独立于买卖合同以外的约定)(self-sufficient instrument),信用证是纯单据业务(pure documentary transaction)。值得注意的是,通过SWIFT网络开立的信用证,即SWIFT信用证,又称"环银电协信用证",因其安全、高效率、低成本等优点,使其在银行间得以广泛使用。

7. UCP600 《跟单信用证统一惯例国际商会第600号出版物》

UCP600(《跟单信用证统一惯例——2007年修订本,国际商会第600号出版物》)共有39个条款,比UCP500减少10条,但却比UCP500更准确、清晰,更易读、易掌握、易操作。它将一个环节涉及的问题归集在一个条款中;将L/C业务涉及的关系方及其重要行为进行了定义,如第二条的14个定义和第三条对具体行为的解释。

UCP600纠正了UCP500造成的许多误解。第一,把UCP500难懂的词语改变为简洁明了的语言,取消了易造成误解的条款,如"合理关注"、"合理时间"、"在其表面"等短语。第二,UCP600取消了无实际意义的许多条款,如"可撤销信用证"、"货运代理提单"、UCP500第5条"信用证完整明确要求"及第12条有关"不完整不清楚指示"的内容也从UCP600中消失。第三,UCP600的新概念描述清楚准确。例如,兑付(Honor)定义了开证行、保兑行、指定行在信用证项下,除议付以外的一切与支付相关的行为;议付(Negotiation)强调对单据(汇票)的买入行为,明确可以垫付或同意垫付给受益人,按照这个定义,远期议付信用证就是合理的。另外还有"相符交单"、"申请人"、"银行日"等。第四,更换了一些定义。例如,对审单作出单证是否相符决定的天数,由"合理时间"变为"最多为收单翌日起第5个工作日"。

又如,“信用证”UCP600 仅强调其本质是“开证行一项不可撤销的明确承诺,即兑付相符的交单”。再如,开证行和保兑行对于指定行的偿付责任,强调是独立于其对受益人的承诺的。第五,方便贸易和操作。UCP600 有些特别重要的改动,如拒付后的单据处理,增加了“拒付后,如果开证行收到申请人放弃不符点的通知,则可以释放单据”;增加了拒付后单据处理的选择项,包括持单候示、已退单、按预先指示行事。这样便利了受益人和申请人及相关银行操作。又如,转让信用证方面,UCP600 强调第二受益人的交单必须经转让行。但当第二受益人提交的单据与转让后的信用证一致,而第一受益人换单导致单据与原证出现不符时,又在第一次要求时不能作出修改的,转让行有权直接将第二受益人提交的单据寄开证行。这项规定保护了正当发货制单的第二受益人的利益。再如,单据在途中遗失,UCP600 强调只要单证相符,即只要指定行确定单证相符,并已向开证行或保兑行寄单,不管指定行是兑付还是议付,开证行及保兑行均对丢失的单据负责。这些条款的规定,都大大便利了国际贸易及结算的顺利运行。

Study Questions

1. What are the legal features of negotiable instruments?
2. What are the differences between UCP500 and UCP600?
3. What are the procedures of D/A and D/P?
4. What are the procedures of the establishment and negotiation of L/C?

Sources of Information and Further Readings

1. http://www.icc.org/
2. http://en.wikipedia.org/wiki/Letter_of_credit
3. http://en.wikipedia.org/wiki/Uniform_Customs_and_Practice_for_Documentary_Credits
4. The Uniform Customs and Practice for Documentary Credits (UCP500, UCP600)
5. http://baike.baidu.com/view/650435.htm
6. Jia, Hao. Comparing UCP 500 and UCP600—an efficient way to learn UCP 600. *LC VIEWS Newsletter* No. 90, January 2007.
7. http://www.itic-insure.com/itic-publications/the-intermediary/article/ucp-500-and-ucp-600-an-update/

Chapter 6

Antidumping Law[1]

Key Concepts

dumping	antidumping duty	unfair competition
normal value	analogue market	countervailing duty

Learning Objectives

1. Understand the definition of "dumping".
2. Be familiar with the methods to determine the normal value of the goods.
3. Understand the concept of "analogue market".
4. Understand the procedures in antidumping investigation and litigation.

Introduction

In international trade, the method of resorting to dumping[2] is frequently adopted by some export-oriented companies so as to expand their business volume and occupy the foreign markets. In essence, dumping is an unfair competition, it may cause injury to the relevant industries of the importing country. Hence, many countries have promulgated antidumping law in order to maintain foreign trade order and fair competition and to protect their domestic industries. According to the antidumping code in WTO, the importing country may impose antidumping tariff, i. e. , a very high and punitive customs duty, upon the dumped imports, if there are sufficient evidences to prove the existence of dumping of the imports.

In economics, "dumping" can refer to any kind of predatory pricing. However, the word is now generally used only in the context of international trade law, where dumping is defined as the act of a manufacturer in one country exporting a product to another country at a price which is either below the price it charges in its home market or if it can be proven that there has been a substantial increase of a specific good; dumping large surpluses into a market will substantially lower the market price as will introducing lower than market priced goods. The term has a negative connotation as advocates of free markets see "dumping" as a form of protectionism. Furthermore, advocates for workers and laborers believe that safeguarding businesses against predatory practices, such as dumping, help alleviate some of the harsher consequences of such practices between economies at different stages of development. The Bolkestein directive, for example, was accused in Europe of being a form of "social dumping", as it favored competition between workers, as exemplified by the Polish Plumber stereotype. While there are very few examples of a national scale dumping that succeeded in producing a national-level monopoly, there are several examples of dumping that produced a monopoly in regional markets for certain industries. Ron Chenow points to the example of regional oil monopolies in Titan: The Life of John D. Rockefeller, Sr. where Rockefeller receives a message from Colonel Thompson outlining an approved strategy where oil in one market, Cincinnati, would be sold at or below cost to drive competition's profits down and force them to exit the market. In another area where other independent businesses were already driven out, namely in Chicago, prices would be increased by a quarter.

A standard technical definition of dumping is the act of charging a lower price for a good in a foreign market than one charges for the same good in a domestic market. This is often referred to as selling at less than "fair value". Under the World Trade Organization (WTO) Agreement, dumping is condemned (but is not prohibited) if it causes or threatens to cause material injury to a domestic industry in the importing country.

Antidumping Actions

Legal Issues

If a company exports a product at a price lower than the price it normally charges in its own home market, it is said to be "dumping" the product. Opinions differ as to whether or not such practice constitutes unfair competition[3], but many governments take action against dumping to protect domestic industry. The WTO Agreement does not pass judgment. Its focus is on how governments can or cannot react to dumping—it disciplines antidumping actions, and it is often called the "antidumping agreement". (This focus only on the reaction to dumping contrasts with the approach of the subsidies and countervailing measures agreement.)

The legal definitions are more precise, but broadly speaking, the WTO Agreement allows governments to act against dumping where there is genuine ("material") injury to the competing domestic industry. To do so, the government has to show that dumping is taking place, calculate the extent of dumping (how much lower the export price is compared to the exporter's home market price), and show that the dumping is causing injury or threatening to cause injury.

Definitions and Extent

While permitted by the WTO, General Agreement on Tariffs and Trade (GATT) (Article VI) allows countries the option of taking action against dumping. The Anti-Dumping Agreement clarifies and expands Article VI, and the two operate together. They allow countries to act in a way that would normally break the GATT principles of binding a tariff and not discriminating between trading partners—typically antidumping action means charging extra import duty on the particular product from the particular exporting country in order to bring its price closer to the "normal value" or to remove the injury to domestic industry in the importing country.

There are many different ways of calculating whether a particular product is being dumped heavily or only lightly. The agreement narrows down the range of possible options. It provides three methods to calculate a product's "normal value". The main one is based on the price in the exporter's domestic market. When this cannot be used, two alternatives are available—the price charged by the exporter in another country, or a calculation based on the combination of the exporter's production costs, other expenses and normal profit margins. And the agreement also specifies how a fair comparison can be made between the export price and what would be a normal price.

Calculating the extent of dumping on a product is not enough. Antidumping measures can only be applied if the dumping is hurting the industry in the importing country. Therefore, a detailed investigation has to be conducted according to specified rules first. The investigation must evaluate all relevant economic factors that have a bearing on the state of the industry in question. If the investigation shows dumping is taking place and domestic industry is being hurt, the exporting company can undertake to raise its price to an agreed level in order to avoid antidumping import duty.

Procedures in Investigation and Litigation

Detailed procedures are set out on how antidumping cases are to be initiated, how the investigations are to be conducted, and the conditions for ensuring that all interested parties are given an opportunity to present evidence. Antidumping measures must expire five years after the date of imposition, unless a review shows that ending the measure would lead to injury.

Antidumping investigations are to end immediately in cases where the authorities determine that the margin of dumping is, *de minimis*, or insignificantly small (defined as less than 2% of the export price of the product). Other conditions are also set. For example, the investigations also have to end if the volume of dumped imports is negligible (i.e., if the volume from one country is less than 3% of total imports of that product—although investigations can proceed if several countries, each supplying less than 3% of the imports, together account for 7% or more of total imports). The agreement says member countries must inform the Committee on Antidumping Practices about all preliminary and final antidumping actions, promptly and in detail. They must also report on all investigations twice a year. When differences arise, members are encouraged to consult each other. They can also use the WTO's dispute settlement procedure.

Actions in the United States

In the United States, domestic firms can file an antidumping petition under the regulations determined by the United States Department of Commerce, which determines "less than fair value" and the International Trade Commission, which determines "injury". These proceedings operate on a timetable governed by US law. The Department of Commerce has regularly found that products have been sold at less than fair value in US markets. If the domestic industry is able to establish that it is being injured by the dumping, then antidumping duties are imposed on goods imported from the dumpers' country at a percentage rate calculated to counteract the dumping margin.

Related to antidumping duties are "countervailing duties"[4]. The difference is that countervailing duties seek to offset injurious subsidization while antidumping duties offset injurious dumping.

Some commentators have noted that domestic protectionism, and lack of knowledge regarding foreign cost of production, lead to the unpredictable institutional process surrounding investigation. Members of the WTO can file complaints against antidumping measures.

Actions in the European Union

European Union antidumping is under the purview of the European Council. It is governed by European Council regulation 384/96. However, implementation of antidumping actions (trade defense actions) is taken after voting by various committees with member state representation.

The bureaucratic entity responsible for advising member states on antidumping actions is the Directorate General Trade (DG Trade), based in Brussels. Community industry can apply to have an antidumping investigation begin. DG Trade first investigates the standing of the complainants. If they are found to represent at least 25% of community industry, the investigation will probably begin. The process is guided by quite specific guidance in the regulations. The DG Trade will make a recommendation to a committee known as the Antidumping Advisory Committee, on which each member state has one vote. Member states abstaining will be treated as if they voted in favor of industrial protection, a voting system which has come under considerable criticism.

As is implied by the criterion for beginning an investigation, EU antidumping actions are primarily considered part of a "trade defense" portfolio. Consumer interests and non-industry related interests ("community interests") are not emphasized during an investigation. An investigation typically looks for damage caused by dumping to community producers, and the level of tariff set is based on the damage done to community producers by dumping.

If consensus is not found, the decision goes to the European Council. If imposed, duties last for five years theoretically. In practice they last at least a year longer, because expiry reviews are usually initiated at the end of the five years, and during the review process the status-quo is maintained.

Analogue Market

The dumping investigation essentially compares domestic prices of the accused dumping nation with prices of the imported product on the European market. However, several rules are applied to the data before the dumping margin is calculated. Most contentious is the concept of "analogue market"[5]. Some exporting nations are not granted "Market Economy Status" by the EU: China is a prime example. In such cases, the DG Trade is prevented from using domestic prices as the fair measure of the domestic price. A particular exporting industry may also lose market status if the DG Trade concludes that this industry receives government assistance. Other tests applied include the application of international accounting standards and bankruptcy laws.

The consequences of not being granted market economy status have a big impact on the investigation. For example, if China is accused of dumping widgets, the basic approach is to consider the price of widgets in China against the price of Chinese widgets in Europe. But China does not have market economy status, so Chinese domestic prices cannot be used as the reference. Instead, the DG Trade must decide upon an analogue market: a market which does have market economy status, and which is similar enough to China. Brazil and Mexico have been used, but the USA is a popular analogue market. In this case, the price of widgets in the USA is regarded as the substitute for the price of widgets in China. This process of choosing an analogue market is subject to the influence of the complainant, which has led to some criticism that it is an inherent bias in the process.

However, China is one of the countries that has the cheapest labor force. Criticisms have argued that it is quite unreasonable to compare China's goods price to the USA's as analogue. China is now developing to a more free and open market, unlike its planned economy in the early 1960s, the market in China is more willing to embrace the global competition. It is thus required to improve its market regulations and conquer the free trade barriers to improve the situation and produce a properly judged pricing level to assess the "dumping" behavior.

Agricultural Support

European Union and Common Agricultural Policy

The Common Agricultural Policy of the European Union has often been accused of dumping though significant reforms were made as part of the Agreement on Agriculture at the Uruguay round of GATT negotiations in 1992 and in subsequent incremental reforms, notably the Luxembourg Agreement in 2003. Initially the CAP sought to increase European agricultural production and provide support to European farmers through a process of market intervention whereby a special fund—the European Agricultural Guidance and Guarantee Fund (EAGGF)—would buy up surplus agricultural produce if the price fell below a certain centrally determined level (the intervention level). Through this measure European farmers were given a "guaranteed" price for their produce when sold in the European community. In addition to this internal measure a system of export reimbursements ensured that European produce sold outside of the European community would sell at or below world prices at no detriment to the European producer. This policy was heavily criticized as distorting world trade and since 1992 the policy has moved away from market intervention and towards direct payments to farmers regardless of production (a process of "decoupling"). Furthermore the payments are generally dependent on the farmer fulfilling certain environmental or animal welfare requirements so as to encourage responsible, sustainable farming in what is termed "multifunctional" agricultural subsidies—that is, the social, environmental and other benefits from subsidies that do not include a simple increase in production.

Antidumping Law in China

Dumping and Injury

Dumping occurs when the export price of an imported product is less than its normal value[6]. Normal value is determined according to the following methods: (1) If products identical with or similar to the imported product have comparable prices in the exporting countries' marketplace, those comparable prices shall be the normal value (2) If products identical with or similar to the imported product do not have comparable prices in the exporting country's marketplace, the normal value shall be either the comparable price of identical or similar products exported to a third country, or the production cost of identical or similar products plus reasonable expenses and profit.

Export price is determined according to the following methods: (1) The price actually paid or the price that should have been paid for the imported product is the export price. (2) If no price is actually paid or should have been paid for the imported product, or its price cannot be determined, the export price shall be the price for which the imported product is resold for the first time to an independent buyer, or the price reconstructed according to a reasonable basis by MOC after consultation with the Customs Bureau.

The dumping margin is the amount by which the imported product's export price is less than its normal value. In determining the dumping margin, the imported product's export price and its normal value should be compared according to fair and reasonable means. Injury includes causing material injury or the threat of material injury to already established corresponding domestic industry or the creation of obstacles to the establishment of corresponding domestic industry by dumping.

In determining injuries cause by dumping to domestic industries, the following matters should be investigated: (1) The quantity of product dumped, including the total quantity of product dumped or the incremental increase in its total quantity relative to identical or similar domestic products and the possibility of large increases therein. (2) The prices of goods dumped, including reductions in the prices of goods dumped or the effect upon the prices of identical or similar domestic products.

(3) The effect of the dumped product on domestic industry. (4) The dumping export company's production capacity, export capacity and inventory.

Antidumping Investigation

Domestic producers of products identical or similar to imported goods, or their related organizations (hereinafter referred to as "the applicant"), may submit a written application for an antidumping investigation to MOC in accordance with the provisions of the relevant regulations. The application should contain the following evidence: (1) The names and addresses of the applicant(s) and the producers it represents. (2) A designation and a description of the imported products, their Import Tariff Code numbers, and a designation and description of the identical or similar domestic products. (3) The imported products' quantity and prices and their effect upon domestic industry. (4) The causal relationship between dumping and injury. (5) Other contents prescribed by MOC. The necessary evidence should be attached to the application form. After receiving an applicant's written application, MOC should examine the application and attached evidence and, after consulting with the State Economic and Trade Commission, should decide whether or not to file the case for investigation. If, under special circumstances, MOC has sufficient evidence to believe that dumping, injury and a causal relationship between the two exists, it may, after consulting with the State Economic and Trade Commission, decide on its own to file a case for investigation. The public announcement of the final ruling in an antidumping investigation must be made within the 12-month period beginning with the date of public announcement of the decision to file the case for investigation. Under special circumstances, that period may be extended to a total of 18 months. MOC should publicly announce its decision whether or not to file a case for investigation and notify the applicant, known exporters and importers, the exporting country's government, and other interested parties.

After the decision to file a case for investigation, MOC and the Customs Bureau shall jointly investigate the existence of dumping and determine the dumping margin, and the State Economic and Trade Commission and the relevant State Council departments shall jointly investigate the existence of injuries and determine the extent of injuries. MOC and the State Economic and Trade Commission shall separately make their initial rulings based upon the results of the investigation. MOC shall publicly announce the initial rulings. If the initial rulings establish the existence of dumping and injury, further investigations shall be made as to the dumping, dumping margin, injuries and extent of injuries in accordance with the provisions of the preceding paragraph. MOC and the State Economic and Trade Commission shall separately make their final rulings based upon the results of the subsequent investigations. MOC shall publicly announce the final rulings.

An antidumping investigation should be terminated and such termination publicly announced by MOC under the following circumstances: (1) The applicant withdraws the application. (2) The initial rulings do not establish the existence of dumping and injury. (3) The final rulings do not establish the existence of dumping and injury. (4) The dumping margin and the dumped product's imported quantity can be ignored.

When MOC and the Customs Bureau or the State Economic and Trade Commission and the relevant department of the State Council jointly investigate, they may distribute interrogatories to interested parties and carry out sample surveys. When requested by an interested party, an opportunity should be provided for it to express its opinion. When MOC believes it is necessary, it may dispatch personnel to the relevant countries to investigate, provided the relevant countries do not object. When MOC and the Customs Bureau or the State Economic and Trade Commission and the relevant department of the State Council jointly investigate, the interested parties shall accurately report the situation and supply the relevant materials. If they do not accurately report the situation and supply the relevant materials, or by other means hinder the investigation, MOC and the State Economic and Trade Commission may make their rulings based upon the materials available to them.

If the initial ruling establishes the existence of dumping and of resultant injuries to corresponding domestic industries, the following temporary antidumping measures may be adopted: (1) According to prescribed procedure, a temporary antidumping tax may be imposed. (2) The provision of a cash deposit or other forms of guarantee may be required. The amount of temporary antidumping tax, cash deposit and other forms of guarantee should be consistent with the dumping margin determined by the initial ruling. MOC may propose and the State Council's Custom Tax Policy Commission shall decide upon the imposition of any temporary antidumping tax. MOC shall decide whether to require the provision of cash deposits and other forms of guarantee. The period for the imposition of antidumping taxes is the 4-month period beginning with the date of public announcement of the decision to impose the temporary measures. Under special circumstances, the period may be extended to a total of 9 months. If the exporter dumping the products or the exporting country's government promises to adopt effective measures to eliminate the injury caused to domestic industry, MOC, after consulting with the State Economic and Trade Commission, may decide to suspend the antidumping investigation. It should publicly announce the decision. If the exporter dumping the product or the exporting country's government fails to fulfill or withdraws the commitments, MOC, after consulting the State Economic and Trade Commission, may decide to resume the antidumping investigation.

If the final ruling establishes the existence of dumping and of the resultant injury to domestic industry, an antidumping tax may be imposed according to prescribed procedures, and MOC shall public announce the decision. MOC may propose, the State Council's Customs Tariff Policy Commission shall decide upon, and the Customs Bureau shall implement the imposition of any antidumping tax. The antidumping taxpayer is the importer of the dumped product. The amount of the antidumping tax must not exceed the dumping margin determined by the final ruling. If the amount of the antidumping tax determined by the final ruling is lower than the amount of the temporary antidumping tax, the excess tax paid shall be refunded. If the amount of the antidumping tax determined by the final ruling is higher than the amount of the temporary antidumping tax, the balance of the two taxes need not be paid. If the final ruling does not impose antidumping tax, the temporary antidumping tax collected, the cash deposit and other forms of guarantee shall be refunded.

When the following two circumstances both exist the State Council's Tariff Policy Commission, based upon MOC proposals, may decide to retroactively impose the antidumping tax on the dumped goods imported within the 90-day period previous to the public announcement of the decision to adopt temporary measures: (1) There is a history of the dumped product causing injury to domestic industry, or the importer of the dumped product knew or should have known that the product's exporter was dumping the product and that the dumping would cause injury to domestic industry. (2) A large quantity of the product dumped was imported within a short period and has already caused injury to domestic industry.

The time period for the imposition of antidumping taxes and price commitments prescribed pursuant to the regulations is five years. Within this time period, MOC, after consulting with the State Economic and Trade Commission, on its own or upon the requests of interested parties, may carry out a reexamination of decisions imposing antidumping taxes. Within a period of 12 months from the date that the reexamination begins, MOC may propose to the State Council's Customs Tariff Policy Commission that the antidumping tax decision be modified, revoked or maintained. The State Council's Custom Tariff Policy Commission shall make the reexamination decision, and MOC shall publicly announce the decision.

Notes

1. Antidumping Law 《反倾销法》

《反倾销法》主要是由一国立法机关制定,由国家行政机关保证执行,为规范进口产品价格秩序,保护国内相关产业,要求进口产品相关者必须遵守的行为规则。《反倾销法》是调整进口国反倾销调查机关在对倾销进行调查、裁定和采取反倾销措施过程中所发生的各种权利与义务关系的法律规范。《反倾销法》的实施属于行政执法,也被称为准司法活动。《反倾销法》通常由国家行政机关实施,如美国的商务部和国际贸易委员会,欧盟的部长理事会和委员会,日本的大藏省和通产省,加拿大的海关和税务部,中国的商务部、海关总署等。反倾销案件直接由有关行政机关受理和裁决,适用的程序是一般行政程序。当然,《反倾销法》这种性质并不排除法院对反倾销程序进行司法审查的可能性,当事人对反倾销行政裁决不服的可以向特定法院提出司法审议的请求,但法院只是对行政机关的行政程序实施审查,而不直接受理当事人的反倾销诉讼,实际上是对行政程序进行法律监督。

本单元主要包括倾销及其界定、倾销构成要件、反倾销调查、美国和欧盟的反倾销措施和程序、中国的反倾销立法等内容,重点应把握倾销的界定、反倾销的异化趋势(西方国家所采用的替代国制度的不合理性、自由裁量权的滥用、从反不正当竞争走向贸易保护主义)以及反倾销法的重新定位。

2. dumping 倾销

依据关贸总协定第6条之规定,一国产品以低于正常价值的价格进入另一国市场,并对该国同类产业造成实质性(material)的损害或威胁,或阻碍其产业的建立,则构成倾销。倾销是一种不正当竞争(unfair competition)手段,但一些发达资本主义国家往往利用反倾销以抵制发展中国家的廉价产品进入其市场,因此反倾销是一种贸易保护主义的手段,也是一种重要的非关税贸易壁垒(non-tariff barrier to trade)。此外,对于出口国是否为市场经济国家,一些发达国家则采取不同的方法来确定产品的正常价值。如果出口国为非市场经济国家,那么就有可能以替代国(substitute nation)的国内销售价格或其产品结构价格(structural price)来代替出口国国内的产品销售价格或其产品结构价格,因替代国往往由进口国来选定,而替代国与出口国之间存在着社会、政治、经济等方面的差异,因此这种方法缺乏公平性,甚至带有一定的歧视性。在反倾销方面,我国出口企业也同样面临着这样的问题。

3. unfair competition 不正当竞争

在国际贸易中,倾销和出口补贴(export subsidy)属于不正当竞争。

4. countervailing duties 抵消性关税

抵消性关税主要是指对直接或间接接受补贴的外国商品进口所征收的一种进口附加税。

5. analogue market 替代市场

在反倾销调查中,如果认为出口国是非市场经济国家,就有可能选定一个经济发展水平与该出口国较为相似的市场经济国家作为其"替代市场"或"替代国"。

6. normal value 正常价值

正常价值是反倾销法中一个重要的概念。正常价值通常是指在出口国的国内市场上,通过正常的销售过程,独立的消费者为该产品支付的价格。如果不存在国内销售价格或不能使用国内销售价格确定正常价值,则可用第三国出口价格或结构价格作为正常价值。第三国出口价格是指相同产品出口到一个合适的第三国,且其出口产品价格具有代表性的可比价格作为正常价值;而结构价格则是指产品在原产地的生产成本基础上加上合理的销售费、管理费及其他费用及利润所形成的价格。

Study Questions

1. What is dumping?
2. What do you think of "analogue market"?
3. Why should the importing nation take measures to stop dumping?
4. How do some Western countries determine the normal price of our exports in dumping investigations?
5. What is the "structural price" of the products?

Case Study

US Steel Files New Antidumping Case

Petitions for Remedies against Surge in Chinese Tubular Goods

(Compiled by Jonathan Katz)

January 7, 2010 United States Steel Corp. said January 7 it has requested more duties on steel imports from China more than a week after the US International Trade Commission determined that imported Chinese steel pipes adversely impacted the domestic steel industry.

This time, US Steel, along with other petitioning parties, filed a " critical circumstances" complaint with the US Commerce Department alleging that certain Chinese seamless steel imports spiked 290% three months after the petitioning parties initially sought antidumping and countervailing duties on seamless standard, line and pressure pipe from China.

In response, US Steel is seeking retroactively imposed duties on certain imports that entered the United States after filing the petitions.

In antidumping and countervailing duty investigations, remedial duties are normally effective when the Commerce Department issues a preliminary unfair trade decision. But under US and international law, duties can be assessed on imports that entered the US market up to 90 days prior to such a decision if evidence shows foreign producers surged into the market in an attempt to avoid tariffs.

If the petitioners are successful, remedial duties could be assessed on imports entering the market within 90 days prior to the preliminary countervailing duty decision, US Steel says. The Commerce Department is scheduled to make its preliminary determination on February 16, 2010.

The move comes just two days after US authorities announced they had slapped tariffs on Chinese wire decking after a preliminary finding that the products were "dumped" at below market value.

About a week earlier, the Trade Commission issued a final decision saying that Chinese steel pipe imports adversely impacted the US steel industry, paving the way for the Commerce Department to impose countervailing duties of up to nearly 16%.

Sources of Information and Further Readings

1. http://en.wikipedia.org/wiki/Dumping
2. http://ec.europa.eu/trade/tackling-unfair-trade/trade-defence/antidumping
3. http://www.customs.gov.au/site/page4227.asp
4. http://www.wto.org/index.htm
5. http://www.commerce.gov/
6. http://www.usitc.gov/

Chapter 7

Contract Law[1]

Key Concepts

contract consideration specific performance damages
offer acceptance misrepresentation

Learning Objectives

1. Understand the concept of "contract".
2. Understand the offer and acceptance in conclusion of the contract.
3. Understand the concept of "consideration".
4. Be familiar with two types of misrepresentation in contract law.

A contract is a legally enforceable agreement between two or more parties with mutual obligations. The remedy at law for breach of contract is "damages" or monetary compensation. In equity, the remedy can be specific performance of the contract[2] or an injunction. Both remedies award the damaged party the "benefit of the bargain" or expectation damages, which are greater than mere reliance damages, as in promissory estoppel.

Origin and Scope

Contract law is based on the principle expressed in the Latin phrase *pacta sunt servanda*, which is usually translated "agreements to be kept" but more literally means "pacts must be kept".

Contract law can be classified, as is habitual in civil law systems, as part of a general law of obligations, along with tort, unjust enrichment, and restitution.

As a means of economic ordering, contract relies on the notion of consensual exchange and has been extensively discussed in broader economic, sociological, and anthropological terms (see "contractual theory" below). In American English, the term extends beyond the legal meaning to encompass a broader category of agreements.

This article mainly concerns the common law. Such jurisdictions usually retain a high degree of freedom of contract, with parties largely at liberty to set their own terms. This is in contrast to the civil law, which typically applies certain overarching principles to disputes arising out of contract, as in the French Civil Code[3].

However, contract is a form of economic ordering common throughout the world, and different rules apply in jurisdictions applying civil law (derived from Roman law principles), Islamic law, socialist legal systems, and customary or local law.

Elements

At common law, the elements of a contract are mutual assent and consideration[4].

Mutual Assent

At common law, mutual assent is typically reached through offer and acceptance, that is, when an offer is met with an acceptance that is unqualified and that does not vary the offer's terms. The latter requirement is known as the mirror image rule[5]. If a purported acceptance does vary the terms of an offer, it is not an acceptance but a counteroffer and, therefore, simultaneously a rejection of the original offer. The Uniform Commercial Code[6] notably disposes of the mirror image rule in 2-207, although the UCC only governs transactions in goods.

Offer and Acceptance[7]

The most important feature of a contract is that one party makes an offer for an arrangement that another accepts. This can be called a concurrence of wills or *consensus ad idem* (meeting of the minds) of two or more parties. The concept is somewhat contested. The obvious objection is that a court cannot read minds and the existence or otherwise of agreement is judged objectively, with only limited room for questioning subjective intention: see Smith v. Hughes. Richard Austen-Baker has suggested that the perpetuation of the idea of "meeting of minds" may come from a misunderstanding of the Latin term *consensus ad idem*, which actually means "agreement to the [same] thing". There must be evidence that the parties had each from an objective perspective engaged in conduct manifesting their assent, and a contract will be formed when the parties have met such a requirement. An objective perspective means that it is only necessary that somebody gives the impression of offering or accepting contractual terms in the eyes of a reasonable person, not that they actually did want to form a contract.

The case of Carlill v. Carbolic Smoke Ball Company is an example of a unilateral contract. Obligations are only imposed upon one party upon acceptance by performance of a condition. In the United States, the general rule is that in "case of doubt, an offer is interpreted as inviting the offeree to accept either by promising to perform what the offer requests or by rendering the performance, as the offeree chooses".

Offer and acceptance does not always need to be expressed orally or in writing. An implied contract is one in which some of the terms are not expressed in words. This can take two forms. A contract which is implied in fact is one in which the circumstances imply that parties have reached an agreement even though they have not done so expressly. For example, by going to a doctor for a checkup, a patient agrees that he will pay a fair price for the service. If one refuses to pay after being examined, the patient has breached a contract implied in fact. A contract which is implied in law is also called a quasi-contract, because it is not in fact a contract; rather, it is a means for the courts to remedy situations in which one party would be unjustly enriched were he or she not required to compensate the other. For example, a plumber accidentally installs a sprinkler system in the lawn of the wrong house.

The owner of the house had learned the previous day that his neighbor was getting new sprinklers. That morning, he sees the plumber installing them in his lawn. Pleased at the mistake, he says nothing, and then refuses to pay when the plumber delivers the bill. Will the man be held liable for payment? Yes, if it could be proven that the man knew that the sprinklers were being installed mistakenly, the court would make him pay because of a quasi-contract. If that knowledge could not be proven, he would not be liable. Such a claim is also referred to as quantum meruit.

Consideration

Consideration is something of value given by a promissor to a promisee in exchange for something of value given by a promisee to a promissor. Typically, the thing of value is an act, such as making a payment, or a forbearance to act when one is privileged to do so, such as an adult refraining from smoking.

Consideration consists of a legal detriment and a bargain. A legal detriment is a promise to do something or refrain from doing something that you have the legal right to do, or actually doing or refraining from doing something that you don't have to do. A bargain is something the promisor (the party making promise or offer) wants, usually being one of the legal detriments. The legal detriment and bargain principles come together in consideration and create an exchange relationship, where both parties agree to exchange something that the other wishes to have.

The purpose of consideration is to ensure that there is a present bargain, that the promises of the parties are reciprocally induced. The classic theory of consideration required that a promise be of detriment to the promissor or benefit to the promisee. This is no longer the case.

Sufficiency

Consideration must be sufficient, but courts will not weight the adequacy of consideration. For instance, agreeing to sell a car for a penny may constitute a binding contract. All that must be shown is that the seller actually wanted the penny. This is known as the peppercorn rule. Otherwise, the penny would constitute nominal consideration, which is insufficient. Parties may do this for tax purposes, attempting to disguise gift transactions as contracts.

Transfer of money is typically recognized as an example of sufficient consideration, but in some cases it will not suffice, for example, when one party agrees to make partial payment of a debt in exchange for being released from the full amount.

Past consideration is not sufficient. Indeed, it is an oxymoron. For instance, in Eastwood v. Kenyon, the guardian of a young girl obtained a loan to educate the girl and to improve her marriage prospects. After her marriage, her husband promised to pay off the loan. It was held that the guardian could not enforce the promise because taking out the loan to raise and educate the girl was past consideration—it was completed before the husband promised to repay it.

The insufficiency of past consideration is related to the preexisting duty rule. The classic instance is Stilk v. Myrick, in which a captain's promise to divide the wages of two deserters among the remaining crew if they would sail home from the Baltic short-handed, was found unenforceable on the grounds that the crew were already contracted to sail the ship through all perils of the sea.

The preexisting duty rule also extends beyond an underlying contract. It would not constitute sufficient consideration for a party to promise to refrain from committing a tort or crime, for example. However, a promise from A to do something for B if B will perform a contractual obligation B owes to C, will be enforceable—B is suffering a legal detriment by making his performance of his contract with A effectively enforceable by C as well as by A.

Consideration must move from the promisee. For instance, it is good consideration for person A to pay person C in return for services rendered by person B. If there are joint promisees, then consideration need only to move from one of the promisees.

Other Jurisdictions

Some common-law and civil-law systems do not require consideration, and some commentators consider it unnecessary—the requirement of intent by both parties to create legal relations by both parties performs the same function under contract. The reason that both exist in common law jurisdictions is thought by leading scholars to be the result of the combining by 19th century judges of two distinct threads: first the consideration requirement was at the heart of the action of assumpsit, which had grown up in the Middle Ages and remained the normal action for breach of a simple contract in England & Wales until 1884, when the old forms of action were abolished; secondly, the notion of agreement between two or more parties as being the essential legal and moral foundation of contract in all legal systems, promoted by the 18th century French writer Pothier in his *Traite des Obligations*, much read (especially after translation into English in 1805) by English judges and jurists. The latter chimed well with the fashionable will theories of the time, especially John Stuart Mill's influential ideas on free will, and got grafted on to the traditional common law requirement for consideration to ground an action in assumpsit.

Civil law systems take the approach that an exchange of promises, or a concurrence of wills alone, rather than an exchange in valuable rights is the correct basis. So if you promised to give me a book, and I accepted your offer without giving anything in return, I would have a legal right to the book and you could not change your mind about giving me it as a gift. However, in common law systems the concept of *culpa in contrahendo*, a form of "estoppel", is increasingly used to create obligations during pre-contractual negotiations. Estoppel is an equitable doctrine that provides for the creation of legal obligations if a party has given another an assurance and the other has relied on the assurance to his detriment. A number of commentators have suggested that consideration be abandoned, and estoppel be used to replace it as a basis for contracts. However, legislation, rather than judicial development, has been touted as the only way to remove this entrenched common law doctrine. Lord Justice Denning famously stated that "The doctrine of consideration is too firmly fixed to be overthrown by a side-wind."

Formation

In addition to the elements of a contract,

- a party must have capacity to contract;
- the purpose of the contract must be lawful;
- the form of the contract must be legal;
- the parties must intend to create a legal relationship; and
- the parties must consent.

As a result, there are a variety of affirmative defenses that a party may assert to avoid his obligation.

Affirmative Defenses

Vitiating factors constituting defences to purported contract formation include:

- mistake;
- incapacity, including mental incompetence and infancy/minority;
- duress;
- undue influence;
- unconscionability;
- misrepresentation[8] / fraud; and
- frustration of purpose.

Such defenses operate to determine whether a purported contract is either void or voidable. Void contracts cannot be ratified by either party. Voidable contracts *can* be ratified.

Freedom to Contract and Hurley v. Eddingfield

In most systems of law, parties have freedom to choose whether or not they wish to enter into a contract, absent superseding duties. In American law, one early case exemplifying this proposition is Hurley v. Eddingfield (1901), in which the Supreme Court of Indiana ruled in favor of a physician who voluntarily decided not to help a patient whom the physician had treated on past occasions, despite the lack of other available medical assistance and the patient's subsequent death.

In addition, for some contracts formalities must be complied with under legislation sometimes called a statute of frauds (especially transactions in real property or for relatively large cash amounts).

Invitation to Treat (Invitation for Offer)

Where a product in large quantities is advertised in a newspaper or on a poster, it generally is not considered an offer but instead will be regarded as an invitation to treat, since there is no guarantee that the store can provide the item for everyone who might want one. This was the basis of the decision in Partridge v. Crittenden a criminal case in which the defendant was charged with "offering for sale" bramble finch cocks and hens. The court held that the newspaper advertisement could only be an invitation to treat, since it could not have been intended as an offer to the world, so the defendant was not guilty of "offering" them for sale. Similarly, a display of goods in a shop window is an invitation to treat, as was held in Fisher v. Bell another criminal case which turned on the correct analysis of offers as against invitations to treat. In this instance the defendant was charged with "offering for sale" prohibited kinds of knife, which he had displayed in his shop window with prices attached. The court held that this was an invitation to treat, the offer would be made by a purchaser going into the shop and asking to buy a knife, with acceptance being by the shopkeeper, which he could withhold. (The law was later amended to "exposing for sale".) A display of goods on the shelves of a self-service shop is also an invitation to treat, with the offer being made by the purchaser at the checkout and being accepted by the shop assistant operating the checkout: Pharmaceutical Society of Great Britain v. Boots Cash Chemists (Southern) Ltd. If the person who is to buy the advertised product is of importance, for instance because of his personality, etc, when buying land, it is regarded merely as an invitation to treat. In Carbolic Smoke Ball, the major difference was that a reward was included in the advertisement, which is a general exception to the rule and is then treated as an offer.

One of the most famous cases on invitation to treat is Carlill v. Carbolic Smoke Ball Company, decided in nineteenth-century England. A medical firm advertised that its new wonder drug, a smoke ball, would prevent those who used it according to the instructions from catching the flu, and if it did not, buyers would receive 100 and said that they had deposited 1,000 in the bank to show their good faith. When sued, Carbolic argued the ad was not to be taken as a serious, legally binding offer. It was merely an invitation to treat, and a gimmick (a "mere puff"). But the court of appeal held that it would appear to a reasonable man that Carbolic had made a serious offer, primarily because of the reference to the 1000 deposited into the bank. People had given good "consideration" for it by going to the "distinct inconvenience" of using a faulty product. "Read the advertisement how you will, and twist it about as you will," said Lindley L. J., "here is a distinct promise expressed in language which is perfectly unmistakable".

Most states consider persons under the age of 18 to be minors. They have the right to cancel the contract at any time before and even after reaching the age of 18. If, however, a minor cancels the contract, the benefits that he or she received must be returned.

Contracts entered into by a minor as one party and an adult as the other party are enforceable if the adult breaches the contract. The minor can enforce the contract and collect damages by the adult's breach. However, if the minor breaches the contract, the adult does not have the legal authority to enforce the contract and cannot collect damages under the bargain principle. Promissory estoppel or unjust enrichment may be available, but generally are not.

Intention to Be Legally Bound

There is a presumption for commercial agreements that parties intend to be legally bound (unless the parties expressly state that they do not want to be bound, like in heads of agreement). On the other hand, many kinds of domestic and social agreements are unenforceable on the basis of public policy, for instance between children and parents. One early example is found in Balfour v. Balfour. Using contract-like terms, Mr. Balfour had agreed to give his wife 30 a month as maintenance while he was living in Ceylon (Sri Lanka). Once he left, they separated and Mr. Balfour stopped payments. Mrs. Balfour brought an action to enforce the payments. At the Court of Appeal, the Court held that there was no enforceable agreement as there was not enough evidence to suggest that they were intending to be legally bound by the promise.

The case is often cited in conjunction with Merritt v. Merritt. Here the court distinguished the case from Balfour v. Balfour because Mr. and Mrs. Merritt, although married again, were estranged at the time the agreement was made. Therefore any agreement between them was made with the intention to create legal relations.

Third Parties

The doctrine of privity of contract means that only those involved in striking a bargain would have standing to enforce it. In general this is still the case, only parties to a contract may sue for the breach of a contract, although in recent years the rule of privity has eroded somewhat and third party beneficiaries have been allowed to recover damages for breaches of contracts they were not party to. In cases where facts involve third party beneficiaries or debtors to the original contracting party have been allowed to be considered parties for purposes of enforcement of the contract. A recent advance has been seen in the case law as well as statutory recognition to the dilution of the doctrine of privity of contract. The recent tests applied by courts have been the test of benefit and the duty owed test. The duty owed test looks to see if the third party was agreeing to pay a debt for the original party [needs elaboration] and whereas the benefit test looks to see if circumstances indicate that the promisee intends to give the beneficiary the benefit of the promised performance. Any defense allowed to parties of the original contract extend to third party beneficiaries. A recent example is in England, where the Contracts (Rights of Third Parties) Act 1999 was introduced.

Formalities and Writing

An unwritten, unspoken contract, also known as "a contract implied by the acts of the parties", which can be either implied in fact or implied in law, may also be legally binding. Contracts implied in fact are "real" contracts, that is, of no different remedy than "benefit of the bargain", as mentioned above. However, contracts implied in law are also known as quasi-contracts, and the remedy is quantum meruit, the fair market value of goods or services rendered.

Oral contracts are ordinarily valid and therefore legally binding. However, in most jurisdictions, certain types of contracts must be reduced to writing to be enforceable. This is to prevent frauds and perjuries, hence the name statute of frauds. For example, an unwritten contract would be unenforceable if for the sale of land.

Contracts that do not meet the requirements of common law or statutory Statutes of frauds are unenforceable, but are not necessarily thereby void. However, a party unjustly enriched by an unenforceable contract may be required to provide restitution for unjust enrichment. Statutes of frauds are typically codified in state statutes covering specific types of contracts, such as contracts for the sale of real estate.

In Australia and many, if not all, jurisdictions which have adopted the common law of England, for contracts subject to legislation equivalent to the Statute of frauds, there is no requirement for the entire contract to be in writing. Although for property transactions there must be a note or memorandum evidencing the contract, which may come into existence after the contract has been formed. The note or memorandum must be signed in some way, and a series of documents may be used in place of a single note or memorandum. It must contain all material terms of the contract, the subject matter and the parties to the contract. In England and Wales, the common law Statute of frauds is only now in force for guarantees, which must be evidenced in writing, although the agreement may be made orally. Certain other kinds of contract must be in writing or they are void, for instance, for sale of land under s. 52, Law of Property Act, 1925.

If a contract is in a written form, and somebody signs it, then the signer is typically bound by its terms regardless of whether he has actually read it, provided the document is contractual in nature. However, affirmative defenses such as duress or unconscionability may enable the signer to avoid his purported obligation. Furthermore, if a party wishes to use a document as the basis of a contract, reasonable notice of its terms must be given to the other party prior to their entry into the contract. This includes such things as tickets issued at parking stations.

Bilateral and Unilateral Contracts

Contracts may be bilateral or unilateral. A bilateral contract is the kind of contract that most people think of when they think "contract" and indeed represents the vast majority of contracts. It is an agreement in which each of the parties to the contract makes a promise or set of promises to the other party or parties. For example, in a contract for the sale of a home, the buyer promises to pay the seller $200,000 in exchange for the seller's promise to deliver title to the property.

In a unilateral contract, only one party to the contract makes a promise. A typical example is the reward contract: A promises to pay a reward to B if B finds A's dog. B is not under an obligation to find A's dog, but A is under an obligation to pay the reward to B if B does find the dog. The consideration for the contract here is B's reliance on A's promise or B giving up his legal right to do whatever he wanted at the time he was engaged in the finding of the dog.

In this example, the finding of the dog is a condition precedent to A's obligation to pay, although it is not a legal condition precedent, because technically no contract here has arisen until the dog is found (because B has not accepted A's offer until he finds the dog, and a contract requires offer, acceptance, and consideration), and the term "condition precedent" is used in contract law to designate a condition of a promise in a contract. For example, if B promised to find A's dog, and A promised to pay B when the dog was found, A's promise would have a condition attached to it, and offer and acceptance would already have occurred. This is a situation in which a condition precedent is attached to a bilateral contract.

Condition precedents can also be attached to unilateral contracts, however. This would require A to require a further condition to be met before he pays B for finding his dog. So, for example, A could say "If anyone finds my dog, and the sky falls down, I will give that person $100." In this situation, even if the dog is found by B, he would not be entitled to the $100 until the sky falls down. Therefore the sky falling down is a condition precedent to A's duty being actualized, even though they are already in a contract, since A has made an offer and B has accepted.

An offer of a unilateral contract may often be made to many people (or "to the world") by means of an advertisement. (The general rule is that advertisements are not offers.) In the situation where the unilateral offer is made to many people, acceptance will only occur on complete performance of the condition (in other words, by completing the performance that the offeror seeks, which is what the advertisement requests from the offerees—to actually find the dog). If the condition is something that only one party can perform, both the offeror and offeree are protected the offeror is protected because he will only ever be contractually obliged to one of the many offerees, and the offeree is protected because if she does perform the condition, the offeror will be contractually obligated to pay her.

In unilateral contracts, the requirement that acceptance be communicated to the offeror is waived unless otherwise stated in the offer. The offeree accepts by performing the condition, and the offeree's performance is also treated as the price, or consideration, for the offeror's promise. The offeror is master of the offer; it is he who decides whether the contract will be unilateral or bilateral. In unilateral contracts, the offer is made to the public at large.

A bilateral contract is one in which there are duties on both sides, rights on both sides, and consideration on both sides. If an offeror makes an offer such as "If you promise to paint my house, I will give you $100", this is a bilateral contract once the offeree accepts. Each side has promised to do something, and each side will get something in return for what they have done.

Uncertainty, Incompleteness and Severance

If the terms of the contract are uncertain or incomplete, the parties cannot have reached an agreement in the eyes of the law. An agreement to agree does not constitute a contract, and an inability to agree on key issues, which may include such things as price or safety, may cause the entire contract to fail. However, a court will attempt to give effect to commercial contracts where possible, by construing a reasonable construction of the contract.

Courts may also look to external standards, which are either mentioned explicitly in the contract or implied by common practice in a certain field. In addition, the court may also imply a term; if price is excluded, the court may imply a reasonable price, with the exception of land, and second-hand goods, which are unique.

If there are uncertain or incomplete clauses in the contract, and all options in resolving its true meaning have failed, it may be possible to sever and void just those affected clauses if the contract includes a severability clause. The test of whether a clause is severable is an objective test—whether a reasonable person would see the contract standing even without the clauses.

Contractual Terms

A contractual term is "any provision forming part of a contract". Each term gives rise to a contractual obligation, breach of which can give rise to litigation. Not all terms are stated expressly and some terms carry less legal weight as they are peripheral to the objectives of the contract.

Boilerplate

As discussed in Tina L. Stark's Negotiating and Drafting Contract Boilerplate, when lawyers refer to a "boilerplate" provision, they are referring to any standardized, "one size fits all" contract provision. But lawyers also use the term in a more narrow context to refer to certain provisions that appear at the end of the contract. Typically, these provisions tell the parties how to govern their relationship and administer the contract. Although often thought to be of secondary importance, these provisions have significant business and legal consequences. Common provisions include the governing law provision, venue, assignment and delegation provisions, waiver of jury trial provisions, notice provisions, and force majeure[9] provisions.

Classification of Term

● Condition or Warranty

Conditions are terms which go to the very root of a contract. Breach of these terms repudiates the contract, allowing the other party to discharge the contract. A warranty is not so imperative so the contract will subsist after a warranty breach. Breach of either will give rise to damages.

It is an objective matter of fact whether a term goes to the root of a contract. By way of illustration, an actress's obligation to perform the opening night of a theatrical production is a condition, whereas a singer's obligation to perform during the first three days of rehearsal is a warranty.

Statute may also declare a term or nature of term to be a condition or warranty; for example the Sale of Goods Act 1979 S15A provides that terms as to title, description, quality and sample (as described in the Act) are conditions save in certain defined circumstances.

● Innominate Term

Lord Diplock, in Hong Kong Fir Shipping Co Ltd. v. Kawasaki Kisen Kaisha Ltd., created the concept of an innominate term, breach of which may or not go to the root of the contract depending upon the nature of the breach. Breach of these terms, as with all terms, will give rise to damages. Whether or not it repudiates the contract depends upon whether legal benefit of the contract has been removed from the innocent party. Megaw L.J., in 1970, preferred the legal certainty of using the classic categories of condition or warranty. This was interpreted by the House of Lords as merely restricting its application in Reardon Smith Line Ltd. v. Hansen-Tangen.

Status as a Term

Status as a term is important as a party can only take legal action for the non fulfillment of a term as opposed to representations or mere puffery. Legally speaking, only statements that amount to a term create contractual obligations. There are various factor that a court may take into account in determining the nature of a statement. In particular, the importance apparently placed on the statement by the parties at the time the contract is made is likely to be significant. In Bannerman v. White it was held a term of a contract for sale and purchase of hops that they had not been treated with sulphur, since the buyer made very explicit his unwillingness to accept hops so treated, saying that he had no use for them. The relative knowledge of the parties may also be a factor, as in Bissett v. Wilkinson in which a statement that farmland being sold would carry 2,000 sheep if worked by one team was held merely a representation (it was also only an opinion and therefore not actionable as misrepresentation). The reason this was not a term was that the seller had no basis for making the statement, as the buyer knew, and the buyer was prepared to rely on his own and his son's knowledge of farming.

Implied Terms

A term may either be express or implied. An express term is stated by the parties during negotiation or written in a contractual document. Implied terms are not stated but nevertheless form a provision of the contract.

Terms Implied in Fact

Terms may be implied due to the facts of the proceedings by which the contract was formed. In the Australian case of BP Refinery Westernport v. Shire of Hastings the UK Privy Council proposed a five stage test to determine situations where the facts of a case may imply terms (this only applies to formal contracts in Australia). However, the English Court of Appeal sounded a note of caution with regard to the BP case in Philips Electronique Grand Public SA v. British Sky Broadcasting Ltd in which the Master of the Rolls described the test as "almost misleading" in its simplicity. The classic tests have been the "business efficacy test" and the "officious bystander test". The first of these was proposed by Lord Justice Bowen in The Moorcock. This test requires that a term can only be implied if it is necessary to give business efficacy to the contract to avoid such a failure of consideration that the parties cannot as reasonable businessmen have intended. But only the most limited term should then be implied—the bare minimum to achieve this goal. The officious bystander test derives its name from the judgment of Lord Justice Mackinnon in

Shirlaw v. Southern Foundries (1926) Ltd. but the test actually originates in the judgment of Lord Justice Scrutton in Reigate v. Union Manufacturing Co (Ramsbottom) Ltd. This test is that a term can only be implied in fact if it is such a term that had an "officious bystander" listening to the contract negotiations suggested that they should include this term the parties would "dismiss him with a common 'Oh of course!'". It is at least questionable whether this is truly a separate test or just a description of how one might go about arriving at a decision on the basis of the business efficacy test.

Some jurisdictions, notably Australia, Israel and India, imply a term of good faith into contracts. A final way in which terms may be implied due to fact is through a previous course of dealing or common trade practice. The Uniform Commercial Code of the United States also imposes an implied covenant of good faith and fair dealing in performance and enforcement of contracts covered by the Code, which cannot be derogated from.

Terms Implied in Law

These are terms that have been implied into standardized relationships. Instances of this are quite numerous, especially in employment contracts and shipping contracts.

Common Law

Liverpool City Council v. Irwin established a term to be implied into all contracts between tenant and landlord in multi-storey blocks that the landlord is obliged to take reasonable care to keep the common areas in a reasonable state of repair.

These terms will be implied into all contracts of the same nature as a matter of law.

Statute Law

The rules by which many contracts are governed are provided in specialized statutes that deal with particular subjects. Most countries, for example, have statutes which deal directly with sale of goods, lease transactions, and trade practices. For example, most American states have adopted Article 2 of the Uniform Commercial Code, which regulates contracts for the sale of goods. The most important legislation implying terms under United Kingdom law are the Sale of Goods Act 1979, the Consumer Protection (Distance Selling) Regulations 2000 and the Supply of Goods and Services Act 1982 which imply terms into all contracts whereby goods are sold or services provided.

Coercive vs. Voluntary Contractive Exchanges

There are a few ways of determining whether a contract has been coerced or is voluntary:

- Moral consideration: Objective consideration of right or wrong outside of the objective cause, or the perceived cause. Example: X (event) occurs everyday at 5 pm. X is wrong. Anything that avoids X is good; allowing X, even if all parties agree, is bad.
- Phenomenological consideration—what models did the participants have which influenced the perception of what was to occur or what had occurred. Example: I observe X, Y (events) every day at 5 pm. I contract against X. Today I did / did not see Y occur.
- Statistical consideration—did the participants have a statistical prediction, likelihood of an event occurring which is covered by the contract. Example: X (event) happens every day at 5 pm, I enter a contract to avoid X. X does or does not occur.

Setting Aside the Contract

There can be four different ways in which contracts can be set aside. A contract may be deemed "void", "voidable", "unenforceable" or "ineffective". Voidness implies that a contract never came into existence. Voidability implies that one or both parties may declare a contract ineffective at their wish. Unenforceability implies that neither party may have recourse to a court for a remedy. Ineffectiveness implies that the contract terminates by order of a court where a public body has failed to satisfy public procurement law. To rescind is to set aside or unmake a contract.

Misrepresentation

Misrepresentation means a false statement of fact made by one party to another party and has the effect of inducing that party into the contract. For example, under certain circumstances, false statements or promises made by a seller of goods regarding the quality or nature of the product that the seller has may constitute misrepresentation. A finding of misrepresentation allows for a remedy of rescission and sometimes damages depending on the type of misrepresentation.

There are two types of misrepresentation in contract law, fraud in the factum and fraud in inducement. Fraud in the factum focuses on whether the party in question knew they were creating a contract. If the party did not know that they were entering into a contract, there is no meeting of the minds, and the contract is void. Fraud in inducement focuses on misrepresentation attempting to get the party to enter into the contract. Misrepresentation of a material fact (if the party knew the truth, that party would not have entered into the contract) makes a contract voidable.

According to Gordon v. Selico it is possible to make a misrepresentation either by words or by conduct, although not everything said or done is capable of constituting a misrepresentation. Generally, statements of opinion or intention are not statements of fact in the context of misrepresentation.

Both an order for specific performance and an injunction are discretionary remedies, originating for the most part in equity. Neither is available as of right and in most jurisdictions and most circumstances a court will not normally order specific performance. A contract for the sale of real property is a notable exception. In most jurisdictions, the sale of real property is enforceable by specific performance. Even in this case the defenses to an action in equity may act as a bar to specific performance.

Related to orders for specific performance, an injunction may be requested when the contract prohibits a certain action. Action for injunction would prohibit the person from performing the act specified in the contract.

Procedure

In the United States, in order to obtain damages for breach of contract or to obtain specific performance or other equitable relief, the aggrieved injured party may file a civil (non-criminal) lawsuit in state court (unless there is diversity of citizenship giving rise to federal jurisdiction). If the contract contains a valid arbitration clause, the aggrieved party must submit an arbitration claim in accordance with the procedures set forth in the clause.

Many contracts provide that all disputes arising thereunder will be resolved by arbitration, rather than litigated in courts. Customer claims against securities brokers and dealers are almost always resolved by arbitration because securities dealers are required, under the terms of their membership in self-regulatory organizations such as the Financial Industry Regulatory Authority (formerly the NASD) or NYSE to arbitrate disputes with their customers. The firms then began including arbitration agreements in their customer agreements, requiring their customers to arbitrate disputes. On the other hand, certain claims have been held to be non-arbitrable if they implicate a public interest that goes beyond the narrow interests of the parties to the agreement (i. e., claims that a party violated a contract by engaging in illegal anti-competitive conduct or civil rights violations). Arbitration judgments may generally be enforced in the same manner as ordinary court judgments. However, arbitral decisions are generally immune from appeal in the United States unless there is a showing that the arbitrator's decision was irrational or tainted by fraud. Virtually all states have adopted the Uniform Arbitration Act to facilitate the enforcement of arbitrated judgments. Notably, New York State, where a sizable portion of major commercial agreements are executed and performed, has not adopted the Uniform Arbitration Act.

In England and Wales, a contract may be enforced by use of a claim, or in urgent cases by applying for an interim injunction to prevent a breach. Likewise, in the United States, an aggrieved party may apply for injunctive relief to prevent a threatened breach of contract, where such breach would result in irreparable harm that could not be adequately remedied by money damages.

Other Contract

Online contracts, which are easily made, are usually valid on a smaller scale for a period of one to three months, while on a larger scale can last about five years. As with all things legal, especially in regards to the ever-evolving Internet, general rules like length of validity have many exceptions. All cases are evaluated on their own merits, and those merits are defined by the facts presented in each instance. It is up to the owner of the site to do what it can to guarantee enforceability of its contracts. Though 90% of people sign online contracts before reading the content, E-signature laws have made the electronic contract and signature as legally valid as a paper contract. It has been estimated that roughly one hundred and ten electronic contracts are signed every second.

Contract Theory

Contract theory is the body of legal theory that addresses normative and conceptual questions in contract law. One of the most important questions asked in contract theory is why contracts are enforced. One prominent answer to this question focuses on the economic benefits of enforcing bargains. Another approach, associated with Charles Fried, maintains that the purpose of contract law is to enforce promises. This theory is developed in Fried's book, *Contract as Promise*. Other approaches to contract theory are found in the writings of legal realists and critical legal studies theorists.

More generally, writers have propounded Marxist and feminist interpretations of contract. Attempts at overarching understandings of the purpose and nature of contract as a phenomenon have been made, notably "relational contract theory" originally developed by US contracts scholars Ian Roderick Macneil and Stewart Macaulay, building at least in part on the contract theory work of US scholar Lon L. Fuller, while US scholars have been at the forefront of developing economic theories of contract focussing on questions of transaction cost and so-called "efficient breach" theory.

Another dimension of the theoretical debate in contract is its place within, and relationship to a wider law of obligations. Obligations have traditionally been divided into contracts, which are voluntarily undertaken and owed to a specific person or persons, and obligations in tort which are based on the wrongful infliction of harm to certain protected interests, primarily imposed by the law, and typically owed to a wider class of persons.

Recently it has been accepted that there is a third category, restitutionary obligations, based on the unjust enrichment of the defendant at the plaintiff's expense. Contractual liability, reflecting the constitutive function of contract, is generally for failing to make things better (by not rendering the expected performance), liability in tort is generally for action (as opposed to omission) making things worse, and liability in restitution is for unjustly taking or retaining the benefit of the plaintiff's money or work.

The common law describes the circumstances under which the law will recognize the existence of rights, privilege or power arising out of a promise.

Notes

1. Contract Law 《合同法》

本单元主要介绍合同的概念和法律性质、要约和承诺、对价、合同形式、合同种类、合同效力、虚假陈述等内容。

2. specific performance of the contract 合同实际履行

实际履行与禁令(injunction)是衡平法的重要违约救济制度,衡平法是为了补充和匡正当时的普通法而产生的。普通法的救济方式主要是金钱赔偿和返还财产,衡平法发展了实际履行和禁令。

3. French Civil Code 《法国民法典》

1804年颁布的《法国民法典》又称《拿破仑法典》,是第一部资本主义国家和以资本主义经济制度为基础的近代民法典。该法典与当时的自由竞争经济条件相适应,体现了"个人最大限度的自由、法律最小限度的干预"这样的立法精神。其基本原则是:全体公民民事权利平等的原则、绝对所有权制度、契约自由及过失责任原则等,这些都是代表着资产阶级的自然法领域中的"天赋人权"理论在此民法典中的体现。而私权神圣的核心就是所有权绝对。由于该法典的系统性、完整性和规范性,因而对后来其他资本主义的立法产生了巨大影响,其内在的价值和思想即使在今天仍具有重要意义。

4. Consideration 对价

对价又称做约因,是英美合同法中的重要概念,也是合同法上的效力原则,其本意是为换取另一个人做某事的允诺某人付出的不一定是金钱的代价。换言之,对价是指当事人一方在获得某种利益时必须给付对方相应的代价。对价的必要条件是:对价必须合法,对价须是待履行或已履行的对价,过去的对价不能构成有效的对价,已经存在的义务和法律义务不能作为对价,对价须具有真实价值(但毋需完全等价),对价必须来自受允诺人包括其代理人,放弃有效的诉权构成对价,部分支付不能作为偿还全部债务的有效对价(但这一规则受到禁反言规则的制约)。

5. mirror image rule 镜像规则

镜像规则是普通法上的传统制度,1887年的Langellier v. Shaefer一案中曾对这一规则作出经典的归纳:"一方对另一方所发出的交易要约施加责任于前者,除非后者根据要约的条款对其予以承诺。任何对这些条款的修改和背离都将使要约无效,除非要约方同意这种修改和背离。"镜像规则要求承诺严格地与要约相符,否则将被视为反要约。美国《统一商法典》(UCC)则在相当的程度上实现了对"镜像规则"的变革,集中体现在UCC第2—207条的规定上。该条第1款规定:明确且及时表示的承诺或者在合理时间内发出的确认书生承诺之效力,即使它规定了与要约条款或双方约定之条款不同的附加条款,但承诺人明确表示其承诺以要约人同意该附加条款或不同条款为条件的除外。这一款的规定废弃了镜像规则中承诺必须与要约相一致的要求,只要是明确及时的非限定性承诺即可生效,使得格式之战下合同的成立较为轻易。UCC考虑到商人很少关心和阅读合同背面的一般条件,视之为陈词滥调，假如买方发出订单，卖方发回销售确认，只要双方文件中的正面条件（品种、数量、价格）相符，即使背面条款不符，合同仍可成立。UCC 的此种考虑在格式之战条件下是有其现实意义的，避免了大量正面条件已达成一致的合同因背面条款相歧而归于不成立，或将它们成立与否归因于此后捉摸不定的当事人行为，缓消了镜像规则所表现出来的僵硬和机械，有利于商业交易的进行。

6. Uniform Commercial Code 《统一商法典》

美国《统一商法典》是在美国统一州法全国委员会和美国法学会联合组织制定的一部示范法，1952 年正式公布。它分为 11 章（Article），以总则（General Provisions）和各分则的形式，对现实中的商事规则和商事惯例进行了归纳和制度层面的架构。基本消除了各州商法对州际交易因规定不同而造成的障碍，实现了美国商法在州际交易范围内，关于销售、票据、担保、信贷各领域规定的统一（除路易斯安那州之外的其他各州采纳了这部法典），并为各类商事交易活动提供了优良的模式，被美国国内乃至国际商事社会广泛采用和吸收，实现了商法的国际性。

7. Offer and Acceptance 要约和承诺

要约是当事人一方向对方发出的希望与对方订立合同的意思表示。发出要约的一方称要约人（offeror），接收要约的一方称受要约人（offeree）。承诺是受要约人同意要约的意思表示，即受约人同意接受要约的全部条件而与要约人订立合同。承诺应当以通知的方式作出，但根据交易习惯或者要约表明可以通过行为作出承诺的除外。承诺的法律效力在于，承诺一经作出并送达要约人，合同即告成立，要约人不得加以拒绝。

8. misrepresentation 虚假陈述

虚假陈述就是主体作出的与事实不符的言词或行为。虚假陈述的情形非常复杂，它可能会诱使他人订立某项合同，也可能对他人的合法权益造成侵害，还有可能是作为违约行为的表现方式。英美法中的虚假陈述通常是指引诱他人订立合同的虚假言词或行为。

9. force majeure 不可抗力

不可抗力条款是规定在合同订立后发生当事人在订合同时不能预见、不能避免、不可控制的意外事故，以致不能履行合同或不能如期履行合同时，遭受不可抗力的一方可以免除履行合同的责任的条款。不可抗力的法律后果是解除合同、延迟履行。不可抗力主要包括以下几种情形：自然灾害（如台风、洪水、地震等）、政府行为（如征收、征用等）、社会事件（如罢工、骚乱等）。

Study Questions

1. What is a contract?
2. How is a contract concluded?
3. How do you understand "consideration"?
4. What do you think of the remedies for breach of contract in equity?

Case Study

Gordon v. Selico (1986) is an English contract law on the subject of misrepresentation by action.

Facts

Mr Gordon and Mrs Teixeira, contracted in November 1978 to purchase a 99-year lease of a flat owned by the defendant, Selico Ltd. The flat was in poor condition, as was the block that contained it, with some evidence of dry rot. Prior to the first inspection by the plaintiffs in about November 1978, the second defendants had instructed some painters to conceal patches of dry rot from view, by painting them. The plaintiffs obtained a detailed survey of the flat in February 1979, which concluded that no dry rot had been found (although only one floorboard had been lifted, and it could not be guaranteed that it did not exist elsewhere in the flat). The plaintiffs moved into their flat on January 1, 1980, and subsequently discovered extensive dry rot in the front bedroom, bathroom, and lavatory.

Judgment

Ordinarily, a misrepresentation is made by a statement of supposed fact, or otherwise a statement of intent. It was held by the Court of Appeal that the painting of dry rot to conceal it amounted to a misrepresentation. The court distinguished the set of facts from other cases, where it was held that reliance on an independent surveyor's findings defeated a claim of misrepresentation:

Furthermore, he observed, the plaintiffs and their surveyor had ample opportunity to inspect the flat, an opportunity of which they availed themselves. In these circumstances, decisions such as Horsfall v. Thomas and Smith v. Hughes, precluded the plaintiffs from complaining of any misrepresentation.

Both these two cases, however, are distinguishable from the present on their facts. In the former, not only was the defect in the gun patent and discoverable on inspection, but the purchaser took no steps to inspect it, so that he did in fact not rely on any misrepresentation as to its condition which might have been made. In the latter case, the vendor did nothing to disguise the character of the oats sold. In the present case, on the learned judge's relevant findings of fact, with which we see no reason to disagree, not only was a fraudulent misrepresentation made, which was intended to mislead prospective purchasers of a lease of the property; the misrepresentation did mislead the purchasers and they acted on it to their detriment. In these circumstances, it is in our judgment no answer in law to the claim in deceit for the defendants to say that the plaintiffs or their surveyor could have discovered the dry rot on a closer inspection of Flat C or were content to purchase without any warranty as to the condition of the property; they and their surveyor were in fact misled by the cover-up operation, as they were intended to be. The general principle caveat emptor has no application where a purchaser has been induced to enter the contract of purchase by fraud. Nor can Clause 4(2)(a) of the Law Society's Conditions of Sale avail a vendor in these circumstances. These subsidiary submissions made by way of defence to the claim based on deceit are not in our judgment well founded.

Sources of Information and Further Readings

1. Mekendrik, Ewan. *Contract Law-Text, Cases and Materials.* Oxford University Press, 2005.
2. Atiyah, P. S. *The Rise and Fall of Freedom of Contract.* Clarendon Press, 1979.
3. Barnett, R. E. *Contracts.* Aspen Publishers, 2003.
4. http://www.expertlaw.com/library/business/contract_law.html
5. http://en.wikipedia.org/wiki/Contract

Chapter 8

United Nations Convention on Contracts for the International Sale of Goods[1]

Key Concepts

offer invitation for offer acceptance anticipatory of the contract
fundamental breach of the contract preservation of the goods

Learning Objectives

1. Understand the concept of "offer" and "acceptance".
2. Understand the differences between withdrawal of an offer and revocation of an offer.
3. Understand the obligations of the seller and the buyer.
4. Understand remedies of the breach of the contract by the seller and the buyer respectively.

Offer

An offer means a proposal for concluding a contract addressed to one or more specific persons. The offer shall be sufficiently definite and indicates the intention of the offeror to be bound in case of acceptance. A proposal is sufficiently definite if it indicates the goods and expressly or implicitly fixes or makes provisions for determining the quantity and the price. So an effective offer shall be in line with the minimum requirements of this convention. An offer becomes effective when it reaches the offeree.

Invitation for Offer[2]

A proposal other than one addressed to one or more specific persons is to be considered merely as an invitation to make offers, unless the contrary is clearly indicated by the person making the proposal. In practice, catalogues of the goods, price list, public announcement of auction or tender, prospectus, commercial advertisements, etc, are usually taken as invitation for offer. In some countries, if the contents of the commercial advertisement are sufficiently definite, and it is made to the public as an offer, it shall constitute an offer. For instance, the commercial advertisement states that it constitutes an offer, or the goods under this advertisement will be sold to those who are the first to pay cash, or open L/C.

Withdrawal and Revocation of an Offer[3]

Withdrawal means that the offeror takes the offer back, making it void, before it reaches the offeree and becomes effective. While revocation means that the offeror revokes it so as to make it void after the offer reaches the offeree, and becomes effective. Withdrawal or revocation has great significance in international trade. The offeror may withdraw or revoke the offer if he makes a mistake in the offer, or due to the fluctuation of the market price. An offer may be revoked if the revocation reaches the offeree before he has dispatched an acceptance. An offer can not be revoked if it states a fixed time for acceptance or otherwise, that it is irrevocable, or if it was reasonable for the offeree to rely on the offer as being irrevocable and the offeree has acted in reliance on the offer. An offer, even if it is irrevocable, may be withdrawn if the withdrawal reaches the offeree before or at the same time as the offer.

Acceptance[4]

An acceptance means a statement made by or other conduct of the offeree indicating assent to an offer. Silence or inactivity does not amount to acceptance. An acceptance of an offer becomes effective at the moment the indication of assent reaches the offeror. An acceptance is not effective if the indication of assent does not reach the offeror within the time he has fixed or, if no time is fixed, within a reasonable time. An oral offer must be accepted immediately unless the circumstances indicate otherwise. The offeree may indicate assent by performing an act, such as one relating to the dispatch of the goods or payment of the price, without notice to the offeror, the acceptance is effective at the moment the act is performed, provided that the act is performed within the period of time.

A reply to an offer which purports to be an acceptance but contains additions, limitations or other modifications is a rejection of the offer and constitute a counteroffer[5]. Nevertheless, if certain additional or different terms in a reply to an offer do not materially alter[6] the terms of the offer, the reply shall constitute an acceptance, unless the offeror, without undue delay, objects orally to the discrepancy or dispatches a notice to that effect. Additional or different terms relating to the price, payment, quality and quantity of the goods, place and time of delivery, extent of one party's liability to the other or the settlement of disputes are considered to alter the terms of the offer materially.

If a notice of acceptance can not be delivered at the address of the offeror on the last day of the period because that day falls on an official holiday or a non-business day at the place of the offeror, the period is extended until the first business day which follows. If its transmission had been normal it would have reached the offeror in due time, the late acceptance is effective as an acceptance unless, without delay, the offeror informs the offeree that he considers his offer as having lapsed. An acceptance may be withdrawn if the withdrawal reaches the offeror before or at the same time as the acceptance would have become effective.

A contract is concluded at the moment when an acceptance of an offer becomes effective in accordance with the provisions of this convention.

Obligations of the Seller

Delivery of the Goods and Handing Over of Documents

The seller must deliver the goods, hand over any documents relating to them and transfer the property in the goods as required by the contract. The seller must deliver the goods at the time required by the contract, or in any other case, within a reasonable time after the conclusion of the contract. If the seller is not bound to deliver the goods at any other particular place, he shall hand the goods over to the first carrier for transmission to the buyer, provided that the contract involves carriage of the goods. If the seller is not bound to effect insurance in respect of the carriage of the goods, he must, at the buyer's request, provide him with all available information necessary to enable him to effect such insurance. If the seller is bound to hand over documents relating to the goods, he must hand them over at the time and place and in the form required by the contract.

Conformity of the Goods and Third Party Claims

The quantity, quality and descriptions of the goods delivered by the seller shall be in conformity with those required by the contract. The goods are contained or packaged in the manner required by the contract. The seller is liable in accordance with the contract for any lack of conformity which exists at the time when the risk passes to the buyer, even though the lack of conformity becomes apparent only after that time. The seller is also liable for any lack of conformity which is due to a breach of his obligations, including a breach of any guarantee that for a period of time the goods will remain fit for their ordinary purpose or for some particular purpose or will retain specified qualities or characteristics.

In any event, the buyer loses the right to rely on a lack of conformity of the goods if he does not give the seller notice thereof at the latest within a period of two years from the date on which the goods were actually handed over to the buyer, unless this time limit is inconsistent with a contractual period of guarantee.

The seller must deliver goods which are free from any right or claim of a third party, unless the buyer agreed to take the goods subject to that right or claim. The seller must deliver the goods which are free from any right or claim of a third party based on industrial property or other intellectual property, of which at the time of the conclusion of the contract the seller knew or could not have been unaware, provided that the right or claim is based on industrial property or other industrial property, (a) under the law of the State where the goods will be resold or otherwise used, if it was contemplated by the parties at the time of the conclusion of the contract that the goods would be resold or otherwise used in that State; (b) in any other case, under the law of the state where the buyer has his place of business. Nevertheless, the seller's obligation is not governed if, at the time of the conclusion of the contract the buyer knew or could not have been unaware of the right or claim; or the right or claim results from the seller's compliance with technical drawings, designs, formulae or other such specifications furnished by the buyer.

Remedies for Breach of the Contract by the Seller[7]

If the seller fails to perform any of his obligations under the contract, the buyer may act as follows:

- The buyer may require performance by the seller of his obligations.
- If the goods do not conform with the contract, the buyer may require delivery of substitute goods only if the lack of conformity constitute a fundamental breach of the contract[8].
- If the goods do not conform with the contract, the buyer may require the seller to remedy the lack of conformity by repair.
- The buyer may declare the contract avoided if the seller's failure to perform any of his obligations under the contract amounts to a fundamental breach of the contract, or in case of non-delivery, if the seller does not deliver the goods within the additional period of time fixed by the buyer.
- If the goods do not conform with the contract and whether or not the price has already been paid, the buyer may reduce the price in the same proportion as the value that the goods actually delivered had at the time of the delivery bears to the value that conforming goods would have had at that time.
- If the seller delivers the goods before the date fixed, the buyer may take delivery or refuse to take delivery.
- If the seller delivers a quantity of the goods greater than that provided for in the contract, the buyer may take delivery or refuse to take delivery of the excess quantity. If the buyer takes delivery of all or part of the excess quantity, he must pay for it at the contract rate.
- The buyer is not deprived of any right he may have to claim damages by exercising his right to other remedies.

Obligations of the Buyer

The buyer must pay the price of the goods and take delivery of them as required by the contract. If the price is fixed according to the weight of the goods, in case of doubt it is to be determined by the net weight. The buyer must pay the price on the date fixed by or determinable from the contract without the need for any request or compliance with any formality on the part of the seller. The buyer's obligation to take delivery consists in doing all the acts which could reasonably be expected of him in order to enable the seller to make delivery, and taking over the goods.

Remedies for Breach of the Contract by the Buyer

If the buyer fails to perform any of his obligations under the contract,

- the seller may require the buyer to pay the price, take delivery or perform his other obligations, unless the seller has resorted to a remedy which is inconsistent with this requirement;
- the seller may fix an additional period of time of reasonable length for performance by the buyer of his obligations;
- the seller may declare the contract avoided if the failure by the buyer to perform any of his obligations under the contract amounts to a fundamental breach of contract; or if the buyer does not perform his obligations within the additional period of time fixed by the seller, or if he declares that he will not do so within the period so fixed;
- the seller is not deprived of any right he may have to claim damages by exercising his right to other remedies;
- no period of grace may be granted to the buyer by a court or arbitral tribunal when the seller resorts to a remedy for breach of contract.

Passing of Risks

Loss of or damages to the goods after the risk has passed to the buyer does not discharge him from his obligation to pay the price, unless the loss or damage is due to an act or omission of the seller.

If the contract of sale involves carriage of the goods and the seller is not bound to hand them over at a particular place, the risk passes to the buyer when the goods are handed over to the first carrier for transmission to the buyer in accordance with the contract. If the seller is bound to hand the goods over to a carrier at a particular place, the risk does not pass to the buyer until the goods are handed over to the carrier at that place. The fact that the seller is authorized to retain documents controlling the disposition of the goods does not affect the passage of the risk. The risk in respect of goods sold in transit passes to the buyer from the time of the conclusion of the contract. Nevertheless, if at the time of the conclusion of the contract the seller knew or ought to have known that the goods had been lost or damaged and did not disclose this to the buyer, the loss or damage is at the risk of the seller. In other cases, the risk passes to the buyer when he takes over the goods or, if he does not do so in due time, from the time when the goods are placed at his disposal and he commits a breach of the contract by failing to take delivery.

Anticipatory Breach[9]

A party may suspend the performance of his obligations if, after the conclusion of the contract, it becomes apparent that the other party will not perform a substantial part of his obligations as a result of a serious deficiency in his ability of performance or in his creditworthiness, or his conduct in preparing to perform or in performing the contract. A party suspending performance, whether before or after dispatch of the goods, must immediately give notice of suspension to the other party and must continue with performance if the other party provides adequate assurance of his performance.

Installment Contract

In the case of the contract for delivery of goods by installments, if the failure of one party to perform any of his obligations in respect of any installment constitutes a fundamental breach of the contract with respect to that installment, the other party may declare the contract avoided with respect to that installment. If one party's failure to perform any of his obligations gives the other party good grounds to conclude that a fundamental breach of contract will occur with respect to future installments, he may declare the contract avoided for the future, provided that he does so within a reasonable time. The buyer who declares the contract avoided in respect of any delivery may, at the same time, declare it avoided in respect of deliveries already made or of future deliveries if, by reason of their interdependence, those deliveries could not be used for the purpose contemplated by the parties at the time of the conclusion of the contract.

Damages

Damages for breach of contract by one party consist of a sum equal to the loss, including loss of profit, suffered by the other party as a consequence of the breach. The party claiming damages may recover the difference between the contract price and the price in the substitute transaction as well as any further damages, such as the loss of profit, or the difference between the price fixed by the contract and the current price at the time of avoidance of the contract under differently circumstances.

The party who relies on a breach a contract must take reasonable measures to mitigate the loss, including the loss of profit, resulting from the breach. If he fails to take such measures, the party in breach may claim a reduction in the damages in the amount by which the loss should have been mitigated.

Furthermore, if a party fails to pay the price or any other sum that is in arrears, the other party is entitled to interest on it, without prejudice to any claim for other damages.

Exemption

A party who is not liable for any failure to perform any of his obligations if he proves that the failure was due to an impediment beyond his control[10] and he could not reasonably be expected to have taken the impediment into account at the time of the conclusion of the contract or to have avoided or overcome it or its consequences. The exemption has effect for the period which the impediment exists.

A party may not rely on a failure of the other party to perform to the extent that such failure was caused by the first party's act or omission.

Effects of Avoidance

Avoidance of the contract releases both parties from their obligations under it, subject to any damages which may be due. A voidance does not affect any provisions of the contract for the settlement of disputes or any other provisions of the contract governing the rights and obligations of the parties consequent upon the avoidance of the contract.

A party who has performed the contract either wholly or in part may claim restitution from the other party of whatever the first party has supplied or paid under the contract. If both parties are bound to make restitution, they must do so concurrently.

If the seller is bound to refund the price, he must also pay interest on it, from the date on which the price was paid.

The buyer must account to the seller for all benefits which he has derived from the goods or part of them if he must make restitution of the goods or part of them.

Preservation of the Goods[11]

If the buyer is in delay in taking delivery of the goods or, where payment of the price and delivery of the goods to be made concurrently, if he fails to pay the price, and the seller is either in possession of the goods or other wise able to control their disposition, the seller must take steps as are reasonable in the circumstances to preserve the goods. He is entitled to retain them until he has been reimbursed for his reasonable expenses by the buyer.

If the buyer has received the goods and intends to exercise the right under the contract or this convention to reject them, he must take such steps to preserve them, and is entitled to retain them until he has been reimbursed his reasonable expenses by the seller.

If the goods dispatched to the buyer have been placed at his disposal at their destination and he exercises the right to reject them, he must take possession of them on behalf of the seller, provided that this can be done without payment of the price and without unreasonable inconvenience or unreasonable expenses. This provision does not apply if the seller or a person authorized to take charge of the goods.

A party who is bound to preserve the goods may deposit them in a warehouse of a third person at the expense of the other party provided that the expense incurred is not unreasonable.

A party who is bound to preserve the goods may sell them by any appropriate means if there has been an unreasonable delay by the other party in taking possession of the goods or in taking them back or in paying the price or the cost of preservation, provided that reasonable notice of the intention to sell has been given to the other party. If the goods are subject to deterioration or their preservation would involve unreasonable expense, a party who is bound to preserve the goods must take reasonable measures to sell them. To the extent possible he must give notice to the other party of his intention to sell.

A party selling the goods has right to retain out of the proceeds of sale an amount equal to the reasonable expenses of preserving the goods and of selling them.

He must account to the other party for the balance.

Notes

1. **United Nations Convention on Contracts for the International Sale of Goods 《联合国国际货物销售合同公约》**

    该公约于1980年通过,并已于1988年1月1日起正式生效。该公约既考虑到大陆法系国家的合同法,亦考虑到英美法系国家的相关法律,是迄今为止关于国际货物买卖的一个最重要的国际公约。至1998年5月31日,已有51个国家加入该公约。我国于1986年加入该公约,但在加入时就合同形式(form of the contract)及适用范围(sphere of its application)作出了保留,即:要求合同采用书面形式;公约的适用范围限于双方的营业地处于不同缔约国的当事人之间所订立的货物买卖合同。

2. **invitation for offer 要约邀请**

    要约邀请是指当事人向他人作出的希望对方向自己发出要约的意思表示。

3. **withdrawal and revocation of an offer 要约撤回和撤销**

    撤回是指要约在生效前收回,而撤销则指的是要约生效后的收回。

4. **acceptance 承诺**

    承诺是指受要约人对要约表示无条件接受的意思表示。

5. **counteroffer 反要约**

    在外贸实务中又称"还盘",反要约应视为一项新要约。

6. **materially alter 实质性变更**

    实质性变更是指对要约中的价格、货物质量、数量、付款、交货时间或地点、赔偿责任、争议解决中的任何一项作出添加或变更。若受要约人对要约作了实质性的变更,那就不能视为对要约的承诺,而是一项反要约。

7. **Remedies for Breach of the Contract by the Seller 对卖方违约的补救方法**

    比如,要求卖方实际履行、减少价款、宣告合同无效、损害赔偿。应注意的是,买方享有要求损害赔偿的权利不因其行使其他救济办法的权利而丧失。

8. **fundamental breach of the contract 根本违约**

    根本违约是指一方违反合同,致使另一方根据合同有权期待得到的东西落空。是否构成根本违约,对当事人采取何种救济措施有直接的关系。如果已构成根本违约,受害方有权宣告撤销合同,反之则不能。

9. **Anticipatory Breach 预期违约**

    预期违约是指履约期限到来之前,一方无正当理由而明确表示将不履行合同(明示毁约),或者其行为表明将不可能履约(默示毁约)。

10. **an impediment beyond his control 非他所能控制的障碍**

    此处实际上指的是"不可抗力"(force majeure),即一方所难以预见、难以避免、难以克服的客观情况。

11. Preservation of the Goods 货物保全

通常在买方迟延收取货物、迟延支付价款时，如货物仍在卖方的掌控中，卖方应采取合理措施以保全货物。如果货物已到达目的地或买方在收到货物后打算退货，买方亦应采取保全措施，如将货物存放在第三方的仓库。而货物保全的合理费用则由另一方承担。

Study Questions

1. What is offer?
2. What is acceptance of an offer?
3. Briefly explain the seller's obligation.
4. How do you think of the transfer of risks to the goods?
5. Are there any stipulations as regard the transfer of ownership in the convention? Why?

Case Study

Carlill v. Carbolic Smoke Ball Company

Facts

The Carbolic Smoke Ball Company made a product called the "smoke ball". It claimed to be a cure for influenza and a number of other diseases; in the context of the 1889 – 1890 flu pandemic which is estimated to have killed 1 million people. The smoke ball was a rubber ball with a tube attached. It was filled with carbolic acid (phenol). The tube was then inserted into the user's nose. It was squeezed at the bottom to release the vapours into the nose of the user. This would cause the nose to run, and hopefully flush out the viral infection.

The Company published advertisements in the *Pall Mall Gazette* and other newspapers on November 13, 1891, claiming that it would pay 100 to anyone who got sick with influenza after using its product according to the instructions set out in the advertisement.

"100 reward will be paid by the Carbolic Smoke Ball Company to any person who contracts the increasing epidemic influenza colds, or any disease caused by taking cold, after having used the ball three times daily for two weeks, according to the printed directions supplied with each ball.

1,000 is deposited with the Alliance Bank, Regent Street, showing our sincerity in the matter.

During the last epidemic of influenza many thousand carbolic smoke balls were sold as preventives against this disease, and in no ascertained case was the disease contracted by those using the carbolic smoke ball.

One carbolic smoke ball will last a family several months, making it the cheapest remedy in the world at the price, 10s. post free. The ball can be refilled at a cost of 5s. Address: "Carbolic Smoke Ball Company, 27, Princes Street, Hanover Square, London."

Mrs. Louisa Elizabeth Carlill saw the advertisement, bought one of the balls and used three times daily for nearly two months until she contracted the flu on January 17, 1892. She claimed 100 from the Carbolic Smoke Ball Company. They ignored two letters from her husband, who had trained as a solicitor. On a third request for her reward, they replied with an anonymous letter that if it is used properly the company had complete confidence in the smoke ball's efficacy, but "to protect themselves against all fraudulent claims" they would need her to come to their office to use the ball each day and be checked by the secretary. Mrs. Carlill brought a claim to court. The barristers representing her argued that the advertisement and her reliance on it was a contract between her and the company, and so they ought to pay. The company argued it was not a serious contract.

Judgment

The Carbolic Smoke Ball Company, despite being represented by HH Asquith, lost its argument at the Queen's Bench. It appealed straight away. The Court of Appeal unanimously rejected the company's arguments and held that there was a fully binding contract for 100 with Mrs. Carlill. Among the reasons given by the three judges were (1) that the advert was a unilateral offer to all the world, (2) that satisfying conditions for using the smoke ball constituted acceptance of the offer, (3) that purchasing or merely using the smoke ball constituted good consideration, because it was a distinct detriment incurred at the behest of the company and, furthermore, more people buying smoke balls by relying on the advert was a clear benefit to Carbolic, and (4) that the company's claim that 1,000 was deposited at the Alliance Bank showed the serious intention to be legally bound.

Sources of Information and Further Readings

1. United Nations Convention on Contracts for the International Sale of Goods (CISG), 1980.
2. August, Ray. *International Business Law*. Pearson Education Ltd, 2004.
3. Mo, J. S. *International Commercial Law*. Lexis Nexis, 2003.
4. http://en.wikipedia.org/wiki/United_Nations_Convention_on_Contracts_for_the_International_Sale_of_Goods
5. http://en.wikipedia.org/wiki/Carlill_v_Carbolic_Smoke_Ball_Company

Chapter 9

Contract Law in China[1]

Key Concepts

standard terms | right of demurrer for concurrent performance
right of demurrer for security | right of subrogation
right of revocation | deposit the object

Learning Objectives

1. Understand the concept of "standard terms".
2. Understand the types of demurrer's rights.
3. Understand the right of subrogation in contract law.
4. Understand the right of revocation in contract law.

The contract law is designed to protect the lawful rights and interests of the parties to the contract, maintain the social economic order and promote the social economic development. The contract refers to an agreement establishing, modifying and/or terminating the civil rights and obligations between subjects of equal status, that is, between natural persons, legal persons or other organizations. The parties to a contract shall have equal legal status, and have the rights to be voluntary to enter into a contract in accordance with the law. No party may impose its will on the other party, and no unit or individual may illegal interfere. In concluding a contract, the parties shall have appropriate civil capacity of right and civil capacity of conduct[2].

The parties may conclude a contract through an agent according to the law. The parties to a contract shall abide by the principle of fairness in defining the rights and obligations, and act in accordance with the principle of good faith in exercising rights or in performing obligations. The contract concluded in accordance with the law is under the protection of the law. In concluding and executing the contract, the parties shall observe the laws and administrative regulations, observe the social ethics. No party may harm the public interests or disrupt the social economic order.

Conclusion of the Contract

Forms of the Contract

The contract may be in written, oral or other forms. Where the laws or administrative regulations require a contract to be concluded in written form, the contract shall be in written form. The written form mean the form which can show the described contents visibly, such as a written contractual agreement, letters, and data-telex (including telegram, telex, fax, EDI and e-mail).

Contents of the Contract

The contents of the contract shall be decided and agreed upon by the parties. In general, the following clauses can be contained:

- title or name and domicile of the parties
- contract object
- quantity
- quality
- price or remuneration
- time limit, place and method of performance
- liability for breach of the contract
- methods to settle disputes

The parties may conclude a contract by reference to the model text of each kind of contract. In practice, the model text of each kind of contract can be adopted by the parties as a reference.

Offer and Acceptance

The parties shall conclude a contract in the form of an offer and acceptance. An offer is a proposal hoping to enter into a contract with other parties. The contents of an offer shall be detailed and definite. An offer indicates the offeror to be bound in case of acceptance of the proposal. An invitation for offer is a proposal for requesting other parties to make offers to the principal. Price list to be mailed, public announcement of auction or tender, commercial advertisements, and prospectus, etc are invitation for offer. Where the contents of a commercial advertisement comply with the terms of the offer, it shall be regarded as offer. An offer becomes effective when it reaches the offeree. An offer may be withdrawn, if the withdrawal notice reaches the offeree before or at the same time when the offer arrives. Theoretically speaking, it does work, but in the present society, an offer is made by means of instantaneous communication, such as telephone, facsimile or e-mail, it is almost impossible to do so in practice. An offer may be revoked, if the revocation reaches the offeree before it has dispatched an acceptance. An offer shall not be revoked if the offeror indicates a fixed time for acceptance or otherwise explicitly states that the offer is irrevocable, or the offeree has reasons to rely on the offer as being irrevocable and has made preparation for performing the contract. An offer shall be null and void[3] under the following circumstances:

- The notice of rejection reaches the offeror;
- The offeror revokes its offer according to the law;
- The offeree fails to make an acceptance within the time limit fixed in the offer;
- The offeree substantially alters the contents of the offer.

An acceptance is a statement made by the offeree indicating assent to an offer. An acceptance shall reach the offeror within the time limit fixed in the offer. Where no time limit is fixed in the offer, the acceptance shall arrive within a reasonable period of time. An acceptance becomes effective when its notice reaches the offeror. If an acceptance needn't be notified, it becomes effective when an act of acceptance is performed in accordance with transaction practice or as required in the offer. A contract is established when the acceptance becomes effective. An acceptance may be withdrawn if a notice of withdrawal reaches the offeror before or at the same time when the notice of acceptance reaches the offeror. Where the offeree makes an acceptance beyond the time limit for acceptance, the acceptance shall be a new offer except that the offoror informs the offeree of the effectiveness of the said acceptance promptly. The contents of an acceptance shall comply with those of the offer. If the offeree substantially modifies the contents of the offer, it shall constitute a new offer. The modification relating to the contract object, quality, quantity, price or remuneration, time limit or place or method of performance, liability for breach of the contract and settlement of disputes, etc shall constitute the substantial modification of an offer. If the acceptance does not substantially modifies the contents of the offer, it shall be effective, and the contents of the contract shall be subject to those of the acceptance, excepted as rejected promptly by the offeror or indicated in the offer that an acceptance shall not modify the offer at all. Where the parties adopt a written contract, the contract is established when both parties sign or affix a seal on it. Where the parties conclude the contract in the form of a letter or data-telex, etc, one party may request to sign a letter of confirmation before the conclusion of the contract. The contract shall be established at the time when the letter of confirmation is signed.

Standard Terms[4]

Standard terms are clauses which are prepared in advance for repeated use by one party and which are not negotiated with the other party in concluding a contract. Where standard terms are adopted in concluding a contract, the party which supplies the standard terms shall follow the principle of fairness in defining the rights and obligations between the parties, and request the other party to note the exclusion or restriction of its liabilities in reasonable ways, and explain the standard terms according to the requirement of the other party. If the dispute over the interpretation of the standard terms occurs, it shall be interpreted according to general understanding. Where there are two or more kinds of interpretations, an interpretation unfavorable to the party supplying the standard terms shall be preferred. Where the standard terms are inconsistent with non-standard terms, the latter shall be adopted.

Effectiveness of the Contract

The contract established in accordance with the law becomes effective when it is established. With regard to contracts which shall be subject to approval or registration as provided for by the laws or administrative regulations, the provisions thereof shall be followed. A contract concluded by a person with limited civil capacity of conduct[5] shall be effective after being ratified afterwards by the person's statutory agent. But a pure profit-making contract or a contract concluded which is appropriate to the person's age, intelligence or mental health conditions need not be ratified by his statutory agent. The counterpart may urge the statutory agent to ratify the contract within one month. It shall be regarded as a refusal of ratification if the statutory agent does not make any expression. A bona-fide counterpart has the right to withdraw it before the contract is ratified. The withdrawal shall be made by means of notice. A contract concluded on behalf of the principal by an actor who has no power of agency, or oversteps the power of agency, or whose power of agency has expired shall have no legally binding force on the principal without ratification by the principal, and the actor shall be held reliable for any consequences arising hereof. But the bona fide counterpart has reason to trust that the actor has the power of agency, the act of agency shall be effective. A contract shall be null and void under any of the following circumstances:

- A contract is concluded through the use of fraud or coercion by one party to harm the interests of the state;
- Malicious collusion is conducted to damage the interests of the state, a collective or a third party;
- An illegal purpose is concealed under the guise of legitimate acts;
- Harming the public interests;
- Violating the compulsory provisions of the laws and administrative regulations.

A party shall have the right to request the court or an arbitration institution to modify or revoke the contract if it is concluded as a result of serious misunderstanding, or due to obvious unfairness at the time when the contract is concluded. Furthermore, if a contract is concluded by one party against the other party's true intentions through the use of fraud, coercion or exploitation of the other party's unfavorable position, the injured party shall have the right to request the court or an arbitration institution to modify or revoke it.

A contract that is null and void or revoked shall have no legally binding force ever from the very beginning. If part of the contract is null and void, the validity of the other parts is not affected, and shall still be valid. If the contract is null and void, revoked or terminated, it shall not affect the validity of the dispute settlement clause which is independently existing in the contract.

Performance of the Contract

The parties shall perform their obligations thoroughly according to the terms of the contract. The parties shall follow the principle of good faith and perform the obligations of notice, assistance and maintaining confidentiality, etc on the basis of the character, purpose or the transaction practices. Where there is no agreement in the contract on the terms regarding price, quality or remuneration and place of performance, etc or such agreement is unclear, the parties conclude supplementary terms through consultation. Where the parties agree that the obligor performs the obligations to a third party, and the obligor fails to do so, or the performance does not meet the terms of the contract, the obligor shall be liable to the obligee for the breach of the contract. Where the parties agree that a third party performs the obligations to the obligee, and the third party fails to do so, or the performance does not meet the terms of the contract, the obligor shall be liable to the obligee for the breach of the contract.

Right of Demurrer for Concurrent Performance[6]

If both parties have obligations towards each other and there is no order of priority in respect of the performance of obligations, the parties shall perform the obligations simultaneously. One party has the right to reject the other party's request for performance before the other party's performance. One party has the right to reject the other party's corresponding request for performance if the other party's performance does not meet the terms of the contract.

Right of Demurrer for Security[7]

One party which shall perform its obligations first, may suspend its performance, if it has conclusive evidence that the other party is under any of the following circumstances:

- Its business conditions are seriously deteriorating;
- It moves away its property and take out its capital secretly to evade debt;
- It loses its commercial credibility;
- Other circumstances showing that it loses or is possible to lose the capacity of credit.

One party to the contract which suspends its performance of the contract in accordance with the above-mentioned conditions, shall promptly inform the other party of such suspension. It shall resume its performance of the contract when the other party provides a sure guarantee (security). After the suspension of the performance, if the other party does not reinstate (resume) its capacity of performance and does not provide with adequate assurance of his performance, the party suspending performance of the contract may rescind the contract.

Right of Subrogation[8]

If the obligor is indolent in exercising its due creditor's right, thus damaging the interests of the obligee, the obligee may request the court for subrogation in its own name, except that the creditor's right exclusively belongs to the obligor. The subrogation shall be exercised within the scope of the creditor's right of the obligee. The necessary expenses caused to the obligee by exercising subrogation shall be borne by the obligor.

Right of Revocation

If the obligor renounces its due creditor's right or transfers its property gratis (free of charge), thus harming the interests of the obligee, the obligee may request the court to revoke the obligor's act. If the obligor transfers its property at an obviously unreasonable low price, thus harming the interests of the obligee, and the transferee knows such situation, the obligee may request the court to revoke the obligor's act.

Modification and Assignment of the Contract

A contract may be modified if the parties reach a consensus through consultation. If the laws or administrative regulations stipulate that a contract to be modified shall be subject to approval and registration, such provisions shall be followed.

The obligee assigning its rights shall notify the obligor. Without notification, the assignment shall not become effective to the obligor. If the obligor assigns its obligations, wholly or in part, to a third party, it shall obtain consent from the obligee first. One party to a contract may assign its rights and obligations under the contract together to a third party with the consent of the other party.

If one party to the contract is merged after the contract has been concluded, the legal person or other organization established after the merger shall exercise the contract rights and perform the contract obligations. If one party is separated after the contract has been concluded, the legal persons or other organizations thus established after separation shall exercise the contract rights or assume the contract obligations

Termination of the Rights and Obligations of the Contract

The rights and obligations of the contract shall be terminated under any of the following circumstances:

- The debt obligations have been performed in accordance with the terms of the contract;
- The contract has been rescinded;
- The debts have been offset against each other;
- The obligor has deposited the object according to the law;
- The debt obligations have been exempted by the obligee;
- The creditor's rights and debt obligations are assumed by the same person.

When the rights and obligations of the contract have been terminated, the parties to the contract shall, following the principle of good faith, perform such obligations as making a notice, providing assistance and maintaining confidentiality according to transaction practices.

The contract may be rescinded if the parties reach a consensus through consultation. The parties to the contract may rescind the contract under any of the following circumstances:

- The purpose of the contract is not able to be realized because of force majeure;
- One party expresses explicitly or indicates through its acts, before the expiry of the performance period, that it will not perform its principal debt obligations;
- One party delays in performing the principal debt obligations and fails, after being urged, to perform them within a reasonable time period;
- One party delays in performing the debt obligations or commits (performs) other acts in breach of the contract so that the purpose of the contract is not able to be realized.

The party to rescind the contract shall give a notice to the other party. The contract shall be rescinded upon the arrival of the notice to the other party.

Deposit the Object[9]

The obligor may deposit the object if the debt obligations are difficult to be performed under any of the following circumstances: (1) the obligee refuses to accept them without justified reasons; (2) the obligee is missing; (3) the obligee is deceased and the heir is not yet determined, or the obligee has lost his capacity of conduct and the guardian is not yet determined. If the object is not fit to be deposited or the deposit expenses are excessively high, the obligor may auction or sell the object and deposit the money obtained therefrom. The deposit departments are usually the courts or notary public.

Liability for Breach of the Contract

Where one party to the contract fails to perform the contract obligations or its performance fails to satisfy the terms of the contract, the party shall bear such liabilities for breach of the contract as to continue to perform its obligations, to take remedial measures, or to compensate for losses.

Where one party to the contract expresses explicitly or indicates through its acts that it will not perform the contract obligations, the other party may demand it to bear the liability for the breach of the contract before the expiry of the performance period.

If the quality fails to satisfy the terms of the contract, the breach of contract the liability for breach of the contract shall be assumed according to the terms of the contract agreed upon by the parties. If there is no such agreement in the contract, in light of the character of the object and degree of losses, the infringed party may request the other party to bear the liabilities for breach of the contract such as repairing, substituting, reworking, returning the goods, or reducing the price or remuneration.

According to the Guaranty Law of PRC, the parties may agree that one party pays a deposit to the other party as the guaranty for the creditor's rights. After the debt obligations are performed by the obligor, the deposit shall be returned or offset against the price. If the party which pays the deposit fails to perform the agreed debt obligations, it shall have no right to reclaim the deposit. If the party that receives the deposit fails to perform the agreed debt obligations, it shall return twice the amount of the deposit.

The parties may agree that one party shall pay a certain amount of penalties for breach of the contract, or may agree upon the calculating method of compensation for losses resulting from the breach of the contract. If the party pays the penalties in respect to the delay in performance, the party in breach shall still perform its obligations after paying the penalties.

Force majeure means the objective circumstances that are unforeseeable, unavoidable and insurmountable. One party that is unable to perform the contract because of force majeure cases, shall give a notice to the other party promptly so as to reduce the probable losses and provide evidence within a reasonable time period.

In case both parties to the contract violate the contract, they shall bear the liabilities respectively.

In case that the breach of the contract by one party infringes upon the other party's personal or property rights, the aggrieved party shall be entitled to request the other party to bear the liability for breach of the contract, or may claim the assumption of the liability of the infringing party according to the other laws.

Notes

1. Contract Law in China 《中国合同法》

《中国合同法》于1999年颁布,主要是平等主体之间的交易关系的法律,它主要规定合同的订立、合同的效力及合同的履行、变更、解除、保全及违约责任等问题。本单元需重点掌握格式条款、同时履行抗辩权、不安抗辩权、代为权、撤销权等概念。

2. civil capacity of right and civil capacity of conduct 民事权利能力和民事行为能力

前者是指自然人依法享有民事权利和承担民事义务的资格;后者则指自然人通过自己的行为来引起民事法律关系产生、变更、消灭,并承担相应法律后果的能力。

3. null and void 无效

近义词并用为英文合同的重要语言特征,再如,terms and conditions, provisions and stipulation,等等。

4. Standard Terms 格式条款

格式条款,主要是指当事人为了重复使用而预先拟定,并在订立合同时未与对方协商的条款。

5. limited civil capacity of conduct 限制民事行为能力

依照我国民法之规定,10周岁以上、18周岁以下的自然人以及不能完全辨认自己行为的精神病人为限制民事行为能力人。

6. Right of Demurrer for Concurrent Performance 同时履行抗辩权

同时履行抗辩权是指双务合同的当事人没有先后履行顺序的,一方在对方未为对待给付以前,可拒绝履行自己债务的权利。而先履行抗辩权则指当事人互负债务,有先后履行顺序的,先履行一方未按约履行之前,后履行的一方有权拒绝其履行请求。

7. Right of Demurrer for Security 不安抗辩权

不安抗辩权成立条件:双方因同一双务合同而互负债务;后给付人的履约能力明显降低,有不能履约之危险;未给付人未提供适当担保。

8. Right of Subrogation 代位权

此处是指因债务人怠于行使其到期债权,对债权人造成损害的债权人可以向法院申请以自己的名义代位行使债务人的债权。

9. Deposit the Object 提存标的物

在债权人无正当理由拒绝受领、债权人下落不明或债权人死亡或丧失行为能力且又未确定继承人或监护人的情形下,债务人将交付的标的物交给提存部门,以使合同权利义务终止。因此,提存的目的在于消灭债务人与债权人之间的合同关系。

Study Questions

1. What are the types of the demurrer's rights?
2. What is the right of subrogation?
3. Under what circumstances may the creditor enjoy the right of revocation?
4. How do you understand "Standard Terms" in the contract?
5. What are the different methods for settlement of contract disputes?

Case Study

试用英文对以下案例进行分析和讨论:

案例 1:国际货物买卖合同的成立

法国公司甲给中国公司乙发盘:"供应 50 台拖拉机,100 匹马力,每台 CIF 北京 4000 美元,合同订立后 3 个月装船,不可撤销即期信用证付款,请电复。"乙还盘:"接受你的发盘,在订立合同后立即装船。"双方的合同是否成立?为什么?(1992 年律师考试法学综合知识试卷简答第 3 题)

案例 2:要约的添加与修改

卖方 A 发出电报于 B:"确认售与你方 A 型起重机一架,请汇 1000 英镑,接款后 20 天内交货。"B 复电:"确认你方电报,我方购买 A 型起重机一架,条件按你方电报的规定,已汇交你方银行 1000 英镑,该款在交货前由银行代你方保管,请确认在本电日期 20 天内交货。"A 方没有回电,却以较高价格卖给第三方。B 遂向法院起诉。试问:A 与 B 双方的合同是否成立?为什么?(2003 年浙江省高等教育自学考试国际经济法概论试题 A 卷案例分析第 1 题)

案例 3:要约的实质性修改

中国山东某公司于 2003 年 6 月 14 日收到甲国某公司来电称:"×××设备 3560 台,每台 270 美元 CIF 青岛,7 月甲国×××港装船,不可撤销即期信用证支付,2003 年 6 月 22 日前复到有效。"中国山东公司于 2003 年 6 月 17 日复电:"若单价为 240 美元 CIF 青岛,可接受 3560 台×××设备;如有争议在中国国际经济贸易仲裁委员会仲裁。"甲国公司于 2003 年 6 月 18 日回电称仲裁条款可以接受,但价格不能减少。此时,该机器价格上涨,中方又于 2003 年 6 月 21 日复电:"接受你 14 日发盘,信用证已经由中国银行福建分行开出。"但甲国公司未予答复并将货物转卖他人。关于该案,依 1980 年《国际货物买卖合同公约》的规定,合同是否成立?(2004 司法考试卷一多选题第 73 题)

案例 4:要约是否一定要向一个或一个以上特定人发出

石炭酸烟丸的药品制造商甲(被告)刊载一则广告,声称:任何人根据指示的方法和在特定期间服用一颗药丸后,如果仍染上流行性感冒,可获得 100 英磅,并称已将 1000 英磅存入 X 银行,以示诚意。购药人(乙,原告)见此广告,信以为真,购买药丸并按说明书指示服用,但结果仍染上流行性感冒,遂向甲(被告)追讨 100 英磅。制药商甲(被告)以种种理由申辩,其中之一是要约不能向公众提出。法院受理该案,并作出了判决。

问:1. 乙提出的要求是否有理?甲应否支付 100 英磅?2. 要约是否可向公众提出?3. 甲的广告是否明确肯定,足以构成一项允诺?(1999 年北京市高等教育自学考试国际经济法概论试卷实例分析第 2 题)

Sources of Information and Further Readings

1. Mckendrick, Ewan. *Contract Law—Text, Cases and Materials.* Oxford University Press, 2005.
2. http://www.lawinfochina.com
3. Barnett, R. E. *Contracts.* Aspen Publishers, 2003.
4. http://www.expertlaw.com/library/business/contract_law.html
5. http://www.chinaiprlaw.com/english/laws/laws2.htm

Chapter 10

Corporate Law[1]

Key Concepts

board of directors
articles of incorporation
closely held corporations
corporate governance
pierce the corporate veil
publicly traded corporations
mercantilism
liquidations

Learning Objectives

1. Understand the history of corporation.
2. Be familiar with different varieties of corporate.
3. Be familiar with the characteristics of corporate.
4. Understand the modern corporate governance.

Introduction

Corporate law, the law of the most dominant kind of business enterprise in the modern world, regulates the formation, registration or incorporation, governance, operations and dissolution of corporations. It is the study of how shareholders, directors, employees, creditors, and other stakeholders such as consumers, the community and the environment interact with one another under the internal rules of the firm.

Corporate law is a part of a broader companies law (or the law of business associations) which is the field of law concerning companies and other business organizations. This includes corporations, partnerships and other associations which usually carry on some form of economic or charitable activity. The most prominent kind of company, usually referred to as a "corporation", is a "juristic person"[2], i. e., it has separate legal personality, and those who invest money into the business have limited liability for any losses the company makes, governed by corporate law. Other types of business associations can include partnerships (in the UK governed by the Partnership Act 1890), or trusts (like a pension fund) or companies limited by guarantee (like some universities or charities). Corporate law is about big business, which has separate legal personality, with limited liability or unlimited liability for its members or shareholders, who buy and sell their stocks depending on the performance of the board of directors. It deals with the firms that are incorporated or registered under the corporate or company law of a sovereign state or their subnational states. The four defining characteristics of the modern corporation are:

- Separate Legal Personality of the corporation (the right to sue and be sued in its own name, i. e., the law treats the company as a human being);
- Limited Liability of the shareholders (so that when the company is insolvent, they only owe the money that they subscribed for in shares);
- Shares (usually on a stock exchange, such as the London Stock Exchange, New York Stock Exchange or Euronext in Paris);
- Delegated Management, in other words, control of the company placed in the hands of a board of directors.

In most developed countries excluding the English speaking world, company boards are appointed as representatives of both shareholders and employees to "codetermine" company strategy. Corporate law is often divided into corporate governance[3] (which concerns the various power relations within a corporation) and corporate finance (which concerns the rules on how capital is used).

Definition of Corporate

A corporation is a legal entity that is created under the laws of a state designed to establish the entity as a separate legal entity having its own privileges and liabilities distinct from those of its members. There are many different forms of corporations, most of which are used to conduct business. Early corporations were established by charter (i. e. , by an *ad hoc* act passed by a parliament or legislature). Most jurisdictions now allow the creation of new corporations through registration.

The word "corporation" is generally synonymous with large publicly owned companies. In the United States, a company may or may not be a separate legal entity, and is often used synonymously with "firm" or "business". A corporation may accurately be called a company; however, a company should not necessarily be called a corporation, which has distinct characteristics. According to *Black's Law Dictionary*, in the US a company means "a corporation—or, less commonly, an association, partnership or union—that carries on industrial enterprise".

The defining feature of a corporation is its legal independence from the people who create it. If a corporation fails, its shareholders will lose their money, and employees will lose their jobs, though disproportionately affecting its workers as opposed to its upper executives. Shareholders, however owning a part piece of the company, are not liable for debts that remain owing to the corporation's creditors. This rule is called limited liability, and it is why corporations end with "Ltd." (or some variant like "Inc." and "plc").

But despite this, corporations are recognized by the law to have rights and responsibilities like actual people. Corporations can exercise human rights against real individuals and the state, and they may be responsible for human rights violations. Just as they are "born" into existence through its members obtaining a certificate of incorporation, they can "die" when they lose money into insolvency. Corporations can even be convicted of criminal offences, such as fraud and manslaughter.

History of Corporation

The word "corporation" derives from *corpus*, the Latin word for body, or a "body of people". Entities which carried on business and were the subjects of legal rights were found in ancient Rome, and the Maurya Empire in ancient India. In medieval Europe, churches became incorporated, as did local governments, such as the Pope and the City of London Corporation. The point was that the incorporation would survive longer than the lives of any particular member, existing in perpetuity. The alleged oldest commercial corporation in the world, the Stora Kopparberg mining community in Falun, Sweden, obtained a charter from King Magnus Eriksson in 1347. Many European nations chartered corporations to lead colonial ventures, such as the Dutch East India Company[4] or the Hudson's Bay Company, and these corporations came to play a large part in the history of corporate colonialism.

During the time of colonial expansion in the 17th century, the true progenitors of the modern corporation emerged as the "chartered company". Acting under a charter sanctioned by the Dutch government, the Dutch East India Company (VOC) defeated Portuguese forces and established itself in the Moluccan Islands in order to profit from the European demand for spices. Investors in the VOC were issued paper certificates as proof of share ownership, and were able to trade their shares on the original Amsterdam stock exchange. Shareholders are also explicitly granted limited liability in the company's royal charter. In the late 18th century, Stewart Kyd, the author of the first treatise on corporate law in English, defined a corporation as a collection of many individuals united into one body, under a special denomination, having perpetual succession under an artificial form, and vested, by policy of the law, with the capacity of acting, in several respects, as an individual, particularly of taking and granting property, of contracting obligations, and of suing and being sued, of enjoying privileges and immunities in common, and of exercising a variety of political rights, more or less extensive, according to the design of its institution, or the powers conferred upon it, either at the time of its creation, or at any subsequent period of its existence.

Mercantilism[5]

A bond issued by the Dutch East India Company, dating from 1623, for the amount of 2,400 florins. Labeled by both contemporaries and historians as "the grandest society of merchants in the universe", the British East India Company would come to symbolize the dazzlingly rich potential of the corporation, as well as new methods of business that could be both brutal and exploitive. On 31 December 1600, the English monarchy granted the company a 15-year monopoly on trade to and from the East Indies and Africa. By 1611, shareholders in the East India Company were earning an almost 150% return on their investment. Subsequent stock offerings demonstrated just how lucrative the Company had become. Its first stock offering in 1613 – 1616 raised by 418,000, and its first offering in 1617 – 1622 raised by 1.6 million.

In the United States, government chartering began to fall out of vogue in the mid-19th century. Corporate law at the time was focused on protection of the public interest, and not on the interests of corporate shareholders. Corporate charters were closely regulated by the states. Forming a corporation usually required an act of legislature. Investors generally had to be given an equal say in corporate governance, and corporations were required to comply with the purposes expressed in their charters. Many private firms in the 19th century avoided the corporate model for these reasons (Andrew Carnegie formed his steel operation as a limited partnership, and John D. Rockefeller set up Standard Oil as a trust). Eventually, state governments began to realize the greater corporate registration revenues available by providing more permissive corporate laws. New Jersey was the first state to adopt an "enabling" corporate law, with the goal of attracting more business to the state. Delaware followed, and soon became known as the most corporation-friendly state in the country after New Jersey raised taxes on the corporations, driving them out. New Jersey reduced these taxes after this mistake was realized, but by then it was too late; even today, most major public corporations in the United States are set up under Delaware law.

By the beginning of the 19th century, government policy on both sides of the Atlantic began to change, reflecting the growing popularity of the proposition that corporations were riding the economic wave of the future. In 1819, the US Supreme Court granted corporations a plethora of rights they had not previously recognized or enjoyed. Corporate charters were deemed "inviolable", and not subject to arbitrary amendment or abolition by state governments. The Corporation as a whole was labeled an "artificial person", possessing both individuality and immortality.

At around the same time, British legislation was similarly freeing the corporation from historical restrictions. In 1844 the British Parliament passed the Joint Stock Companies Act, which allowed companies to incorporate without a royal charter or an Act of Parliament. Ten years later, limited liability, the key provision of modern corporate law, passed into English law: in response to increasing pressure from newly emerging capital interests, Parliament passed the Limited Liability Act of 1855, which established the principle that any corporation could enjoy limited legal liability on both contract and tort claims simply by registering as a "limited" company with the appropriate government agency.

This prompted the English periodical *The Economist* to write in 1855 that "never, perhaps, was a change so vehemently and generally demanded, of which the importance was so much overrated". The glaring inaccuracy of the second part of this judgment was recognized by the same magazine more than 75 years later, when it claimed that, "the economic historian of the future ... may be inclined to assign to the nameless inventor of the principle of limited liability, as applied to trading corporations, a place of honor with Watt and Stephenson, and other pioneers of the Industrial Revolution."

Modern Corporations

By the end of the 19th century the Sherman Act[6], New Jersey allowing holding companies, and mergers resulted in larger corporations with dispersed shareholders. (See The Modern Corporation and Private Property The well-known Santa Clara County v. Southern Pacific Railroad decision began to influence policymaking and the modern corporate era had begun.)

The 20th century saw a proliferation of enabling law across the world, which helped to drive economic booms in many countries before and after World War I. Starting in the 1980s, many countries with large state-owned corporations moved toward privatization, the selling of publicly owned services and enterprises to corporations. Deregulation (reducing the regulation of corporate activity) often accompanied privatization as part of a laissez-faire policy[7]. Another major postwar shift was toward the development of conglomerates, in which large corporations purchased smaller corporations to expand their industrial base. Japanese firms developed a horizontal conglomeration model, the keiretsu, which was later duplicated in other countries as well.

Corporate Formation

Historically, corporations were created by a charter granted by government. Today, corporations are usually registered with the state, province, or national government and regulated by the laws enacted by that government. Registration is the main prerequisite to the corporation's assumption of limited liability. The law sometimes requires the corporation to designate its principal address, as well as a registered agent (a person or company designated to receive legal service of process). It may also be required to designate an agent or other legal representative of the corporation.

Generally, a corporation files articles of incorporation[8] with the government, laying out the general nature of the corporation, the amount of stock it is authorized to issue, and the names and addresses of directors. Once the articles are approved, the corporation's directors meet to create bylaws that govern the internal functions of the corporation, such as meeting procedures and officer positions.

The law of the jurisdiction in which a corporation operates will regulate most of its internal activities, as well as its finances. If a corporation operates outside its home state, it is often required to register with other governments as a foreign corporation, and is almost always subject to laws of its host state pertaining to employment, crimes, contracts, civil actions, and the like.

Corporate Personality

One of the key legal features of corporations is their separate legal personality, also known as "personhood" or being "artificial persons". However, the separate legal personality was not confirmed under English law until 1895 by the House of Lords in Salomon v. Salomon & Co. Separate legal personality often has unintended consequences, particularly in relation to smaller, family companies. In B v. B [1978] Fam 181 it was held that a discovery order obtained by a wife against her husband was not effective against the husband's company as it was not named in the order and was separate and distinct from him. And in Macaura v. Northern Assurance Co Ltd. a claim under an insurance policy failed where the insured had transferred timber from his name into the name of a company wholly owned by him, and it was subsequently destroyed in a fire; as the property now belonged to the company and not to him, he no longer had an "insurable interest" in it and his claim failed.

However, separate legal personality does allow corporate groups a great deal of flexibility in relation to tax planning, and also enables multinational companies to manage the liability of their overseas operations. For instance in Adams v. Cape Industries plc it was held that victims of asbestos poisoning at the hands of an American subsidiary could not sue the English parent in tort. There are certain specific situations where courts are generally prepared to "pierce the corporate veil"[9], to look directly at, and impose liability directly on the individuals behind the company. The most commonly cited examples are:

- where the company is a mere (or facade);
- where the company is effectively just the agent of its members or controllers;
- where a representative of the company has taken some personal responsibility for a statement or action;
- where the company is engaged in fraud or other criminal wrongdoing;
- where the natural interpretation of a contract or statute is as a reference to the corporate group and not the individual company;
- where permitted by statute (for example, many jurisdictions provide for shareholder liability where a company breaches environmental protection laws);
- in many jurisdictions, where a company continues to trade despite foreseeable bankruptcy, the directors can be forced to account for trading losses personally.

Capacity and Powers

Historically, because companies are artificial persons created by operation of law, the law prescribed what the company could and could not do. Usually this was an expression of the commercial purpose which the company was formed for, and came to be referred to as the company's objects, and the extent of the objects are referred to as the company's capacity. If an activity fell outside of the company's capacity it was said to be *ultra vires* (or beyond strength) and void.

By way of distinction, the organs of the company were expressed to have various corporate powers. If the objects were the things that the company was able to do, then the powers were the means by which it could do them. Usually expressions of powers were limited to methods of raising capital, although from earlier times distinctions between objects and powers have caused lawyers difficulty. Most jurisdictions have now modified the position by statute, and companies generally have capacity to do all the things that a natural person could do, and power to do it in any way that a natural person could do it.

However, references to corporate capacity and powers have not quite been consigned to the dustbin of legal history. In many jurisdictions, directors can still be liable to their shareholders if they cause the company to engage in businesses outside of its objects, even if the transactions are still valid as between the company and the third party. And many jurisdictions also still permit transactions to be challenged for lack of "corporate benefit", where the relevant transaction has no prospect of being for the commercial benefit of the company or its shareholders.

As artificial persons, companies can only act through human agents. The main agent who deals with the company's management and business is the board of directors, but in many jurisdictions other officers can be appointed too. The board of directors is normally elected by the members, and the other officers are normally appointed by the board. These agents enter into contracts on behalf of the company with third parties.

Although the company's agents owe duties to the company (and, indirectly, to the shareholders) to exercise those powers for a proper purpose, generally speaking third parties' rights are not impugned if it transpires that the officers were acting improperly. Third parties are entitled to rely on the ostensible authority of agents held out by the company to act on its behalf. A line of common law cases reaching back to Royal British Bank v. Turquand established in common law that third parties were entitled to assume that the internal management of the company was being conducted properly, and the rule has now been codified into statute in most countries.

Accordingly, companies will normally be liable for all the act and omissions of their officers and agents. This will include almost all torts, but the law relating to crimes committed by companies is complex, and varies significantly between countries.

Corporate Governance

Corporate governance is primarily the study of the power relations between the board of directors and those who elect them (shareholders in the "general meeting" and employees). It also concerns other stakeholders, such as creditors, consumers, the environment and the community at large. One of the main differences between different countries in the internal form of companies is between a two-tier and a one-tier board. The United Kingdom, the United States, and most Commonwealth countries have single unified boards of directors. In Germany, companies have two tiers, so that shareholders (and employees) elect a "supervisory board", and then the supervisory board chooses the "management board". There is the option to use two tiers in France, and in the new European Companies (Societas Europea).

Recent literature, especially from the United States, has begun to discuss corporate governance in the terms of management science. While post-war discourse centred on how to achieve effective "corporate democracy" for shareholders or other stakeholders, many scholars have shifted to discussing the law in terms of principal-agent problems. On this view, the basic issue of corporate law is that when a "principal" party delegates his property (usually the shareholder's capital, but also the employee's labour) into the control of an "agent" (i. e., the director of the company) there is the possibility that the agent will act in his own interests, be "opportunistic", rather than fulfill the wishes of the principal. Reducing the risks of this opportunism, or the "agency cost", is said to be central to the goal of corporate law.

Corporate Constitution

The rules for corporations derive from two sources. These are the country's statutes (in the US, usually the Delaware General Corporation Law (DGCL); in the UK, the Companies Act 2006 (CA 2006); in Germany, the Aktiengesetz (AktG) and the Gesetz betreffend die Gesellschaften mit beschr nkter Haftung (GmbH-Gesetz, GmbHG)). The law will set out which rules are mandatory, and which rules can be derogated from. Examples of important rules which cannot be derogated from would usually include how to fire the board of directors, what duties directors owe to the company or when a company must be dissolved as it approaches bankruptcy. Examples of rules that members of a company would be allowed to change and choose could include, what kind of procedure general meetings should follow, when dividends get paid out, or how many members (beyond a minimum set out in the law) can amend the constitution. Usually, the statute will set out model articles, which the corporation's constitution will be assumed to have if it is silent on a bit of particular procedure.

The United States, and a few other common law countries, split the corporate constitution into two separate documents (the UK got rid of this in 2006). The memorandum of Association (or articles of incorporation) is the primary document, and will generally regulate the company's activities with the outside world. It states which objects the company is meant to follow (e. g., "this company makes automobiles") and specifies the authorised share capital of the company. The articles of association (or by-laws) is the secondary document, and will generally regulate the company's internal affairs and management, such as procedures for board meetings, dividend entitlements etc In the event of any inconsistency, the memorandum prevails and in the United States only the memorandum is publicised. In civil law jurisdictions, the company's constitution is normally consolidated into a single document, often called the charter.

It is quite common for members of a company to supplement the corporate constitution with additional arrangements, such as shareholders' agreements, whereby they agree to exercise their membership rights in a certain way. Conceptually a shareholders' agreement fulfills many of the same functions as the corporate constitution, but because it is a contract, it will not normally bind new members of the company unless they accede to it somehow. One benefit of shareholders' agreement is that they will usually be confidential, as most jurisdictions do not require shareholders' agreements to be publicly filed. Another common method of supplementing the corporate constitution is by means of voting trusts, although these are relatively uncommon outside of the United States and certain offshore jurisdictions. Some jurisdictions consider the company seal to be a part of the "constitution" (in the loose sense of the word) of the company, but the requirement for a seal has been abrogated by legislation in most countries.

Balance of Power

Adolf Berle in *The Modern Corporation and Private Property* argued that the separation of control of companies from the investors who were meant to own them endangered the American economy and led to a mal-distribution of wealth.

The most important rules for corporate governance are those concerning the balance of power between the board of directors and the members of the company. Authority is given or "delegated" to the board to manage the company for the success of the investors. Certain specific decision rights are often reserved for shareholders, where their interests could be fundamentally affected. There are necessarily rules on when directors can be removed from office and replaced. To do that, meetings need to be called to vote on the issues. How easily the constitution can be amended and by who necessarily affects the relations of power.

It is a principle of corporate law that the directors of a company have the right to manage. This is expressed in statute in the DGCL, where 141 (a) states, the business and affairs of every corporation organized under this chapter shall be managed by or under the direction of a board of directors, except as may be otherwise provided in this chapter or in its certificate of incorporation.

In Germany, 76 AktG says the same for the management board, while under 111 AktG the supervisory board's role is stated to be to "oversee" (*berwachen*). In the United Kingdom, the right to manage is not laid down in law, but is found in Art. 2 of the Model Articles. This means it is a default rule, which companies can opt out of (s. 20 CA 2006) by reserving powers to members, although companies rarely do. UK law specifically reserves shareholders right and duty to approve "substantial non cash asset transactions" (s. 190 CA 2006), which means those over 10% of company value, with a minimum of 5,000 and a maximum of 100,000. Similar rules, though much less stringent, exist in 271 DGCLand through case law in Germany under the so called Holzm ller-Doktrin.

Probably the must fundamental guarantee that directors will act in the members' interests is that they can easily be sacked. During the Great Depression, two Harvard scholars, Adolf Berle and Gardiner Means wrote *The Modern Corporation and Private Property*, an attack on American law which failed to hold directors to account, and linked the growing power and autonomy of directors to the economic crisis. In the UK, the right of members to remove directors by a simple majority is assured under s. 168 CA 2006 Moreover, Art. 21 of the Model Articles requires a third of the board to put themselves up for re-election every year (in effect creating maximum three year terms). 10% of shareholders can demand a meeting any time, and 5% can if it has been a year since the last one (s. 303 CA 2006). In Germany, where employee participation creates the need for greater boardroom stability, 84(3) AktG states that management board directors can only be removed by the supervisory board for an important reason (*ein wichtiger Grund*) though this can include a vote of no-confidence by the shareholders. Terms last for five years, unless 75% of shareholders vote otherwise. 122 AktG lets 10% of shareholders demand a meeting. In the US, Delaware lets directors enjoy considerable autonomy. 141 (k) DGCL states that directors can be removed without any cause, unless the board is "classified", meaning that directors only come up for re-appointment on different years. If the board is classified, then directors cannot be removed unless there is gross misconduct. Director's autonomy from shareholders is seen further in 216 DGCL, which allows for plurality voting and 211 (d) which states shareholder meetings can only be called if the constitution allows for it. The problem is that in America, directors usually choose where a company is incorporated and 242(b)(1) DGCL says any constitutional amendment requires a resolution by the directors. By contrast, constitutional amendments can be made at any time by 75% of shareholders in Germany (179 AktG) and the UK (s. 21 CA 2006).

Director's Duties

In most jurisdictions, directors owe strict duties of good faith, as well as duties of care and skill, to safeguard the interests of the company and the members.

The standard of skill and care that a director owes is usually described as acquiring and maintaining sufficient knowledge and understanding of the company's business to enable him to properly discharge his duties.

Directors are also strictly charged to exercise their powers only for a proper purpose. For instance, were a director to issue a large number of new shares, not for the purposes of raising capital but in order to defeat a potential takeover bid, that would be an improper purpose.

Directors have a duty to exercise reasonable skill care and diligence—This right enables the company to seek compensation from its director if it can be proved that he hasn't shown reasonable skill or care which in turn has caused the company to incur a loss.

Directors also owe strict duties not to permit any conflict of interest or conflict with their duty to act in the best interests of the company. This rule is so strictly enforced that, even where the conflict of interest or conflict of duty is purely hypothetical, the directors can be forced to disgorge all personal gains arising from it. In Aberdeen Ry v. Blaikie (1854) 1 Macq HL 461 Lord Cranworth stated in his judgment that, "A corporate body can only act by agents, and it is, of course, the duty of those agents so to act as best to promote the interests of the corporation whose affairs they are conducting. Such agents have duties to discharge of a fiduciary nature towards their principal. And it is a rule of universal application that no one, having such duties to discharge, shall be allowed to enter into engagements in which he has, or can have, a personal interest conflicting or which possibly may conflict, with the interests of those whom he is bound to protect ... So strictly is this principle adhered to that no question is allowed to be raised as to the fairness or unfairness of the contract entered into ... "

However, in many jurisdictions the members of the company are permitted to ratify transactions which would otherwise fall foul of this principle. It is also largely accepted in most jurisdictions that this principle should be capable of being abrogated in the company's constitution.

Corporate Litigation

Members of a company generally have rights against each other and against the company, as framed under the company's constitution. In relation to the exercise of their rights, minority shareholders usually have to accept that, because of the limits of their voting rights, they cannot direct the overall control of the company and must accept the will of the majority (often expressed as majority rule). However, majority rule can be iniquitous, particularly where there is one controlling shareholder.

Accordingly, a number of exceptions have developed in law in relation to the general principle of majority rule.

- Where the majority shareholder(s) are exercising their votes to perpetrate a fraud on the minority, the courts may permit the minority to sue.
- members always retain the right to sue if the majority acts to invade their personal rights, e. g., where the company's affairs are not conducted in accordance with the company's constitution (this position has been debated because the extent of a personal right is not set in law). Macdougall v. Gardiner and Pender v. Lushington present irreconcilable differences in this area.
- in many jurisdictions it is possible for minority shareholders to take a representative or derivative action in the name of the company, where the company is controlled by the alleged wrongdoers.

Corporate Finance

Shares and Share Capital

Companies generally raise capital for their business ventures either by debt or equity. Capital raised by way of equity is usually raised by issued shares (sometimes called "stock" (not to be confused with stock-in-trade)) or warrants.

A share is an item of property, and can be sold or transferred. Holding a share makes the holder a member of the company, and entitles them to enforce the provisions of the company's constitution against the company and against other members. Shares also normally have a nominal or par value, which is the limit of the shareholder's liability to contribute to the debts of the company on an insolvent liquidation.

Shares usually confer a number of rights on the holder. These will normally include:

- voting rights;
- rights to dividends (or payments made by companies to their shareholders) declared by the company;
- rights to any return of capital either upon redemption of the share, or upon the liquidation of the company;
- in some countries, shareholders have preemption rights, whereby they have a preferential right to participate in future share issues by the company.

Many companies have different classes of shares, offering different rights to the shareholders. For example, a company might issue both ordinary shares and preference shares, with the two types having different voting and/or economic rights. For example, a company might provide that preference shareholders shall each receive a cumulative preferred dividend of a certain amount per annum, but the ordinary shareholders shall receive everything else.

The total number of issued shares in a company is said to represent its capital. Many jurisdictions regulate the minimum amount of capital which a company may have, although some countries only prescribe minimum amounts of capital for companies engaging in certain types of business (e.g., banking, insurance etc).

Similarly, most jurisdictions regulate the maintenance of capital, and prevent companies returning funds to shareholders by way of distribution when this might leave the company financially exposed. In some jurisdictions this extends to prohibiting a company from providing financial assistance for the purchase of its own shares.

Liquidations[10]

Liquidation is the normal means by which a company's existence is brought to an end. It is also referred to (either alternatively or concurrently) in some jurisdictions as winding up and/or dissolution.

Liquidations generally come in two forms, either compulsory liquidations (sometimes called creditors' liquidations) and voluntary liquidations (sometimes called members' liquidations, although a voluntary liquidation where the company is insolvent will also be controlled by the creditors, and is properly referred to as a creditors' voluntary liquidation).

As its names imply, applications for compulsory liquidation are normally made by creditors of the company when the company is unable to pay its debts. However, in some jurisdictions, regulators have the power to apply for the liquidation of the company on the grounds of public good, i. e., where the company is believed to have engaged in unlawful conduct, or conduct which is otherwise harmful to the public at large.

Voluntary liquidations occur when the company's members decide voluntarily to wind up the affairs of the company. This may be because they believe that the company will soon become insolvent, or it may be on economic grounds if they believe that the purpose for which the company was formed is now at an end, or that the company is not providing an adequate return on assets and should be broken up and sold off.

Some jurisdictions also permit companies to be wound up on "just and equitable" grounds. Generally, applications for just and equitable winding-up are brought by a member of the company who alleges that the affairs of the company are being conducted in a prejudicial manner, and asking the court to bring an end to the company's existence. For obvious reasons, in most countries, the courts have been reluctant to wind up a company solely on the basis of the disappointment of one member, regardless of how well-founded that member's complaints are. Accordingly, most jurisdictions which permit just and equitable winding up also permit the court to impose other remedies, such as requiring the majority shareholder(s) to buy out the disappointed minority shareholder at a fair value.

Where a company goes into liquidation, normally a liquidator is appointed to gather in all the company's assets and settle all claims against the company. If there is any surplus after paying off all the creditors of the company, this surplus is then distributed to the members.

Types of Corporations

Most corporations are registered with the local jurisdiction as either a stock corporation or a non-stock corporation. Stock corporations sell stock to generate capital. A stock corporation is generally a for-profit corporation. A non-stock corporation does not have stockholders, but may have members who have voting rights in the corporation.

Some jurisdictions (Washington, D. C., for example) separate corporations into for-profit and non-profit, as opposed to dividing into stock and non-stock.

Several states also allow a variation of the corporation for use by professionals (i. e., those individuals typically considered as professionals who require a license from the state to conduct business). In some states, such as Georgia, these corporations are known as "professional corporations".

For-Profit and Non-Profit

In modern economic systems, conventions of corporate governance commonly appear in a wide variety of business and non-profit activities. Though the laws governing these creatures of statute often differ, the courts often interpret provisions of the law that apply to profit-making enterprises in the same manner (or in a similar manner) when applying principles to non-profit organizations—as the underlying structures of these two types of entity often resemble each other.

Closely Held Corporations and Publicly Traded Corporations[11]

The institution most often referenced by the word "corporation" is a publicly traded corporation, the shares of which are traded on a public stock exchange (for example, the New York Stock Exchange or Nasdaq in the United States) where shares of stock of corporations are bought and sold by and to the general public. Most of the largest businesses in the world are publicly traded corporations. However, the majority of corporations are said to be closely held, privately held or close corporations, meaning that no ready market exists for the trading of shares. Many such corporations are owned and managed by a small group of businesspeople or companies, although the size of such a corporation can be as vast as the largest public corporations.

Closely held corporations do have some advantages over publicly traded corporations. A small, closely held company can often make company-changing decisions much more rapidly than a publicly traded company. A publicly traded company is also at the mercy of the market, having capital flow in and out based not only on what the company is doing but the market and even what the competitors are doing. Publicly traded companies also have advantages over their closely held counterparts. Publicly traded companies often have more working capital and can delegate debt throughout all shareholders. This means that people invested in a publicly traded company will each take a much smaller hit to their own capital as opposed to those involved with a closely held corporation. Publicly traded companies though suffer from this exact advantage. A closely held corporation can often voluntarily take a hit to profit with little to no repercussions (as long as it is not a sustained loss). A publicly traded company though often comes under extreme scrutiny if profit and growth are not evident to stock holders, thus stock holders may sell, further damaging the company. Often this blow is enough to make a small public company fail.

Often communities benefit from a closely held company more so than from a public company. A closely held company is far more likely to stay in a single place that has treated them well, even if going through hard times. The shareholders can incur some of the damage the company may receive from a bad year or slow period in the company profits. Closely held companies often have a better relationship with workers. In larger, publicly traded companies, often when a year has gone badly the first area to feel the effects are the work force with lay offs or worker hours, wages or benefits being cut. Again, in a closely held business the shareholders can incur this profit damage rather than passing it to the workers.

The affairs of publicly traded and closely held corporations are similar in many respects. The main difference in most countries is that publicly traded corporations have the burden of complying with additional securities laws, which (especially in the US) may require additional periodic disclosure (with more stringent requirements), stricter corporate governance standards, and additional procedural obligations in connection with major corporate transactions (for example, mergers) or events (for example, elections of directors).

A closely held corporation may be a subsidiary of another corporation (its parent company) , which may itself be either a closely held or a public corporation. In some jurisdictions, the subsidiary of a listed public corporation is also defined as a public corporation (for example, Australia) .

Mutual Benefit Corporations

A mutual benefit nonprofit corporation is a corporation formed in the United States solely for the benefit of its members. An example of a mutual benefit nonprofit corporation is a golf club. Individuals pay to join the club, memberships may be bought and sold, and any property owned by the club is distributed to its members if the club dissolves. The club can decide, in its corporate bylaws, how many members to have, and who can be a member. Generally, while it is a nonprofit corporation, a mutual benefit corporation is not a charity. Because it is not a charity, a mutual benefit nonprofit corporation cannot obtain 501 (c) (3) status. If there is a dispute as to how a mutual benefit nonprofit corporation is being operated, it is up to the members to resolve the dispute since the corporation exists to solely serve the needs of its membership and not the general public.

Corporations Globally

Following on the success of the corporate model at a national level, many corporations have become transnational or multinational corporations: growing beyond national boundaries to attain sometimes remarkable positions of power and influence in the process of globalizing.

The typical "transnational" or "multinational" may fit into a web of overlapping shareholders and directorships, with multiple branches and lines in different regions, many such sub-groupings comprising corporations in their own right. Growth by expansion may favor national or regional branches; growth by acquisition or merger can result in a plethora of groupings scattered around and/ or spanning the globe, with structures and names which do not always make clear the structures of shareholder ownership and interaction.

In the spread of corporations across multiple continents, the importance of corporate culture has grown as a unifying factor and a counterweight to local national sensibilities and cultural awareness.

Corporations & Corporate Laws in Different Countries

Australia

In Australia corporations are registered and regulated by the Commonwealth Government through the Australian Securities and Investments Commission. Corporations law has been largely codified in the Corporations Act 2001.

Brazil

In Brazil there are many different types of corporations (sociedades), but the two most common ones commercially speaking are: (i) *sociedade limitada*, identified by Ltda. after the company's name, equivalent to the British limited company, and (ii) *sociedade an nima* or *companhia*, identified by *SA* or Companhia in the company's name, equivalent to the British public limited company. The *Ltda.* is mainly governed by the new Civil Code, enacted in 2002, and the *SA* by the Law 6.404 dated 15 December 1976.

Canada

In Canada both the federal government and the provinces have corporate statutes, and thus a corporation may have a provincial or a federal charter. Many older corporations in Canada stem from Acts of Parliament passed before the introduction of general corporation law. The oldest corporation in Canada is the Hudson's Bay Company; though its business has always been based in Canada, its Royal Charter was issued in England by King Charles II in 1670, and became a Canadian charter by amendment in 1970 when it moved its corporate headquarters from London to Canada. Federally recognized corporations are regulated by the Canada Business Corporations Act.

China

In China, the Corporate Law mainly regulates two forms of corporations: limited liability company or joint stock limited company.

German-Speaking Countries

Germany, Austria, Switzerland and Liechtenstein recognize two forms of corporation: the Aktiengesellschaft (AG), analogous to public corporations in the English-speaking world, and the Gesellschaft mit beschr nkter Haftung (GmbH), similar to (and an inspiration for) the modern limited liability company.

Italy

The Italian Republic recognizes three types of company with limited liability: *S. r. l.*, or *Societ a responsabilit limitata* (a private limited company), *S. p. A.* or *Societ per Azioni* (a joint-stock company, similar to a Public Limited Company in the United Kingdom), and *S. a. p. a.* ("Societ in Accomandita per Azioni"). The latter is a hybrid form that involves two categories of shareholders, some with and some without limited liability, and is rarely used in practice.

Japan

In Japan, both the state and local public entities under the Local Autonomy Law (prefectures and municipalities) are considered to be corporations. Non-profit corporations may be established under the Civil Code.

The term "company" is used to refer to business corporations. The predominant form is the *kabushiki kaisha*, used by public corporations as well as smaller enterprises. *Mochibun kaisha*, a form for smaller enterprises, are becoming increasingly common. Between 2002 and 2008, the intermediary corporation existed to bridge the gap between for-profit companies and non-governmental and non-profit organizations.

Spain

In Spain there are two types of companies: with limited liability called *S. L.*, or *Sociedad Limitada* (a private limited company) and *S. A.* or *Sociedad An nima* (similar to a Public Limited Company).

United Kingdom

In the United Kingdom, "corporation" most commonly refers to a body corporate formed by Royal Charter or by statute, of which few now remain. The BBC is the oldest and best known corporation within the UK that is still in existence. Others, such as the British Steel Corporation, were privatized in the 1980s.

In the private sector, corporations are referred to as companies, and are regulated by the Companies Act 2006 (or the Northern Ireland equivalent). The most common type of company is the private limited company ("Limited" or "Ltd."). Private limited companies can either be limited by shares or by guarantee. Other corporate forms include the public limited company ("plc") and the private unlimited company, and companies limited by guarantee.

A special type of corporation is a corporation sole, which is an office held by an individual natural person (the incumbent), but which has a continuing legal entity separate from that person: an example is a Church of England bishopric

US Corporate Law

ABA—Model Business Corporations Act

The laws governing every aspect of a corporation exist within the Model Business Corporation Act. The law lays out in detail the steps required to form a corporation and the reasons for which a corporation may be formed. In addition, the MBCA describes various voting procedures for making decisions and provides insight on the rights of shareholders and directors. The code provides for the rules that govern mergers and acquisitions as well as the sale and issuance of stock. The act itself has 17 chapters and covers almost 200 pages.

Corporate Law—Definition

Corporate law in the United States is a collection of 50 different systems of corporate law, or one law for each state. Two sources of law are, however particularly important. Firstly, the Model Business Corporation Act (MBCA), which is drafted by the American Bar Association was influential and adopted by twenty four states. Secondly, because, under the US Constitution, companies are free to incorporate in any state, regardless of whether they are doing any business there or have their headquarters there, states have competed on various rules to attract business, and many corporations found Delaware's laws and specialized courts attractive. More than half of US corporations are incorporated under the Delaware General Corporation Law (DGCL), and Delaware corporate law is particularly influential.

Corporations—Overview

A corporation is a legal entity created through the laws of its state of incorporation. Individual states have the power to promulgate laws relating to the creation, organization and dissolution of corporations. Many states follow the Model Business Corporation Act.

Delaware General Corporation Law (DGCL)

The Delaware General Corporation Law (Title 8, Chapter 1 of the Delaware Code) is the statute governing corporate law in the state of Delaware. Delaware is well known as a corporate haven. Over 50% of US publicly-traded corporations and 60% of the Fortune 500 companies are incorporated in that state.

Different Types of Corporations

Anyone who operates a business, alone or with others, may incorporate. This is also true for anyone or any group engaged in religious, civil, non-profit or charitable endeavors. You do not have to be a business giant to be able to have the financial and other benefits of operating a corporation. Given the right circumstances, the owner(s) of a business of any size can benefit from incorporating.

Uniform Commercial Code

The Uniform Commercial Code (UCC) is a set of suggested laws relating to commercial transactions. The UCC was one of many uniform codes that grew out of a late nineteenth-century movement toward uniformity among state laws.

Notes

1. Corporate Law 《公司法》

《公司法》是指规定公司的设立、组织、活动、解散及其他对内对外关系的法律规范的总称。本单元主要介绍公司的概念、公司的发展历史、公司的特点、公司的设立、现代公司治理以及不同国家公司立法情况。我国《公司法》于 1993 颁布,2005 年修订。《公司法》中所称公司有其特定适用范围:依据属地主义原则,为依照《公司法》在中国境内设立的公司;组织形式仅限于有限责任公司和股份有限公司。

2. juristic person 法人

法人是具有民事权利能力和民事行为能力、依法独立享有民事权利和承担民事义务的组织,是社会组织在法律上的人格化。法人是相对于自然人而言,自然人是以生命为存在特征的个人。

3. corporate governance 公司治理

公司治理是现代企业制度中最重要的组织架构。狭义而言,公司治理主要是指公司的股东、董事及经理层之间的关系;广义而言,公司治理还包括公司与利益相关者(如员工、客户、供应商、债权人、社会公众)之间的关系及有关法律、法规等。20 世纪 90 年代以来,公司治理在发达国家成为一个引起人们持续关注的问题,超产权理论、两权分离理论、委托代理理论和利益相关者理论构成了公司治理结构的主要理论基础。

4. Dutch East India Company 荷兰东印度公司

荷兰东印度公司是 1602 年荷兰建立的具有国家职能、向东方进行殖民掠夺和垄断东方贸易的商业公司,1799 年解散。这是世界上第一家跨国公司,也是第一个发行股票的公司。这也是世界上第一个特大公司,政府持有股份,并具有与外国签订条约、铸造货币、建立殖民地等权利,在近 200 年的时间里,在世界贸易中有重要影响力。

5. Mercantilism 重商主义

重商主义是封建主义解体之后的 16—17 世纪西欧资本原始积累时期的一种经济理论或经济体系,反映资本原始积累时期商业资产阶级利益的经济理论和政策体系。该理论认为,一国积累的金银越多,就越富强;主张国家干预经济生活,禁止金银输出,增加金银输入。

6. Sherman Act 《谢尔曼法案》

1890 年美国联邦政府通过了第一个联邦反垄断法,称为《谢尔曼法案》,以后在 1914 年、1936 年、1950 年多次修订补充这些法律。该法案规定,不允许一家公司独霸市场,也禁止几家大企业暗中达成协议,逃避竞争。

7. laissez-faire policy 自由放任政策

自由放任经济体制的基本特征主要有:自由竞争、消费者主权、政府的天职是"守夜人"。自由放任的经济活动和资源的配置完全由市场机制来推动,国家或政府的经济职能仅限于保护自由竞争,保障私有财产,建立某些必要的公共事业和公共设施。

8. articles of incorporation 公司章程

公司章程是指公司依法制定的、规定公司名称、住所、经营范围、经营管理制度等重大事项的基本文件。公司章程是公司组织和活动的基本准则，是公司的宪章。公司章程是关于公司组织和行为的基本规范。公司章程不仅是公司的自治法规，而且是国家管理公司的重要依据。

9. pierce the corporate veil 揭开公司面纱

揭开公司面纱，即所谓的公司人格否定(disregard of corporate personality)，当公司的独立人格和股东有限责任被公司背后的股东滥用时，就具体法律关系中的特定事实，将公司与其背后的股东视为一体并追究其共同的连带法律责任，以保护公司债权人或其他相关利害关系群体的利益。"揭开公司面纱"的直接后果是追偿股东之责任。

10. Liquidations 破产清算

破产清算是指公司宣告破产后，由清算组接管公司，对破产财产进行清算、评估和处理、分配。

11. Closely Held Corporations and Publicly Traded Corporations 有限责任公司和股份有限公司

有限责任公司是指股东人数较少、不发行股票、股份不得随意转让、股东对公司承担有限责任的公司。股份有限公司是指全部资本划分成等额的股份，其股份以股票形式依法公开发行和自由转让的一种公司形式。

Study Questions

1. What are the main characteristics of corporate?
2. What do you think of "pierce the corporate veil" or "disregard of corporate personality"?
3. What are the differences between closely held corporations and publicly traded corporations?
4. How do you understand the modern corporate governance?

Case Study

Salomon v A Salomon & Co Ltd. [1897] AC 22 is a landmark UK company law case. The effect of the Lords' unanimous ruling was to uphold firmly the doctrine of corporate personality, as set out in the Companies Act 1862, so that creditors of an insolvent company could not sue the company's shareholders to pay up outstanding debts.

Facts

Mr Aron Salomon was a leather boot and shoe manufacturer. His firm was in Whitechapel High Street, with warehouses and a large establishment. He had it for 30 years and "he might fairly have counted upon retiring with at least 10,000 in his pocket". His sons wanted to become business partners, so he turned the business into a limited company.

His wife and five eldest children became subscribers and two eldest sons also directors. Mr Salomon took 20,001 of the company's 20,007 shares. The price fixed by the contract for the sale of the business to the company was 39,000.

According to the court, this was "extravagent" and not "anything that can be called a business like or reasonable estimate of value". Transfer of the business took place on June 1, 1892. The purchase money for the business was paid, totalling 20,000, to Mr Salomon. 10,000 was paid in debentures to Mr Salomon as well (i. e., Salomon gave the company a loan, secured by a charge over the assets of the company). The balance paid went to extinguish the business's debts (1,000 of which was cash to Salomon).

Soon after Mr Salomon incorporated his business, however, a series of strikes in the shoe industry led the government, Salomon's main customer, to split its contracts among more firms (the government wanted to diversify its supply base to avoid the risk of its few suppliers being crippled by strikes). His warehouse was full of unsold stock. He and his wife lent the company money. He cancelled his debentures. But the company needed more money, and they sought 5,000 from a Mr Edmund Broderip. He assigned Broderip his debenture, the loan with 10% interest and secured by a floating charge. But Salomon's business still failed, and he could not keep up with the interest payments. In October 1893 Mr Broderip sued to enforce his security. The company was put into liquidation. Broderip was repaid his 5,000, and then the debenture was reassigned to Salomon, who retained the floating charge over the company.

The company's liquidator met Broderip's claim with a counter claim, joining Salomon as a defendant, that the debentures were invalid for being issued as fraud. The liquidator claimed all the money back that was transferred when the company was started: rescission of the agreement for the business transfer itself, cancellation of the debentures and repayment of the balance of the purchase money.

Judgment

- **High Court**

At first instance, the case entitled Broderip v. Salomon Vaughan Williams J. said Mr Broderip's claim was valid. It was undisputed that the 20,000 shares were fully paid up. He said the company had a right of indemnity against Mr. Salomon. He said the signatories of the memorandum were mere dummies, the company was just Mr. Salomon in another form, an alias, his agent. Therefore, it was entitled to indemnity from the principal. The liquidator amended the counter claim, and an award was made for indemnity.

- **Court of Appeal**

The Court of Appeal confirmed Vaughan Williams J.'s decision against Mr. Salomon, though on the grounds that Mr. Salomon had abused the privileges of incorporation and limited liability, which Parliament had intended only to confer on "independent bona fide shareholders, who had a mind and will of their own and were not mere puppets". Lindley L. J. (an expert on partnership law) held that the company was a trustee for Mr Salomon, and as such was bound to indemnify the company's debts.

"Lindley L. J. was the leading expert on partnerships and company law.

The incorporation of the company cannot be disputed. (See s. 18 of the Companies Act 1862.) Whether by any proceeding in the nature of a scire facias the Court could set aside the certificate of incorporation is a question which has never been considered, and on which I express no opinion; but, be that as it may, in such an action as this the validity of the certificate cannot be impeached. The company must, therefore, be regarded as a corporation, but as a corporation created for an illegitimate purpose. Moreover, there having always been seven members, although six of them hold only one 1l. share each, Mr. Aron Salomon cannot be reached under s. 48, to which I have already alluded. As the company must be recognised as a corporation, I feel a difficulty in saying that the company did not carry on business as a principal, and that the debts and liabilities contracted in its name are not enforceable against it in its corporate capacity. But it does not follow that the order made by Vaughan Williams J. is wrong. A person may carry on business as a principal and incur debts and liabilities as such, and yet be entitled to be indemnified against those debts and liabilities by the person for whose benefit he carries on the business. The company in this case has been regarded by Vaughan Williams J. as the agent of Aron Salomon. I should rather liken the company to a trustee for him—a trustee improperly brought into existence by him to enable him to do what the statute prohibits. It is manifest that the other members of the company have practically no interest in it, and their names have merely been used by Mr. Aron Salomon to enable him to form a company, and to use its name in order to screen himself from liability. This view of the case is quite consistent with In re George Newman & Co. In a strict legal sense the business may have to be regarded as the business of the company; but if any jury were asked, Whose business was it? They would say Aron Salomon's, and they would be right, if they meant that the beneficial interest in the business was his. I do not go so far as to say that the creditors of the company could sue him. In my opinion, they can only reach him through the company. Moreover, Mr. Aron Salomon's liability to indemnify the company in this case is, in my view, the legal consequence of the formation of the company in order to attain a result not permitted by law. The liability does not arise simply from the fact that he holds nearly all the shares in the company. A man may do that and yet be under no such liability as Mr. Aron Salomon has come under. His liability rests on the purpose for which he formed the company, on the way he formed it, and on the use which he made of it. There are many small companies which will be quite unaffected by this decision. But there may possibly be some which, like this, are mere devices to enable a man to carry on trade with limited liability, to incur debts in the name of a registered company, and to sweep off the company's assets by means of debentures which he has caused to be issued to himself in order to defeat the claims of those who have been incautious enough to trade with the company without perceiving the trap which he has laid for them.

It is idle to say that persons dealing with companies are protected by s. 43 of the Companies Act, 1862, which requires mortgages of limited companies to be registered, and entitles creditors to inspect the register. It is only when a creditor begins to fear he may not be paid that he thinks of looking at the register; and until a person is a creditor he has no right of inspection. As a matter of fact, persons do not ask to see mortgage registers before they deal with limited companies; and this is perfectly well known to every one acquainted with the actual working of the Companies Acts and the habits of business men. Mr Aron Salomon and his advisers, who were evidently very shrewd people, were fully alive to this circumstance. If the legislature thinks it right to extend the principle of limited liability to sole traders it will no doubt do so, with such safeguards, if any, as it may think necessary. But until the law is changed such attempts as these ought to be defeated whenever they are brought to light. They do infinite mischief; they bring into disrepute one of the most useful statutes of modern times, by perverting its legitimate use, and by making it an instrument for cheating honest creditors. Mr. Aron Salomon's scheme is a device to defraud creditors."

Lopes L. J. and Kay L. J. variously described the company as a myth and a fiction and said that the incorporation of the business by Mr. Salomon had been a mere scheme to enable him to carry on as before but with limited liability.

- **House of Lords**

The House of Lords unanimously overturned this decision, rejecting the arguments from agency and fraud. They held that there was nothing in the Act about whether the subscribers (ie the shareholders) should be independent of the majority shareholder. The company was duly constituted in law and it was not the function of judges to read into the statute limitations they themselves considered expedient. Lord Halsbury LC stated that the statute "enacts nothing as to the extent or degree of interest which may be held by each of the seven [shareholders] or as to the proportion of interest or influence possessed by one or the majority over the others". His judgment continued.

"Lord Halsbury LC, a conservative peer and author of Halsbury's Laws took strict literalist approach to legislative interpretation.

I have no right to add to the requirements of the statute, nor to take from the requirements thus enacted. The sole guide must be the statute itself ...

Either the limited company was a legal entity or it was not. If it was, the business belonged to it and not to Mr. Salomon. If it was not, there was no person and no thing to be an agent at all; and it is impossible to say at the same time that there is a company and there is not.

Lindley L. J. on the other hand, affirms that there were seven members of the company; but he says it is manifest that six of them were members simply in order to enable the seventh himself to carry on business with limited liability. The object of the whole arrangement is to do the very thing which the Legislature intended not to be done.

It is obvious to inquire where is that intention of the Legislature manifested in the statute. Even if we were at liberty to insert words to manifest that intention, I should have great difficulty in ascertaining what the exact intention thus imputed to the Legislature is, or was. In this particular case it is the members of one family that represent all the shares; but if the supposed intention is not limited to so narrow a proposition as this, that the seven shareholders must not be members of one family, to what extent may influence or authority or intentional purchase of a majority among the shareholders be carried so as to bring it within the supposed prohibition? It is, of course, easy to say that it was contrary to the intention of the Legislature—a proposition which, by reason of its generality, it is difficult to bring to the test; but when one seeks to put as an affirmative proposition what the thing is which the Legislature has prohibited, there is, as it appears to me, an insuperable difficulty in the way of those who seek to insert by construction such a prohibition into the statute."
Lord Herschell noted the potentially "far-reaching" implications of the Court of Appeal's logic and that in recent years many companies had been set up in which one or more of the seven shareholders were "disinterested persons" who did not wield any influence over the management of the company. Anyone dealing with such a company was aware of its nature as such, and could by consulting the register of shareholders become aware of the breakdown of share ownership among the shareholders.

Lord Macnaghten asked what was wrong with Mr. Salomon taking advantage of the provisions set out in the statute, as he was perfectly legitimately entitled to do. It was not the function of judges to read limitations into a statute on the basis of their own personal view that, if the laws of the land allowed such a thing, they were "in a most lamentable state", as Malins V-C had stated in an earlier case in point, In Re Baglan Hall Colliery Co, which had likewise been overturned by the House of Lords. The key parts of his judgment were as follows.

"Lord Macnaghten.

When the memorandum is duly signed and registered, though there be only seven shares taken, the subscribers are a body corporate "capable forthwith", to use the words of the enactment, "of exercising all the functions of an incorporated company". Those are strong words. The company attains maturity on its birth. There is no period of minority—no interval of incapacity. I cannot understand how a body corporate thus made "capable" by statute can lose its individuality by issuing the bulk of its capital to one person, whether he be a subscriber to the memorandum or not. The company is at law a different person altogether from the subscribers to the memorandum; and, though it may be that after incorporation the business is precisely the same as it was before, and the same persons are managers, and the same hands receive the profits, the company is not in law the agent of the subscribers or trustee for them. Nor are the subscribers as members liable, in any shape or form, except to the extent and in the manner provided by the Act. That is, I think, the declared intention of the enactment. If the view of the learned judge were sound, it would follow that no common law partnership could register as a company limited by shares without remaining subject to unlimited liability ...

... Among the principal reasons which induce persons to form private companies, as is stated very clearly by Mr. Palmer in his treatise on the subject, are the desire to avoid the risk of bankruptcy, and the increased facility afforded for borrowing money. By means of a private company, as Mr. Palmer observes, a trade can be carried on with limited liability, and without exposing the persons interested in it in the event of failure to the harsh provisions of the bankruptcy law. A company, too, can raise money on debentures, which an ordinary trader cannot do. Any member of a company, acting in good faith, is as much entitled to take and hold the company's debentures as any outside creditor. Every creditor is entitled to get and to hold the best security the law allows him to take.

If, however, the declaration of the Court of Appeal means that Mr. Salomon acted fraudulently or dishonestly, I must say I can find nothing in the evidence to support such an imputation. The purpose for which Mr. Salomon and the other subscribers to the memorandum were associated was "lawful". The fact that Mr. Salomon raised 5,000l, for the company on debentures that belonged to him seems to me strong evidence of his good faith and of his confidence in the company. The unsecured creditors of A. Salomon and Company, Limited, may be entitled to sympathy, but they have only themselves to blame for their misfortunes. They trusted the company, I suppose, because they had long dealt with Mr Salomon, and he had always paid his way; but they had full notice that they were no longer dealing with an individual, and they must be taken to have been cognisant of the memorandum and of the articles of association. For such a catastrophe as has occurred in this case some would blame the law that allows the creation of a floating charge. But a floating charge is too convenient a form of security to be lightly abolished. I have long thought, and I believe some of your Lordships also think, that the ordinary trade creditors of a trading company ought to have a preferential claim on the assets in liquidation in respect of debts incurred within a certain limited time before the winding-up. But that is not the law at present. Everybody knows that when there is a winding-up debenture-holders generally step in and sweep off everything; and a great scandal it is.

It has become the fashion to call companies of this class "one man companies". That is a taking nickname, but it does not help one much in the way of argument. If it is intended to convey the meaning that a company which is under the absolute control of one person is not a company legally incorporated, although the requirements of the Act of 1862 may have been complied with, it is inaccurate and misleading: if it merely means that there is a predominant partner possessing an overwhelming influence and entitled practically to the whole of the profits, there is nothing in that that I can see contrary to the true intention of the Act of 1862, or against public policy, or detrimental to the interests of creditors. If the shares are fully paid up, it cannot matter whether they are in the hands of one or many. If the shares are not fully paid, it is as easy to gauge the solvency of an individual as to estimate the financial ability of a crowd. One argument was addressed to your Lordships which ought perhaps to be noticed, although it was not the ground of decision in either of the Courts below. It was argued that the agreement for the transfer of the business to the company ought to be set aside, because there was no independent board of directors, and the property was transferred at an overvalue. There are, it seems to me, two answers to that argument. In the first place, the directors did just what they were authorized to do by the memorandum of association. There was no fraud or misrepresentation, and there was nobody deceived. In the second place, the company have put it out of their power to restore the property which was transferred to them. It was said that the assets were sold by an order made in the presence of Mr Salomon, though not with his consent, which declared that the sale was to be without prejudice to the rights claimed by the company by their counter-claim. I cannot see what difference that makes. The reservation in the order seems to me to be simply nugatory.

- **Significance**

In the decades since Salomon's case, various exceptional circumstances have been delineated, both by legislatures and the judiciary, in England and elsewhere (including

Ireland) when courts can legitimately disregard a company's separate legal personality, such as where crime or fraud has been committed. Although Salomon's case is cited in court to this day, it has met with considerable criticism. For example, Otto Kahn-Freund called the decision "calamitous" in his article published at [1944] 7 MLR 54. In that article, the author also called for the abolition of private companies. There is therefore much debate as to whether the same decision would be reached if the same facts were considered in the modern legal environment, given the House of Lords' decisions in Pepper v. Hart and Re Spectrum Plus Ltd. and the Privy Council in AG of Belize v. Belize Telecom Ltd. that require a purposive approach to interpreting legislation.

Sources of Information and Further Readings

1. Kershaw, David. *Company Law in Context.* Oxford University Press, 2009.
2. Gower, LCB. Some contrasts between British and American Corporation Law (1956) 69(8). *Harvard Law Review*, 1369.
3. Kraakman, Reinier H. *et al.* (2004). *Anatomy of Corporate Law: A Comparative and Functional Approach.* Oxford University Press.
4. Lowry, John & Alan Dignam. *Company Law.* Oxford University Press, 2006.
5. http://en.wikipedia.org/wiki/Corporate_law
6. http://www.hg.org/corporate-law.html

Chapter 11

The Law of Partnerships[1]

Key Concepts

general partnership	limited partnership	partnership agreement
general partners	silent partners	limited partners

Learning Objectives

1. Understand the definition of "partnership".
2. Be familiar with the types of partnership.
3. Understand the formation of a partnership.
4. Understand the rights and obligations of partners.
5. Understand the advantages and disadvantages of a partnership.

Types of Partnerships

General Partnership[2]

In this standard form of partnership, all of the partners are equally responsible for the business's debts and liabilities. In addition, all partners are allowed to be involved in the management of the company. In fact, in the absence of a statement to the contrary in the partnership agreement, each partner has equal rights to control and manage the business. Therefore, unanimous consent of the partners is required for all major actions undertaken. Be advised, though, that any obligation made by one partner is legally binding on all partners, whether or not they have been informed.

Limited Partnership[3]

In a limited partnership, one or more partners are general partners, and one or more are limited partners. General partners are personally liable for the business's debts and judgments against the business; they can also be directly involved in the management. Limited partners are essentially investors (silent partners, so to speak) who do not participate in the company's management and who are also not liable beyond their investment in the business. State laws determine how involved limited partners can be in the day-to-day business of the firm without jeopardizing their limited liability. This business form is especially attractive to real estate investors, who benefit from the tax incentives available to limited partners, such as being able to write off depreciating values.

Forming a Partnership

The first step in creating a partnership is reserving a name, which must be done with the secretary of state's office or its equivalent. Most states require that the words "Company" or "Associates" be included in the name to show that more than one partner is involved in the business. In all states, though, the name of the partnership must not resemble the name of any other corporation, limited liability company, partnership, or sole proprietorship that is registered with the state.

A partnership can be formed in essentially two ways: by verbal or written agreement. A partnership that is formed at will, or verbally, can also be dissolved at will. In the absence of a formal agreement, state laws (the Uniform Partnership Act, except in Louisiana) will govern the business. These laws specify that without an agreement, all partners share equally in the profits and losses of the partnership and that partners are not entitled to compensation for services. If you would like to structure your partnership differently, you will need to write a partnership agreement. It may be advisable to consult a lawyer before drafting the agreement, but you should at least research the issue on your own. A thorough partnership agreement should generally cover the following areas:

- Name and address
- Duration of partnership—You can specify a finite date on which all business will terminate or you can include a general clause that explains the partnership will exist until all partners agree to dissolve it or a partner dies.
- Purpose of business.
- Partners' contributions—These may be in cash, property or services. Be sure to determine the value of all non-cash contributions.
- Partners' compensation—Determine how profits will be split up and how often. Also decide if any of the partners will receive a salary.
- Management authority—Will partners be able to make some decisions on their own? Which decisions will require the unanimous consent of all partners?
- Work hours and vacation.
- Kinds of outside business activities that will be allowed for partners.
- Partner withdrawal—Decide how the death, retirement, withdrawal, disability, or death of a partner will be handled through a buy-sell agreement. Also determine whether or not a partner who has simply withdrawn will be allowed to operate a competing business.
- Disposition of the partnership's name if a partner leaves.

Decide whether or not mediation or arbitration will be provided for in the case of disputes that cannot be resolved amongst the partners. This is a way to avoid costly litigation.

Rights and Responsibilities of Partners

The Uniform Partnership Act[4] defines the basic rights and responsibilities of partners. Some of these can be changed by the partnership agreement, except, as a general rule, those laws that govern the partners' relationships with third parties. In the absence of a written agreement, then, the following rights and responsibilities apply:

Rights

- All partners have an equal share in the profits of the partnership and are equally responsible for its losses.

- Any partner, who makes a payment for the partnership beyond its capital, or makes a loan to the partnership, is entitled to receive interest on that money.
- All partners have equal property rights for property held in the partnership's name. This means that the use of the property is equally available to all partners for the purpose of the partnership's business.
- All partners have an equal interest in the partnership, or share of its profits and assets.
- All partners have an equal right in the management and conduct of the business.
- All partners have a right to access the books and records of the partnership's accounts and activities at all times. (This does not apply to limited partners.)
- No partner may be added without the consent of all other partners.

Responsibilities

- Partners must report and turn over to the partnership any income they have derived from use of the partnership's property.
- Partners are not allowed to conduct business that competes with the partnership.
- Each partner is responsible for contributing his or her full time and energy to the success of the partnership.
- Any property that a partner acquires with the intention of it being the partnership's property must be turned over to the partnership.
- Any disputes shall be decided by a majority vote.

Advantages of a Partnership

Collaboration

As compared to a sole proprietorship, which is essentially the same business form but with only one owner, a partnership offers the advantage of allowing the owners to draw on the resources and expertise of the co-partners. Running a business on your own, while simpler, can also be a constant struggle. But with partners to share the responsibilities and lighten the workload, members of a partnership often find that they have more time for the other activities in their lives.

Tax Advantages

The profits of a partnership pass through to its owners, who report their share on their individual tax returns. Therefore, the profits are only taxed once (at the personal level of its owners) rather than twice, as is the case with corporations, which are taxed at the corporate level and then again at the personal level when dividends are distributed to the shareholders. The benefits of single taxation can also be secured by forming an S corporation (although some ownership restrictions apply) or by forming a limited liability company (a new hybrid of corporations and partnerships that is still evolving).

Simple Operating Structure

A partnership, as opposed to a corporation, is fairly simple to establish and run. No forms need to be filed or formal agreements drafted (although it is advisable to write a partnership agreement in the event of future disagreements). The most that is ever required is perhaps filing a partnership certificate with a state office in order to register the business's name and securing a business license. As a result, the annual filing fees for corporations, which can sometimes be very expensive, are avoided when forming a partnership.

Flexibility

Because the owners of a partnership are usually its managers, especially in the case of a small business, the company is fairly easy to manage, and decisions can be made quickly without a lot of bureaucracy. This is not the case with corporations, which must have shareholders, directors, and officers, all of whom have some degree of responsibility for making major decisions.

Uniform Laws

One of the drawbacks of owning a corporation or limited liability company is that the laws governing those business entities vary from state to state and are changing all the time. In contrast, the Uniform Partnership Act provides a consistent set of laws about forming and running partnerships that make it easy for small business owners to know the laws that affect them. And because these laws have been adopted in all states but Louisiana, interstate business is much easier for partnerships than it is for other forms of businesses.

Acquisition of Capital

Partnerships generally have an easier time acquiring capital than corporations because partners, who apply for loans as individuals, can usually get loans on better terms. This is because partners guarantee loans with their personal assets as well as those of the business. As a result, loans for a partnership are subject to state usury laws, which govern loans for individuals. Banks also perceive partners to be less of a risk than corporations, which are only required to pledge the business's assets. In addition, by forming a limited partnership, the business can attract investors (who will not be actively involved in its management and who will enjoy limited liability) without having to form a corporation and sell stock.

Disadvantages of a Partnership

Conflict with Partners

While collaborating with partners can be a great advantage to a small business owner, having to actually run a business from day to day with one or more partners can be a nightmare. First of all, you have to give up absolute control of the business and learn to compromise. And when big decisions have to be made, such as whether and how to expand the business, partners often disagree on the best course and are left with a potentially explosive situation. The best way to deal with such predicaments is to anticipate them by drawing up a partnership agreement that details how such disagreements will be dealt with.

Authority of Partners

When one partner signs a contract, each of the other partners is legally bound to fulfill it. For example, if Anthony orders $10,000 of computer equipment, it is as if his partners, Susan and Jacob, had also placed the order. And if their business cannot afford to pay the bill, then the personal assets of Susan and Jacob are on the line as well as those of Anthony. And this is true whether the other partners are aware of the contract or not. Even if a clause in the partnership agreement dictates that each partner must inform the other partners before any such deals are made, all of the partners are still responsible if the other party in the contract (the computer company) was not aware of such a stipulation in the partnership agreement. The only recourse the other partners have is to sue.

The Uniform Partnership Act does specify some instances in which full consent of all partners is required:

- Selling the busigood will
- Decisions that would compromise the busiability to function normally
- Assign partnership property in trust for a creditor or to someone in exchange for the payment of the partnership's debts
- Admission of liability in a lawsuit
- Submission of a partnership claim or liability to arbitration

Unlimited Liability[5]

As the previous example illustrated, the personal assets of the partnership's members are vulnerable because there is no separation between the owners and the business. The primary reason many businesses choose to incorporate or form limited liability companies is to protect the owners from the unlimited liability that is the main drawback of partnerships or sole proprietorships. If an employee or customer is injured and decides to sue, or if the business runs up excessive debts, then the partners are personally responsible and in danger of losing all that they own. Therefore, if considering a partnership, determine your assets that will be put at risk. If you possess substantial personal assets that you will not invest in the company and do not want to put in jeopardy, a corporation or limited liability company may be a better choice. But if you are investing most of what you own in the business, then you don't stand to lose any more than if you incorporated. Then if your business is successful, and you find at a later date that you now possess extensive personal assets that you would like to protect, you can consider changing the legal status of your business to secure limited liability.

Vulnerability to Death or Departure

Unlike corporations, which exist perpetually, regardless of ownership, general partnerships dissolve if one of the partners dies, retires, or withdraws. (In limited partnerships, the death or withdrawal of the limited partner does not affect the stability of the business.) Even though this is the law governing partnerships, the partnership agreement can contain provisions to continue the business. For example, a provision can be made allowing a buy out of a partner's share if he or she wants to withdraw or if the partner dies.

Limitations on Transfer of Ownership

Unlike corporations, which exist independently of their owners, the existence of partnerships is dependent upon the owners. Therefore, the Uniform Partnership Act stipulates that ownership may not be transferred without the consent of all the other partners. (Once again, a limited partner is an exception: his or her interest in the company may be sold at will.)

Partnerships in Civil Law

A partnership is a nominate contract between individuals who, in a spirit of cooperation, agree to carry on an enterprise; contribute to it by combining property, knowledge or activities; and share its profit. Partners may have a partnership agreement, or declaration of partnership and in some jurisdictions such agreements may be registered and available for public inspection. In many countries, a partnership is also considered to be a legal entity, although different legal systems reach different conclusions on this point.

Germany

Partnerships may be formed in forms of the General Partnership or Limited Partnership. A partnership can be formed by only one person. In the General Partnership, all partners are fully liable for the partnership's debts, whereas in the Limited Partnership there are general partners with unlimited liability and limited partners whose liability is restricted to their fixed contributions to the partnership. Although a partnership itself is not a legal entity, it may acquire rights and incur liabilities, acquire title to real estate and sue or be sued.

China

In mainland China, a partnership enterprise encompasses two types of partnerships: general partnerships and limited partnerships. A general partnership comprises general partners who bear joint and several liabilities for the debts of the partnership enterprise. There is a special general partnership which can be employed by professional service providers such as accountant firms and law firms. A limited partnership enterprise includes general partners and limited partners where the limited partners are liable only to the extent of their capital contributions.

Japan

The Japanese civil code provides for partnerships by contract, which are commonly known as voluntary partnerships. A more recent statute has allowed for the creation of limited liability partnerships.

One form of partnership unique to Japan is the anonymous partnership, in which partners have limited liability so long as they remain anonymous in their capacity as partners and do not participate in the operation of the partnership. Japan provides for partnership-like corporations called mochibun kaisha.

Partnerships in Common Law

Under common law legal systems, the basic form of partnership is a general partnership, in which all partners manage the business and are personally liable for its debts. Two other forms which have developed in most countries are the limited partnership (LP), in which certain limited partners relinquish their ability to manage the business in exchange for limited liability for the partnership's debts, and the limited liability partnership (LLP), in which all partners have some degree of limited liability.

There are two types of partners. General partners have an obligation of strict liability to third parties injured by the Partnership. General partners may have joint liability or joint and several liability depending upon circumstances. The liability of limited partners is limited to their investment in the partnership.

A silent partner[6] is one who still shares in the profits and losses of the business, but who is uninvolved in its management, and/or whose association with the business is not publicly known; these partners usually provide capital.

China's Hong Kong

A partnership in China's Hong Kong is a business entity formed by China's Hong Kong Partnerships Ordinance, which defines a partnership as "the relation between persons carrying on a business in common with a view of profit" and is not a joint stock company or an incorporated company. If the business entity registers with the Registrar of Companies it takes the form of a limited partnership defined in the Limited Partnerships Ordinance. However, if this business entity fails to register with the Registrar of Companies, then it becomes a general partnership as a default.

Australia

Summarizing the Partnership Act 1958, for a partnership in Australia to exist, four main criteria must be satisfied. They are:

- Valid Agreement between the parties
- To carry on a business—this is defined as "any trade, occupation or profession"
- In Common—meaning there must be some mutuality of rights, interests and obligations
- View to Profit—thus charitable organizations cannot be partnerships (charities are typically incorporated associations under Associations Incorporations Act 1981 (Vic))

Partners share profits and losses. A partnership is basically a settlement between two or more groups or firms in which profit and loss are equally divided.

United Kingdom

United Kingdom partnership law refers to the rules under which partnerships are governed in the United Kingdom. Partnerships are a form of business association, which arises automatically when people carry on business with a view to a profit. Partners are jointly and severally liable, just as they own the property in common. A limited partnership, under the Limited Partnerships Act 1907 may have sleeping partners, who if they do not partake in any business management will not be liable beyond their investments. A partnership' under the Limited Liability Partnerships Act 2000 is now considered a separate legal person with limited liability, though it is treated as a partnership for tax, and is not subject to so much regulation as would be a company. There must, however, be at least two partners.

Section one of Partnership Act 1890 states the relationship which subsists between persons carrying on a business in common with a view of profit. This can come about by oral agreement, written document or conduct. The minimum membership is two and the maximum since 2002 is unlimited. Unless a partnership expressly excludes the Act it applies. Each partner is entitled to participate in management, get an equal share of profit, an indemnity in respect of liabilities assumed in the course of business and the right to not be expelled by other partners. A partnership ends on the death of a partner. A partner is jointly and severally liable for others debts, so there is no limited liability. Under Limited Partnership Act 1907, only sleeping partners may have limited liability, and it is not possible to have a partnership made up all of limited partners. Under Limited Liability Partnerships Act 2000, such partnerships are deemed to have legal personality. It allows limited liability for general trading debts, but individual partners cannot limit personal liability for negligence. It was introduced to allow some protection against large negligence actions, where the risks were felt to be excessive.

A limited partnership in the United Kingdom consists of:

- One or more people called general partners, who are liable for all debts and obligations of the firm; and
- One or more people called limited partners, who contribute a sum/sums of money as capital, or property valued at a stated amount. Limited partners are not liable for the debts and obligations of the firm beyond the amount contributed.

Limited partners may not:

- Draw out or receive back any part of their contributions to the partnership during its lifetime; or
- Take part in the management of the business or have power to bind the firm.

If they do, they become liable for all the debts and obligations of the firm up to the amount drawn out or received back or incurred while taking part in the management, as the case may be.

India and Pakistan

According to section 4 of the Partnership Act of 1932, which applies in both India and Pakistan, "Partnership is defined as the relation between two or more persons who have agreed to share the profits and losses according to their ratio of business run by all or any one of them acting for all." This definition superseded the previous definition given in section 239 of Indian Contract Act 1872 as "Partnership is the relation which subsists between persons who have agreed to combine their property, labour, skill in some business, and to share the profits thereof between them". The 1932 definition added the concept of mutual agency.

A partnership firm is not a legal entity apart from the partners constituting it. It has limited identity for the purpose of tax law as per Section 4 of the Partnership Act of 1932.

USA

The federal government of the United States does not have specific statutory law governing the establishment of partnerships. Instead, each of the fifty states as well as the District of Columbia has its own statutes and common law that govern partnerships. These states largely follow general common law principles of partnerships whether a general partnership, a limited partnership or a limited liability partnership. In the absence of applicable federal law, the National Conference of Commissioners on Uniform State Laws has issued non-binding models laws (called uniform act) in which to encourage the adoption of uniformity of partnership law into the states by their respective legislatures. This includes the Uniform Partnership Act and the Uniform Limited Partnership Act. Although the federal government does not have specific statutory law for establishing partnerships, it has an extensive and hyper detailed statutory scheme for the taxation of partnerships in the Internal Revenue Code. The IRC is Title 26 of the United States Code wherein Subchapter K of Chapter 1 creates tax consequences of such great scale and scope that it effectively serves as a federal statutory scheme for governing partnerships.

Notes

1. The Law of Partnerships 《合伙企业法》

《合伙企业法》主要介绍合伙企业的概念和法律特征、合伙企业类型、合伙企业设立、合伙人的权利和义务、合伙企业的优点和缺点、大陆法与普通法国家的合伙企业立法介绍等内容。

2. General Partnership 普通合伙企业

普通合伙企业由普通合伙人组成,合伙人对合伙企业债务承担无限连带责任。

3. Limited Partnership 有限合伙企业

依据我国合伙企业法的规定，有限合伙企业由普通合伙人和有限合伙人组成，普通合伙人对合伙企业债务承担无限连带责任，有限合伙人以其认缴的出资额为限对合伙企业债务承担责任。

4. The Uniform Partnership Act 《统一合伙法》

美国《统一合伙法》由美国统一州法全国委员会于1914年制定，作为示范法对美国各州的合伙制企业立法产生了很大的推动作用，目前，几乎所有的州都参照相关的示范法制定了本州的各类合伙企业法。

5. Unlimited Liability 无限责任

无限责任是指责任人以其所有的全部财产承担民事责任。有限责任是指责任人以其出资财产承担民事责任，比如，有限责任公司的股东仅以其出资对公司债务所承担的责任。区分有限责任和无限责任的意义在于：承担无限责任的财产范围不受责任人的出资或者特定财产的限制，更有利于保护受害人或者权利人的利益。

6. silent partner 隐名合伙人

隐名合伙人是指没有参与经营管理的合伙人。

Study Questions

1. What are the main differences between general partnership and limited partnership?
2. How can a partnership be formed?
3. What are the rights and obligations of partners?
4. What are the advantages and disadvantages of a partnership?
5. Are there any differences concerning the partnership in civil law and common law?

Case Study 1

Green v. Bellerive Condominiums Limited Partnership Carlton M. Green, Receiver, v. Bellerive Condonimiums Limited Partnership

2149, Sept. Term, 1999. No.

—November 3, 2000

Argued before MURPHY, Chief Judge, EYLER and ADKINS, JJ.

Carlton M. Green (Samuel C. Steelman, Jr. and Green, Leitch & Steelman, on the brief), College Park, for appellant. Monica M. Haley-Pierson (Knight, Manzi, Nussbaum & LaPlaca, P. A., on the brief), Upper Marlboro, for appellee.

Affirming the trial court, we hold that general partners of a limited partnership do not have a duty to notify a charging creditor about that partnership opportunity, and that the charging creditor does not have standing to assert the debtor partners' management rights to participate in or object to such a purchase. In this appeal, we again consider the nature and extent of rights conferred by a charging order against a limited partnership interest. The new question presented by this case is whether a receiver with a charging order against limited partnership interests has a right to be notified of a partnership opportunity—in this case, an opportunity to purchase the partnership's debt.

Facts and Background

The other two general partners were Capital Management and Development Corporation ("Capital Management"), a Delaware corporation controlled by its president, Bechara Nammour, and Express Development Corporation, a New York corporation controlled by its president, Richard J. Seikaly. In 1988, Arnold D. Wolfe co-founded Bellerive Condominiums Limited Partnership ("Bellerive" or the "Partnership"), appellee. A corporation controlled by Wolfe, US Investment Group, Inc. ("USIG"), was one of Bellerive's three general partners.

The Partnership's business plan was to develop and sell the property as condominiums. In turn, the Partnership used the funds to put a deposit on real property in Anne Arundel County. Wolfe borrowed $50,000 from Richard C. Beavers and Richard P. Beavers, and contributed the funds to the Partnership.

As a result of the $50,000 capital contribution, Wolfe also became one of eight limited partners in Bellerive. Like Wolfe, Nammour and Seikaly also held both general and limited partnership interests through their business entities. Under the terms of Bellerive's Partnership Agreement, as amended (the "Partnership Agreement"), Wolfe had priority to the first $50,000 in Partnership profits.

The Partnership operated at a loss, despite capital calls and loans from its partners. But the development plans did not proceed as the Bellerive partners had planned. The Loan was increased to $400, 000 in November 1989. A $300,000 loan was evidenced by a September 24, 1988 note and deed of trust on the property (the "Loan", "Note", and "Deed of Trust"). To complete the purchase and develop the property, the Partnership borrowed from the National Bank of Washington ("NBW").

In November, the Partnership was advised of the Charging Order. On October 28, 1993, the Circuit Court for Anne Arundel County entered a charging order (the "Charging Order") appointing Green as the receiver for any share of Partnership profits payable to either Wolfe or USIG, and for "any other money that is or becomes due to said judgment debtors by reason of their partnership interest". Green sought a charging order against

Wolfe's interest as a limited partner and USIG's interest as a general partner. In his collection efforts, Green became aware that Wolfe's priority right to Partnership profits might be used to satisfy the judgment, and that there might be profits if the Partnership's development and sale plans were successful. Attorney Carlton M. Green, appellant, represented the Beavers in that action. In May 1991, the Beavers obtained a judgment against Wolfe and USIG, in the amount of $124,040.74. With no Partnership profits from which to pay the Beavers, Wolfe defaulted on his repayment obligation.

The FDIC scheduled a foreclosure sale for July 19, 1994. Meanwhile, unable to develop and sell the property as planned, the Partnership defaulted on the Note. At about the same time, NBW was dissolved, and the FDIC acquired the Note. By April 1994, the Loan balance exceeded $590,000.

On May 31, 1994, the FDIC agreed to sell the Note for $375,000. Seeking to avoid foreclosure, Seikaly and Nammour negotiated with the FDIC to purchase the Note at a discount. If settlement did not occur by July 19th, the FDIC planned to proceed with foreclosure scheduled for that date. Seikaly and Nammour entered into an agreement to purchase the Note from the FDIC. The scheduled settlement date was July 15th.

At the end of the letter, there were lines to indicate whether the partner "acknowledged, accepted and agreed" or "decline[d] the offer to purchase a share of the Note". The letter further stated that if payment was not made by July 1, Messrs. Nammour and Seikaly "shall assume you choose not to participate in the Note purchase?" The letter specified the amount each partner would have to contribute, and included payment instructions. Seikaly and Nammour then invited all of the Bellerive partners to participate in the purchase of the Note. In a letter dated June 11, 1994, they informed the partners about the opportunity to purchase the Partnership's Note at a discount, and invited each partner to participate pro rata in the purchase.

No notice of the opportunity to purchase the Note was sent to the receiver. But both letters were returned, marked "moved, not forwardable". The notice letters for Wolfe and USIG were sent via certified mail to the most recent address specified for Partnership correspondence. Seikaly testified that USIG "went out of business so they ceased to be a general partner". By this time, neither Wolfe nor USIG was active in Partnership affairs.

All but three of the partners participated in purchasing the Note at the discounted price. The FDIC required the consent of the Partnership to the purchase and assignment of the Note. The partners other than Wolfe and USIG consented to the Note purchase. Those efforts included redesigning the development concept as townhomes, and remarketing the property. With the Note and Deed of Trust now held in friendly hands, the Partnership continued efforts to develop and market the property.

Shortly after filing the complaint, the receiver learned about the discounted Note purchase. The purpose of the petition was to force a sale of the property and distribution of the proceeds in accordance with the Partnership Agreement. He alleged that it was not reasonable to carry on the business at a loss, and that Capital Management had acted unreasonably and had failed to account to the Partnership for any income or expenses. In June 1996, the receiver filed a complaint for dissolution of the Partnership. In January, April, and October, 1995, the receiver wrote to the Partnership's counsel to inquire about the status of the Partnership, but received no response. By Consent Order dated December 20, 1996, the receiver agreed to stay his dissolution efforts in order to give the Partnership more time to sell the property.

There was an additional balance due on the Note. As a result of the discount purchase, the sale of the property, and repayment of the Note three and a half years later, each of the Purchasing Partners benefitted. On December 30, 1997, $676,374.45 of the settlement proceeds was used toward paying off the Note at its full face value, with none of the loan discount passed through to the Partnership. A Consent Order authorized the sale, but required escrow of $60,000 of the settlement proceeds pending judicial determination of the receiver's claims. In December 1997, the Partnership was able to sell the property under the redesigned development concept, at a contract price of $825,000.

If the amount of the Loan discount were credited back to the Partnership, the receiver argued, there would be ample Partnership profit from which to make the priority repayment of Wolfe's $50,000. He asserted that because Wolfe and USIG had not consented to the Note purchase, the Purchasing Partners held any monies they made on the Note for the benefit of the Partnership. He complained that the Purchasing Partners had breached their fiduciary duties by (1) failing to notify him of the opportunity to purchase the Note, and (2) failing to obtain the consent of Wolfe or USIG to the purchase. After settlement, the receiver sought repayment of the $50,000 owed to Wolfe from the $60,000 in escrowed funds.

The receiver's motion for reconsideration of the Order was denied. The court also ruled that $37,500 in settlement proceeds had been improperly paid to Express Development for work to redesign the project concept, and ordered that amount to be credited back to the Partnership. The court ruled inter alia that the receiver was not entitled to notice of the Note purchase, that the Purchasing Partners were not obligated to credit any proceeds from the Partnership's repayment of the Note back to the Partnership, and that any benefit that the Purchasing Partners made on the Note was not "Partnership profit". After an evidentiary hearing, Judge Joseph P. Manck of the Circuit Court for Anne Arundel County rejected the receiver's contentions in a written Memorandum Opinion and Order dated June 18, 1998 (the "Order").

The receiver filed this appeal. On October 14, 1999, the court ordered distribution of the escrowed funds as recommended in the Murphy Report and entered a final order in accordance with its previous Order. Murphy recommended that the escrowed $60,000, plus the $37,500 credited back to the Partnership as a result of the Order, should be used inter alia to pay the remaining debt to the Purchasing Partners on the Note. Because the debt on the Note exceeded the total amount available for distribution, Murphy concluded that there were no Partnership profits, and thus, that there was no "profit" with which to pay the receiver's priority claim. On July 14, 1999, Tim Murphy, CPA, submitted his report and recommendations (the "Murphy Report"). The court subsequently ordered an accounting.

Discussion

I. Standard of Review

See Heat "The clearly erroneous standard for appellate review does not apply to a trial court's determinations of legal questions or conclusions of law based on findings of fact." See In re Michael G., 107 Md. App. 257, 265, 667 A. 2d 956 (1995). If the issue to which appellant excepts, and on which the court ruled, is a purely legal issue, our review is expansive. Md. Rule 8-131(c). In an appeal from a bench trial, we "review the case on both the law and the evidence." & Power Corp. v. Air Prods. & See id. at 592, 578 A. 2d 1202. Because there is no dispute over the trial court's findings of fact in this case, and the issues raised by appellant involve only legal questions, we must determine whether the trial court was "legally correct". Chems., Inc., 320 Md. 584, 591, 578 A. 2d 1202 (1990).

II. Receiver's Rights under the Charging Order

A. Collection Rights

Bank of Bethesda, 44 Md. App. at 354, 408 A. 2d 767. Indeed, we have characterized a charging order against a limited partnership interest as "nothing more than a legislative means of providing a creditor some means of getting at a debtor 'sill-defined interest in a statutory bastard, surnamed partnership', but corporately protecting participants by limiting their liability as are corporate shareholders". See id. They are purely statutory tools that judgment creditors use to reach partnership interests of indebted partners. Charging orders originated as a statutory solution to cumbersome common law collection procedures "that were ill-suited for reaching partnership interests". 91st Street Joint Venture v. Goldstein, 114 Md. App. 561, 567, 691 A. 2d 272 (1997) (detailing development of charging orders and relevant case law and commentary). See Bank of Bethesda v. Koch, 44

Md. App. 350, 354, 408 A. 2d 767 (1979). Although it has some characteristics of both an assignment and an attachment, it is neither. A charging order is a unique tool.

Charging orders against a limited partnership interest are governed by Title 10 of the Corporations and Associations Article ("CA"), known as the Revised Uniform Limited Partnership Act (RULPA). See Lauer Construction v. Schrift, 123 Md. App. 112, 116, 716 A. 2d 1096, cert. denied sub nom. Gibson's Lodging v. Lauer, 352 Md. 310, 721 A. 2d 989 (1998). Under Section 10-705, judgment creditors may obtain a charging order against the partnership interest of either a general or limited partner of a limited partnership.

Section 10-705 restricts the rights conferred under a charging order against an interest in a limited partnership. A charging order gives the charging creditor only limited access to the partnership interest of the indebted partner.

To the extent so charged, the judgment creditor has only the rights of an assignee of the partnership interest. On application to a court of competent jurisdiction by any judgment creditor of a partner, the court may charge the partnership interest of the partner with payment of the unsatisfied amount of the judgment with interest.

Under Section 10-702, the rights of an assignee of a limited partnership interest are also explicitly limited by design. 10-705 (emphasis added). CA §

Unless otherwise provided in the partnership agreement, an assignment entitles the assignee to receive, to the extent assigned, only the distributions to which the assignor would be entitled. An assignment of a partnership interest does not dissolve a limited partnership or entitle the assignee to become a partner or, unless otherwise provided in the partnership agreement, exercise any rights of a partner.

10-703(a). See CA § An assignee of a limited partnership interest generally cannot become a partner without the consent of all other partners. 10-702 (emphasis added). CA §

That alternative is "the ultimate transfer of the debtor partner's interest". Id. We recognized that the court's powers to appoint a receiver, to order an accounting, and to make other orders as "the circumstances of the case may require" are merely "subsidiary aids to the collecting process", which the court may exercise in its discretion. Id. (quoting Gose, supra cor above). Id. (quoting Gose, The Charging Order Under the Uniform Partnership Act, 28 Wash. L. Rev. 1, 10 (1953)). "If this method is ineffectual there is another more drastic course of action." See id. The preferred collection method is to use a charging order to divert the debtor partner's right to partnership profits to the judgment creditor. See id. at 572, 691 A. 2d 272. We outlined the two basic methods by which a creditor may proceed to collect from an indebted partner. See 91st Street, 114 Md. App. at 570, 691 A. 2d 272. In 91st Street Joint Venture, supra, we addressed for the first time the scope of judicial authority to fashion relief under a charging order. In two recent decisions, this Court has examined limitations on the rights conferred by a charging order against a partnership interest.

Examining cases from other jurisdictions, we held that under section 9-505 of the Revised Uniform Partnership Act, See id. at 573, 576-78, 691 A. 2d 272. Accordingly, we held that a receiver must obtain judicial permission for such a forced transfer of the debtor partner's interest, and that a receiver with a charging order against an interest in a general partnership is not entitled to assign the charged partnership interest without court order or the consent of the remaining partners. Id. at 577, 691 A. 2d 272. "the ordering of a sale is [also] something that the trial court may do as a supplement to charging the interest of the partnership and appointing a receiver for profits", but that "any transfer of the debtor partner's interest is to take place pursuant to the rules governing judicial sales".

We based our decision on the absence of explicit enforcement or collection mechanisms in Section 10-705 and similarities in the right to receive partnership distributions under both RULPA and RUPA. See Lauer Construction, 123 Md. App. at 119,716 A. 2d 1096. We held that creditors with a charging order against a limited partnership interest are entitled to the same collection remedy as creditors with a charging order against a general partnership interest, with the same limitations. Id. at 570 n. 2, 691 A. 2d 272. The next year, in Lauer Construction, supra, we addressed for the first time the nature and extent of those rights. But we also noted in 91st Street that under Section 10-705, the rights of a creditor against a limited partnership interest are "more limited than that provided for in the UPA and ULPA" governing general partnerships.

We address that question now. In addressing the collection rights of a charging creditor, neither case addressed whether the charging creditor may exercise the management rights of the debtor partner. In examining these judicially supervised collection methods, we were not presented with, and therefore did not address, whether a creditor also could use the same charging order as a tool to demand information about partnership debt, partnership opportunities, or other partnership affairs, or to participate in the partnership's decisions regarding those matters. Both cases concluded that these collection rights may be exercised only through the courts, and must be judicially determined on a case by case basis. Both cases considered how a creditor could use his unique charging order tool to collect the debt by reaching the indebted partner's financial interest in the partnership. But our holdings in both 91st Street and Lauer Construction addressed only the scope of a creditor's "collection remedy", i. e., a creditor's right to "liquidate" the debtor partner's financial interest in the partnership, because that partner's right to partnership distributions "collateralizes" the judgment debt as a result of a charging order.

B. Management Rights

After an evidentiary hearing, the trial court concluded that the receiver "was not entitled to any notice" of the Note purchase or any credit for the difference between the amount that the Purchasing Partners paid for the Note and the amount they received at the December 1997 settlement. In the trial court, he asserted that by virtue of the Charging Order, he had the same right as USIG and Wolfe to be notified of the opportunity to purchase the Note, and that he was entitled to "stand in the shoes" of Wolfe and USIG to demand that the amount of the loan discount be credited back to the Partnership because the Purchasing Partners did not obtain their consent to the Note purchase. In this case, the receiver seeks more than the collection rights that we addressed in 91st Street and Lauer Construction.

As authority for his consent argument, he relied on Section 9-404, which provides that the receiver moved to reconsider, arguing that the real issue was not whether the receiver received notice of the opportunity, but whether the debtor partners had consented to the Note purchase.

[e]very partner must account to the partnership for any benefit, and hold as trustee for it any profits derived by him without the consent of the other partners from any transaction connected with the formation, conduct, or liquidation of the partnership or from any use by him of its property.

The trial court issued a second written opinion and order, finding inter alia that "the partners discharged their fiduciary duty to Mr Wolfe and USI[G] by offering [them] the opportunity to join in the purchase of the note". The Partnership argued that the partners' fiduciary duty was to disclose and offer the opportunity to the other partners, that Section 9-404 does not require "literal consent", and that even if it did, the receiver had no standing to assert the rights of the debtor partners under Section 9-404. At a hearing on the motion to reconsider, counsel for the Partnership responded that the duty of general partners under Section 9-404 is to "fully disclose and give the opportunity to the partners", and that is exactly what the Bellerive general partners had done. 9-404. CA § court also stated that it was "not convinced that [p]laintiff, as receiver, has a right to challenge the purchase of the note".

See Leventhal, 84 Md. App. at 606, 581 A. 2d 449. Relying on Section 9-404 and language in Rector v. Azzato, 74 Md. App. 684, 539 A. 2d 1162 (1988), and Leventhal v. Five Seasons Partnership, 84 Md. App. 603, 581 A. 2d 449 (1990), the receiver repeatedly asserts that he was entitled to notice of the purchase and to assert the debtor partners' rights under Section 9-404, because the Charging Order placed him "in the shoes of the debtor" and entitled him "to do that which the debtor/partner could have done". On appeal, the receiver renews his notice and consent arguments.

Cf. Rector, supra (judgment creditor of assignee of limited partnership interest may obtain charging order against that interest); Leventhal, supra (receiver with charging order against interests in general partnership may petition for dissolution of general partnership). In fact, neither case involved a partnership opportunity, and Leventhal did not even involve a limited partnership. Neither case involved the debtor partner's right to receive information about limited partnership opportunities, or to participate in limited partnership affairs. Neither case held that a receiver with a charging order against limited partnership interests stands in the debtor partners' shoes for all purposes. Neither Rector nor Leventhal defined the nature and scope of the charging creditor's rights so broadly. The receiver's reliance on this language is misplaced.

We decline the receiver's request to expand the rights conferred by a charging order beyond the collection rights we discussed in Lauer Construction to include the management rights of a debtor partner. Distilled to its essence, the receiver's argument is that the Charging Order operated as either a judicial assignment of the debtor partners' management rights in the Partnership, or as a judicial substitution of the receiver for the debtor partners for all purposes. Like the trial court, we reject the receiver's "substituted shoes" argument, because it is contrary to unambiguous statutory limitations on a charging order against a limited partnership interest and to sound principles of limited partnership law.

We explain. Instead, we conclude that these rights are fundamental "management rights of a partner" that were not transferred to the receiver by the Charging Order. These rights are not analogous to "distribution" or "collection" rights, nor are they merely incidental or ancillary to the receiver's right to receive the debtor partner's distributions. The "rights of a partner" include the right to information and the right to participate in partnership decisions that the receiver is demanding in this instance. 10-702 (emphasis added). When read in pari materia, these sections make it clear that a charging order against a limited partnership interest does not entitle the creditor "to become a partner, or exercise any rights of a partner". As reflected in the unambiguous language of Section 10-702, 10-703, and 10-705, a charging order against a limited partnership interest does not operate as an unlimited assignment of all partnership rights, or as a judicial "swap" of the creditor for the debtor partner.

As a limited partner, Wolfe had only the right to request information. Thus, in the context of this dispute, USIG, as one of Bellerive's three general partners, had the right to request information about Partnership debt and opportunities, and a right to participate in making decisions regarding those matters as a minority of the three general partners. All matters relating to the Partnership's debt were defined as "Major Decisions". It specifically provided that no "'Major Decisions' will be made, taken or implemented by the general partners without the prior concurrence of two-thirds of the general partners". (Emphasis added). It provided that the three general partners "ha[d] full power and authority to manage the business, property and affairs of the Partnership", and that they would "keep all partners reasonably informed, upon their request, as to the business of the Partnership". The Agreement, however, also prohibited the limited partners from voting on or participating in "major decisions". The Partnership Agreement reflected the characteristic management relationship between general and limited partners. The Charging Order in this case covered the limited partnership interests of both a general partner (USIG) and a limited partner (Wolfe). The question raised by the receiver is whether the Charging Order entitled him to exercise any of those rights.

We agree with the trial court's conclusion that the receiver had no right to demand or receive notice of the opportunity to purchase the Note. Under RULPA, among those "rights of a partner" that may not be exercised by a creditor with a charging order against a limited partnership interest is the right to demand and receive information about partnership transactions. Information regarding partnership transactions includes information regarding partnership property and partnership opportunities. 19 (official comment). 10-118, supra (emphasis added); see ULPA § The RULPA drafters' official comment to section 10-702 states that the language prohibiting transferees from "exercis[ing] the rights of a partner" is derived from the following sentence in ULPA: "An assignee who does not become a substituted limited partner has no right to require any information or account of the partnership transactions." §19. 10-118 of the Corporations and Associations Article; ULPA § See Md. Code (1975), §Our construction of RULPA is based on language in its statutory predecessor. Because the receiver had only the rights of an assignee, and such rights do not include the right to demand or receive information regarding partnership opportunities, the trial court was legally correct in ruling that the receiver was not entitled to separate notice of the opportunity to purchase the Note.

We also conclude that the receiver had no standing to assert any right that the debtor partners may have had to consent to or challenge the Note purchase under Section 9-404. Prohibiting a third party creditor from exercising the debtor partner's management rights reflects the fundamental principle that under Sections 10-702 and 10-705, partners whose partnership interests have been assigned or charged remain partners and may continue to exercise their rights as a partner. We think that, like rights to obtain partnership information, rights under Section 9-404 are fundamental "rights of a partner" that are not transferred to a creditor by a charging order.

The principle is not violated by the transfer of purely financial rights through the assignment of a partner's interest in the partnership, but it would be violated by the admission of a new speaking and voting member into the closely knit arrangement that typifies the partnership. partners should be able to choose their associates.

3.05(c)(3)(vi)(4), at 3:86. Bromberg and Ribstein, *supra*, §

Here, the debtor partners neither objected to the Note purchase nor sought to assert rights under like the right to information about partnership opportunities, a partner's right to consent to another partner's pursuit of a partnership opportunity is a management right of a partner that remains with the indebted partner after his right to receive distributions in the limited partnership has been transferred via a charging order. In the context of a proposal to purchase partnership debt, the right to consent under Section 9-404 is essentially a right to participate in the decision regarding whether the partnership should commit its resources to pursue the partnership opportunity. Section 9-404.

We recognize the heightened fairness concerns when the partnership opportunity at issue is the purchase of the partnership's debt. We decline to do so. Adopting exceptions for partnership debt or partnership opportunity cases would be nothing less than judicially amending the language of Sections 10-702, 10-703, and 10-705. We are not free to simply ignore that RULPA prohibits a charging creditor from exercising such fundamental rights of a partner. But we decline to create an exception to Section 10-702 and 10-705 that would allow a receiver with a charging order to assert the rights of the indebted partner under Section 9-404 in matters involving information and decisions about the Partnership's debt and about opportunities and plans to purchase that debt. and that decisions regarding the partnership's debt may have a substantial impact on the financial interests of all partners.

By expanding the rights conferred by a charging order beyond the judicially supervised collection rights of a creditor that we have addressed in our previous decisions, we would defeat one of the primary purposes and benefits of having a uniform limited partnership act—to provide the clarity, predictability, and certainty that facilitate limited partnership investment and business. Thus, a "partnership debt/partnership opportunity" exception would be difficult to interpret, enforce, and limit. Similarly, most management decisions have the potential to affect the partnership's debt. Indeed, it could be argued that most management decisions involve a "partnership opportunity" of one sort or another. Even if we could create a partnership debt/partnership opportunity exception for charging orders, we would not, because such an exception would "swallow the rule" and undermine the important purpose of RULPA's limitation on the rights conferred by a charging order.

See Gilman Paint Instead, restricting the rights conferred by a charging order under Section 10-705 promotes the general purpose of limited partnership acts, which is not primarily to protect or assist creditors, but to encourage investing by enabling limited partners to invest money and to share in the profits, but without risking more than the amount they contributed. In particular, this limitation prevents third party creditors from using a charging order as a license to "squeeze" other limited partners into paying off obligations of the debtor partner, as the necessary cost of eliminating the risk of such interference. By limiting a creditor's right to exercise the debtor partner's management rights, we ensure that creditors of a limited partner cannot disrupt partnership business or interfere with the management rights of other partners. Lauer Construction, 123 Md. App. at 115, 716 A. 2d 1096. In Lauer Construction, supra, we explicitly recognized that limiting a creditor's rights under a charging order "protect[s] the partnership business and prevent[s] the disruption that would result if creditors of a partner executed directly on partnership assets". Varnish Co. v. Legum, 197 Md. 665, 670, 80 A. 2d 906 (1951); Klein, 284 Md. at 51, 395 A. 2d 126.

Undoubtedly, investors contemplating a limited partnership opportunity would be discouraged by the possibility of having to satisfy or deal with creditors of each partner. If a charging creditor is permitted to exercise management rights of the debtor partners in matters pertaining to partnership debt or partnership opportunities, that third party creditor is in an enhanced position to wield any of the debtor partner's management rights as a tool to obtain payment of the judgment debt. These reasons for excluding third party creditors from a seat at the partnership's management table are no less applicable-and perhaps are even more applicable—when the issue under consideration is what to do about partnership debt or about a partnership opportunity.

The Agreement also provides that "if the general partners do not elect to lend such funds to the Partnership, or to borrow such funds, all as determined by the affirmative vote of two-thirds of the general partners the Managing Partner shall call upon all of the partners (general and limited) to invest proportionately". Thus, it is clear that the general partners could choose to lend to the Partnership themselves, rather than make a capital call on all the partners. The Partnership Agreement allows the general partners to "lend to the partnership" any amount required for "additional funds for partnership purposes", and to "charge interest therefore at such rate of interest as the general partners may from time to time determine". We are not convinced that the provision of the Partnership Agreement cited by the receiver mandates a capital call. The receiver complains that the general partners failed to make a capital call, and that they were obligated to do so when the Partnership had insufficient funds to make the mortgage payments.

The purpose of the purchase was to avoid the scheduled foreclosure of the Partnership's sole asset, and the Note purchase "bought time" for the Partnership to obtain a return on its investment by having the Purchasing Partners hold the Partnership's debt and assume all risk of nonpayment for a period of more than three years. Not only did the general partners have authority under the Partnership Agreement to assume the Loan, but their decision to do so benefitted the Partnership. In this context, we do not see a difference between lending directly, and purchasing an outstanding loan made by a third party.

Nor does it prohibit the indebted partner from keeping the charging creditor informed about partnership affairs. Moreover, the receiver seems to forget that a charging order does not prevent indebted partners from participating in partnership affairs, at least to the extent an applicable partnership agreement allows. There is no evidence that he even attempted to do so. 10-703. See § As RULPA and the Partnership Agreement make clear, if the receiver wished to become a substituted partner, he was obligated to apply for and obtain the consent of all other partners. The fact is that the receiver held only a charging order against limited partnership interests, and not a full partnership interest with its concomitant management rights. None of these factors changes our analysis or our decision. We have also considered the receiver's argument that the Purchasing Partners knew about the receiver and the Charging Order before they sent notice of the purchase opportunity, knew that the receiver had asked for information regarding Partnership developments, and knew that the notices sent to the debtor partners had been returned.

Simply stated, lenders should not rely on a charging order as a post hoc substitute for other forms of security that might have been available at the time credit was extended. 13.07(a), at 13:43. "Credit extenders who look to a partner's interest in a partnership as a possible source of satisfaction are well advised to take and perfect a security interest rather than rely on a charging order [because a] partnership interest is not very good collateral." IV Bromberg and Ribstein, *supra*, at § Like other well-informed creditors, they presumably knew that partnership interests are notoriously poor security for the repayment of a debt. We do not think that the receiver or judgment creditors are burdened unfairly by the denial of these management rights.

CONCLUSION

As a result of our holding regarding the receiver's limited rights and standing under the

Charging Order, we will not address the receiver's derivative contentions of error The trial court was legally correct in ruling that the receiver had no right to notice of the opportunity to purchase the Loan. The receiver had no standing to assert any right that the debtor partners may have had to challenge the Note purchase under Section 9-404. regarding the escrowed funds, the interest rate, and the trial court's adoption of the Murphy Report, except to affirm that distribution of the escrowed funds, as recommended in the Murphy Report and approved by the trial court, may proceed.

Costs to be paid by appellant. judgment affirmed.

ADKINS, Judge.

Case Study 2

试用英文对以下案例进行分析和讨论：

孙某、于某和廖某欲合伙从事茶叶销售业务，经商量达成一致意见，已在合伙协议书上签名、盖章后，寻找经营场地、置办设施，并将该合伙企业取名为松竹梅有限责任公司。两年后，廖某因该合伙企业经营状况不佳，决意退出该合伙企业，并按规定通知了孙某与于某，这期间，孙某以该合伙企业名义与新林玉露公司签定了代销信阳毛尖的合同。

鲁某自以为有经营之道，要求加入该合伙企业，提出只负责销售，并须给其一定的利润提成，其他合伙人口头表示认可，从此鲁某便以该合伙企业的名义到处活动。廖某在办理退伙事宜时，因合伙企业与新林玉露公司代销信阳毛尖的合同刚签订不久，故未将此合同有关事宜进行结算，廖某退伙后，即去外地经商，该合伙企业在后来的经营过程中，因违法经营问题严重，被工商部门依法吊销营业执照，导致该合伙企业解散，新林玉露公司得知该合伙企业解散的消息后，即向法院起诉，请求该合伙企业偿还其代销信阳毛尖的款项。

现问：

（1）该合伙企业名称是否合法？为什么？

（2）廖某对合伙企业的债务是否还应承担责任？为什么？

（3）在该案的诉讼活动中，鲁某可否被列为被告？为什么？

（4）设孙某、于某和廖某在合伙协议书中约定对合伙企业事务作出决议时，不论各投资的份额大小，均实行一人一票的表决办法。该约定是否符合法律规定？

（5）设孙某、于某和廖某未就利润分配作出约定，则三人应如何分配利润？

（6）设孙某、于某和廖某决定由孙某一人负责执行合伙企业事务，则于某、廖某对合伙企业经营活动享有哪些权利？

（选自合伙企业案例分析：ttp://china. findlaw. cn/gongsifalv/hehuojiameng/hhqyal/51409. html）

Sources of Information and Further Readings

1. http://en.wikipedia.org/wiki/Partnership
2. Clifford, Denis. *The Partnership Book: How to Write a Partnership Agreement.* (5th edition). Nolo Press, 1997.
3. *Edwards, Paul. Teaming Up: The Small-Business Guide to Collaborating with Others to Boost Your Earnings and Expand Your Horizons.* G. P. Putnam's Sons, 1997.
4. Fay, Jack R. What form of ownership is best? *CPA Journal*, August 1998.
5. Haman, Edward A. *How to Write Your Own Partnership Agreement.* Sphinx Publishing, 1993.
6. Handmaker, Stuart A. *Choosing a Legal Structure for Your Business.* Prentice Hall, 1997.
7. Steingold, Fred S. *The Legal Guide for Starting and Running a Small Business.* (2nd edition). Nolo Press, 1995.

Chapter 12

The Law of Agency[1]

Key Concepts

agency of necessity
agency by estoppels
apparent agency
agency by ratification
breach of implied warranty of authority

Learning Objectives

1. Understand how an agency relationship is created.
2. Be familiar with different varieties of agency.
3. Understand the duties of the agent and the principal and their liabilities to the third party.

Introduction

The agency relationship is one of the most common and important legal relationships. It is widely used in both domestic and international business environment. In international business trade, many business activities are conducted by means of agents, such as the foreign trade agent, forwarding agent, insurance agent, international settlement agent, and so on. A transaction can hardly be completed without the involvement of these agents.

Agency relationships are common in many professional areas such as:

- employment procurement.

- real estate transactions (real estate brokerage, mortgage brokerage). In real estate brokerage, the buyers or sellers are the Principals themselves and the broker or his/her salesperson who represents each Principal is his/her Agent.
- financial advice (insurance agency, stock brokerage, accountancy).
- contract negotiation and promotion (business management) such as for publishing, fashion model, music, movies, theatre, show business, and sport.

An Agent in Commercial Law (also referred to as a manager) is a person who is authorized to act on behalf of another (called the principal or client) to create a legal relationship with a third party.

The law of agency is an area of commercial law dealing with a contractual or quasi-contractual, or non-contractual set of relationships when an agent is authorized to act on behalf of another (called the Principal) to create a legal relationship with a Third Party. Succinctly, it may be referred to as the relationship between a principal and an agent whereby the principal, expressly or impliedly, authorizes the agent to work under his control and on his behalf. The agent is, thus, required to negotiate on behalf of the principal or bring him and third parties into contractual relationship. This branch of law separates and regulates the relationships between:

- agents and principals;
- agents and the third parties with whom they deal on their Principals' behalf; and
- principals and the third parties when the agents purport to deal on their behalf.

Authority[2]

An agent who acts within the scope of authority conferred by her principal binds the principal in the obligations she creates against third parties. There are essentially two kinds of authority recognized in the law: actual authority (whether express or implied) and apparent authority.

Actual Authority

Actual authority can be of two kinds. Either the principal may have expressly conferred authority on the agent, or authority may be implied. Authority arises by consensual agreement, and whether it exists is a question of fact. An agent, as a general rule, is only entitled to indemnity from the principal if she has acted within the scope of her actual authority, and may be in breach of contract, and liable to a third party for breach of the implied warranty of authority.

Implied Actual Authority

Implied actual authority, also called "usual authority", is authority an agent has by virtue of being reasonably necessary to carry out his express authority. As such, it can be inferred by virtue of a position held by an agent. For example, partners have authority to bind the other partners in the firm, their liability being joint and several, and in a corporation, all executives and senior employees with decision-making authority by virtue of their position have authority to bind the corporation.

Apparent Authority

Apparent authority (also called "ostensible authority") exists where the principal's words or conduct would lead a reasonable person in the third party's position to believe that the agent was authorized to act, even if the principal and the purported agent had never discussed such a relationship. For example, where one person appoints a person to a position which carries with it agency-like powers, those who know of the appointment are entitled to assume that there is apparent authority to do the things ordinarily entrusted to one occupying such a position. If a principal creates the impression that an agent is authorized but there is no actual authority, third parties are protected so long as they have acted reasonably. This is sometimes termed "agency by estoppel"[3] or the "doctrine of holding out", where the principal will be estopped from denying the grant of authority if third parties have changed their positions to their detriment in reliance on the representations made.

Rama Corporation Ltd. v. Proved Tin and General Investments Ltd. [1952] 2 QB 147, Slade J., "Ostensible or apparent authority ... is merely a form of estoppel, indeed, it has been termed agency by estoppel and you cannot call in aid an estoppel unless you have three ingredients: (1) a representation, (2) reliance on the representation, and (3) an alteration of your position resulting from such reliance."

In the case of Watteau v. Fenwick, Lord Coleridge C.J. on the Queen's Bench concurred with an opinion by Wills J. that a third party could hold personally liable a principal who he did know about when he sold cigars to an agent that was acting outside of its authority. Wills J. held that "the principal is liable for all the acts of the agent which are within the authority usually confided to an agent of that character, notwithstanding limitations, as between the principal and the agent, put upon that authority". This decision is heavily criticised and doubted, though not entirely overruled in the UK. It is sometimes referred to as "usual authority" (though not in the sense used by Lord Denning M. R. in Hely-Hutchinson, where it is synonymous with "implied actual authority"). It has been explained as a form of apparent authority, or "inherent agency power".

Authority by virtue of a position held to deter: fraud and other harms that may befall individuals dealing with agents, there is a concept of Inherent Agency power, which is power derived solely by virtue of the agency relation. For example, partners have apparent authority to bind the other partners in the firm, their liability being joint and several, and in a corporation, all executives and senior employees with decision-making authority by virtue of their declared position have apparent authority to bind the corporation.

Even if the agent does act without authority, the Principal may ratify an unauthorized agreement entered into by an agent. It is called agency by ratification[4]. Ratification means that after the unauthorized act, the principal may agree to that act making it binding on the third party. This may be express or implied from the principal's behavior, e. g., if the agent has purported to act in a number of situations and the principal has knowingly acquiesced, the failure to notify all concerned of the agent's lack of authority is an implied ratification to those transactions and an implied grant of authority for future transactions of a similar nature.

Agency by Estoppel is an agency that is not created as an actual agency by a principal and an agent but that is imposed by law when a principal acts in such a way as to lead a third party to reasonably believe that another is the principal's agent and the third party is injured by relying on and acting in accordance with that belief. A principal has a duty to correct a third party's mistaken belief in an agent's authority to act on the principal's behalf. If the principal could have corrected the misunderstanding but failed to do so, he or she is estopped from denying the existence of the agency and is bound by the agent's acts in dealing with the third party.

Apparent Agency[5]

It is a legal concept in civil law system. A legal principle that an agent is deemed to have whatever power or authority a person would reasonably infer, either from the principal's representations concerning an agent's authority or from the agent's holding himself out as having proper authority. The principal may be obligated as if it had expressly granted the authority to the agent. Situation wherein the agent's conduct causes a client or prospective insured reasonably to believe that the agent has the authority to sell an insurance policy and contract on behalf of the insurance company. For example, if an agent continues to use insurance company documents, such as its application forms, rate manuals, stationery, and emblems on the door, the client has every reason to believe that the agent does in fact continue to represent the insurance company.

Agency of Necessity[6]

The origins of the doctrine of necessitous intervention by someone who is in a legal relationship with the defendant lie in the principle of agency of necessity, where an agent went beyond his or her authority by intervening on behalf of the principal in an emergency. Because of the circumstances of necessity, particularly the impracticability of the agent communicating with the principal, the courts were prepared to treat the agent as though he or she had the necessary authority to do what was reasonably necessary to save the principal's property. If an agency of necessity was established, the agent would be reimbursed for the expense incurred in rescuing the principal's property.

The doctrine of agency of necessity was initially relevant only in respect of the carriage of goods by sea, where the master took action to save the ship or cargo in an emergency. It was then extended to those cases which concerned the carriage of goods by land. This is illustrated by the Great Northern Railway Co. v. Swaffield where the plaintiff railway company had transported a horse to a station on behalf of the defendant. When the horse arrived there was nobody to collect it, so the plaintiff sent it to a stable. A number of months later the plaintiff paid the stabling charges and then sought to recover what it had paid from the defendant. The plaintiff's claim succeeded even though this involved the extension of the doctrine of agency of necessity to include carriers of goods by land. There was an agency of necessity because the plaintiff was found to have had no choice but to arrange for the proper care of the horse.

Before any agency can be created by necessity, three conditions must be satisfied:

- It must be impossible to get the principal's instructions.
- There must be an actual and definite commercial necessity for the creation of the agency. Generally, there is no agency of necessity unless there is a real emergency, such as may arise out of the possession of perishable goods or of livestock requiring to be fed.
- The agent of necessity must act bona fide in the interests of all parties concerned.

Breach of Implied Warranty of Authority[7]

A persons who professes to act as agent, but has no authority from the alleged principal or has exceeded his authority, is liable in an action for breach of warranty of authority at the suit of the party with whom he professed to make the contract. The action is based, not on the original contract, but on the implied representation by the agent that he had authority to make the original contract. Points to note:

- The action can only be brought by the third party, not by the principal.
- The agent is liable whether he has acted fraudulently or innocently, and even if his authority has been terminated, without his knowledge, by death or mental disorder of the principal.
- The agent is not liable if his lack of authority was known to the third party, or if it was known that he did not warrant his authority or if the contract excludes his liability.
- If the principal gives ambiguous instructions and the agent acts on them bona fide[8] and in a reasonable way, he will not be liable in an action for breach of warranty of authority even if he has interpreted them wrongly.
- The agent warrants his authority not only when he purports to contract on behalf of another but also when, purporting to act as an agent, he induces a third party to enter into any transaction with him on the faith of such agency.
- The measure of damages for breach of warranty of authority is the actual loss sustained.

Liabilities

Liability of Agent to Third Party

If the agent has actual or apparent authority, the agent will not be liable for acts performed within the scope of such authority, so long as the relationship of the agency and the identity of the principal have been disclosed. When the agency is undisclosed or partially disclosed, however, both the agent and the principal are liable. Where the principal is not bound because the agent has no actual or apparent authority, the purported agent is liable to the third party for breach of the implied warranty of authority.

Liability of Agent to Principal

If the agent has acted without actual authority, but the principal is nevertheless bound because the agent had apparent authority, the agent is liable to indemnify the principal for any resulting loss or damage.

Liability of Principal to Agent

If the agent has acted within the scope of the actual authority given, the principal must indemnify the agent for payments made during the course of the relationship whether the expenditure was expressly authorized or merely necessary in promoting the principal's business.

Duties

Duties of Agent to Principal

- **Fiduciary Duty of Loyalty**

The agent owes a fiduciary duty of good faith and utmost loyalty to the principal. The agent must conduct the principal's business with integrity. Therefore, the agent may not have any adverse personal financial interest in the principal's transactions during the agency. Some aspects of this duty persist even after the agency is terminated. Although the duty of loyalty may seem vague, it becomes more precise as it is applied to more specific situations. The fiduciary duty is a most basic ethical matter applicable to nearly all persons in business and government.

The ancient proviso that no person can serve two masters is at the heart of the prohibition against an agent simultaneously serving two principals in the same transaction. This would be a dual or double agency, and the agent would be unable to serve either principal fully. If the agent negotiates gains for one principal, the gains necessarily come as losses to the other. Also, dual agents are often given confidential information by either or both principals concerning key terms and the principal's willingness to sell or buy at the maximum or minimum price stated. Conflicts of interest are not always so obvious. Sometimes a full-time agent for one party may be paid a secret bribe, gratuity, gift, or kickback by the other party. The law presumes these payments exert some influence on the agents' judgment and thereby harm the principal.

Self-dealing is another type of unethical conflict of interest in which the agent's own personal financial interests directly conflict with the principal's financial interests. Agents may not have any undisclosed, unapproved personal financial interest in a transaction in which the principal has a financial interest. The self-dealing prohibition also requires agents to refrain from competing directly with the principal while the agency is in effect. Most firms' employees are prohibited from working for competing firms or personally competing against the principal during their employment.

- **Duty of Care**

Agents must use reasonable skill and care in conducting the principals' business. They must use all the skill they possess plus any skills the agent claims and any additional skills specified in the employment contract. It is probably unethical for an agent to claim skills he or she does not really possess. Such false bravado is often the basis for liability and ethical abuse.

Professional agents such as accountants, brokers, or attorneys must exercise skill equal to other similar professionals in that region. However, the law does not imply that the agent guarantees success unless the agent specifically makes that promise. However, when an agent's negligent performance causes damage to the principal, liability questions arise. An agent may be released from liability for negligence in the employment contract.

- **Obedience**

Agents must generally obey any reasonable directions the principal provides that will impact the principal's business. Even agents given broad discretion must obey the principal's directives. Of course, an agent need not obey orders that are illegal, immoral, or unreasonable. The agent may in good faith interpret vague commands or be disobedient during an emergency if obedience would damage the principal. However, in an emergency during which the principal is unavailable for consultation, the agent could disobey the principal's directive and do as the emergency requires in good faith.

• **Accounting**

The agent's fiduciary duty requires that all property and funds belonging to the principal be accounted for adequately. This is the duty to account or provide an accounting. It requires the agent to keep accurate records and keep the agent's individual property separate from the principal's property. Upon demand, the agent must produce accurate records of receipts and disbursements to the principal. Any commingling of funds belonging to the principal and agent makes it difficult to determine the true ownership. Commingling is a fundamental ethical abuse discovered among professional agents such as accountants, real estate brokers, investment professionals, and attorneys.

• **Communication**

Agents must communicate to the principal all relevant information and notices they receive in the course of performing the principal's business. Agents are often the principal's most visible communicator because they regularly receive or provide information to third parties about the principal's business. It is probably unethical for an agent to withhold information from the principal either in sympathy for the third party or to conceal the agent's poor performance.

An agent authorized to transact the principal's business generally has authority to receive information from third parties. When third parties provide information to the agent, the law presumes the agent will comply with the duty to communicate. Knowledge or notice received by the agent is therefore imputed to the principal. After the third party gives notice to the agent, the third party is relieved from repeating the communication to the principal or to any other agent who might later replace the original agent. The principal and agent are treated as one party after information is communicated to the agent.

Duties of Principal to Agent

• **Duty to Compensate**

Normally, a duty to pay the agent is implied unless special circumstances or the relationship of the parties suggest that a gratuitous agency was intended. The agency agreement should specify the amount of compensation for the agent and when it has been earned. Many disputes arise because no clear agreement has been reached. In the absence of agreement, the agent is entitled to the customary or reasonable value of the services performed. Custom is sometimes quite clear. For example, in most communities, real estate brokers all charge the same commission rate. If there is no clear custom and the amount is in dispute, expert witnesses may testify as to what a reasonable amount would be.

- **Duty to Reimburse and Indemnify**

Sometimes agents make advances from their own funds in conducting the principal's business. If the agent is acting within the scope of her authority, the principal has a duty to reimburse the agent for expenses incurred for the principal. Also, if the agent suffers losses while acting for the principal within the scope of the agent's authority, the principal has a duty to indemnify the agent. For example, suppose David is a salesperson for a company. He is in Chicago when he is asked to go to a foreign trade show. He uses his own funds to pay workers to set up the company's booth at the show. The company has a duty to reimburse him for his expenses. However, if some fault of the agent causes a loss, the principal will not be required to indemnify the agent for the amount of the loss. And, of course, the principal is not liable for unauthorized expenses incurred by the agent.

Termination

An agent's authority can be terminated at any time. If the trust between the agent and principal has broken down, it is not reasonable to allow the principal to remain at risk in any transactions that the agent might conclude during a period of notice.

An agency may come to an end in a variety of ways:

- By the principal revoking the agency—however, principal cannot revoke an agency coupled with interest to the prejudice of such interest. Such Agency is coupled with interest. An agency is coupled with interest when the agent himself has an interest in the subject-matter of the agency, e. g., where the goods are consigned by an upcountry constituent to a commission agent for sale, with poor to recoup himself from the sale proceeds, the advances made by him to the principal against the security of the goods; in such a case, the principal cannot revoke the agent's authority till the goods are actually sold, nor is the agency terminated by death or insanity.
- By the agent renouncing the business of agency.

- By the business of agency being completed.
- By the principal being adjudicated insolvent.

The principal also cannot revoke the agent's authority after it has been partly exercised, so as to bind the principal, though he can always do so, before such authority has been so exercised.

Further, if the agency is for a fixed period, the principal cannot terminate the agency before the time expired, except for sufficient cause. If he does, he is liable to compensate the agent for the loss caused to him thereby. The same rules apply where the agent, renounces an agency for a fixed period. Notice in this connection that want of skill continuous disobedience of lawful orders, and rude or insulting behavior has been held to be sufficient cause for dismissal of an agent. Further, reasonable notice has to be given by one party to the other; otherwise, damage resulting from want of such notice, will have to be paid. The revocation or renunciation of an agency may be made expressly or impliedly by conduct. The termination does not take effect as regards the agent, till it becomes known to him and as regards third party, till the termination is known to them.

When an agent's authority is terminated, it operates as a termination of subagent also.

This has become a more difficult area as states are not consistent on the nature of a partnership. Some states opt for the partnership as no more than an aggregate of the natural persons who have joined the firm. Others treat the partnership as a business entity and, like a corporation, vest the partnership with a separate legal personality. Hence, for example, in English law, a partner is the agent of the other partners whereas, in Scots law where there is a separate personality, a partner is the agent of the partnership. This form of agency is inherent in the status of a partner and does not arise out of a contract of agency with a principal. In the English Partnership Act 1890 provides that a partner who acts within the scope of his actual authority (express or implied) will bind the partnership when he does anything in the ordinary course of carrying on partnership business. Even if that implied authority has been revoked or limited, the partner will have apparent authority unless the third party knows that the authority has been compromised. Hence, if the partnership wishes to limit any partner's authority, it must give express notice of the limitation to the world. However, there would be little substantive difference if

English law was amended (See Law Commission Report 283): partners will bind the partnership rather than their fellow partners individually. For these purposes, the knowledge of the partner acting will be imputed to the other partners or the firm if a separate personality. The other partners or the firm are the principal and third parties are entitled to assume that the principal has been informed of all relevant information. This causes problems when one partner acts fraudulently or negligently and causes loss to clients of the firm. In most states, a distinction is drawn between knowledge of the firm's general business activities and the confidential affairs as they affect one client. Thus, there is no imputation if the partner is acting against the interests of the firm as a fraud. There is more likely to be liability in tort if the partnership benefited by receiving fee income for the work negligently performed, even if only as an aspect of the standard provisions of vicarious liability. Whether the injured party wishes to sue the partnership or the individual partners is usually a matter for the Plaintiff since, in most jurisdictions, their liability is joint and several[9].

Notes

1. **The Law of Agency 《代理法》**

《代理法》主要介绍代理的概念、代理权产生的方式、无权代理、代理的内部关系(代理人义务、本人义务)、代理的外部关系(本人、代理人与第三人之间的关系)、代理关系终止等内容。

2. **Authority 授权**

授权为英美法中的概念,可分为明示授权(express authority)和默示授权(implied authority)。前者是指本人以明示的方式指定他人为代理人;后者是指通过对本人行为的推定而确定其存在的授权。明示授权和默示授权称为实际授权(actual authority),与实际授权相对应的则是表面授权(apparent authority),表面授权也是产生代理权的原因之一。

3. **agency by estoppel 不容否认的代理**

不容否认的代理为英美法概念,是指本人以其言词或行为使善意第三人相信某人是其代理人,且第三人基于这种相信而改变了自己的经济地位,本人就不得否认其代理的存在,并受第三人与代理人所订合同或交易的约束。

4. **agency by ratification 经追认的代理**

经追认的代理是指无权代理人以本人的名义实施的民商事行为、经本人追认的代理行为。经追认的代理是一种无权代理,经本人追认后该代理行为有效。

5. **Apparent Agency 表见代理**

表见代理是指行为人虽无代理权,但善意第三人有理由相信该行为人有代理权的,该代理行为有效。表见代理实质上是无权代理,若无权代理行为均由被代理人(本人)追认决定其效力的话,会给善意第三人造成损害,因此在表见的情形之下,规定由被代理人承担表见代理行为的法律后果,更有利于保护善意第三人的利益,维护交易安全。

6. Agency of Necessity　客观必需的代理

客观必需的代理主要是在一个人受托照管另一个人的财产,为了保护这种财产而必须采取某种行动时而产生的,尽管没有得到采取这种行动的授权,但客观情况的必需视为具有此种授权。

7. Breach of Implied Warranty of Authority　违反有代理授权的默示担保

依据英美法的解释,当代理人与第三人订立合同时,代理人对第三人有一项默示的担保,即保证他是有代理权的。值得注意的是,违反有代理授权的默示担保,该诉讼只能有第三人提起。

8. bona fide　善意的,真诚的

例如,善意第三人(bona fide third party)、善意持票人(bona fide holder)、善意受让人(bona fide transferee)等。

9. joint and several liability　连带责任

负有连带义务的每个债务人都负有清偿全部债务的义务,履行义务的人有权要求其他负连带义务的人偿付他应当承担的份额。或言之,连带责任人承担了连带债务后,依法可以向其他负有连带责任的人追偿。

Study Questions

1. How can an agency relationship be created under common law system?
2. How to interpret "the agency without authority" under common law system and civil law system respectively?
3. What are the duties of the agent to the principal?
4. How to understand the legal relations between the agent, the principal and the third party?

Case Study 1

Facts

Mr. Freeman and Mr. Lockyer sued Buckhurst Park Ltd. and its director, Shiv Kumar Kapoor, for unpaid fees for their architecture work on developing the Buckhurst Park Estate in Sunninghill, Berkshire. The company's articles said that all four directors of the company (another Mr. Hoon, who was never there, and two nominees) were needed to constitute a quorum. Originally the company planned to simply buy and resell the land, but that fell through. Kapoor had acted alone (as if he were a managing director) in engaging the architects, without proper authority. The company argued it was not bound by the agreement.

Judge Herbert at Westminster County Court held the company was bound, and the company appealed.

Judgment

Diplock L. held the judge was right and the company was bound to pay Freeman and Lockyer for their architecture work. He noted that if actual authority is conferred by the board without a formal resolution, this renders the board liable for a fine. If a person has no actual authority to act on a company's behalf, then a contract can still be enforced if an agent had authority to enter contracts of a different but similar kind, the person granting that authority itself had authority, the contracting party was induced by these representations to enter the agreement and the company had the capacity to act. All those conditions were fulfilled on the facts, because (1) the board knew about Kapoor's general activities and permitted him to engage in these kinds of activities; such conduct represented his authority to contract for these kinds of things, (2) the articles conferred full power to the board, (3) Freeman and Lockyer were induced to contract by these representations' and (4) the company had capacity.

An "actual" authority is a legal relationship between principal and agent created by a consensual agreement to which they alone are parties. Its scope is to be ascertained by applying ordinary principles of construction of contracts, including any proper implications from the express words used, the usages of the trade, or the course of business between the parties. To this agreement the contractor is a stranger; he may be totally ignorant of the existence of any authority on the part of the agent. Nevertheless, if the agent does enter into a contract pursuant to the "actual" authority, it does create contractual rights and liabilities between the principal and the contractor. It may be that this rule relating to "undisclosed principals", which is peculiar to English law, can be rationalized as avoiding circuity of action, for the principal could in equity compel the agent to lend his name in an action to enforce the contract against the contractor, and would at common law be liable to indemnify the agent in respect of the performance of the obligations assumed by the agent under the contract.

An "apparent" or "ostensible" authority, on the other hand, is a legal relationship between the principal and the contractor created by a representation, made by the principal to the contractor, intended to be and in fact acted upon by the contractor, that the agent has authority to enter on behalf of the principal into a contract of a kind within the scope of the "apparent" authority, so as to render the principal liable to perform any obligations imposed upon him by such contract. To the relationship so created the agent is a stranger. He need not be (although he generally is) aware of the existence of the representation but he must not purport to make the agreement as principal himself. The representation, when acted upon by the contractor by entering into a contract with the agent, operates as an estoppel, preventing the principal from asserting that he is not bound by the contract. It is irrelevant whether the agent had actual authority to enter into the contract.

In ordinary business dealings the contractor at the time of entering into the contract can in the nature of things hardly ever rely on the "actual" authority of the agent. His information as to the authority must be derived either from the principal or from the agent or from both, for they alone know what the agent's actual authority is. All that the contractor can know is what they tell him, which may or may not be true. In the ultimate analysis he relies either upon the representation of the principal, that is, apparent authority, or upon the representation of the agent, that is, warranty of authority.

The representation which creates "apparent" authority may take a variety of forms of which the commonest is representation by conduct, that is, by permitting the agent to act in some way in the conduct of the principal's business with other persons. By so doing the principal represents to anyone who becomes aware that the agent is so acting that the agent has authority to enter on behalf of the principal into contracts with other persons of the kind which an agent so acting in the conduct of his principal's business has usually "actual" authority to enter into.

In applying the law as I have endeavored to summarise it to the case where the principal is not a natural person, but a fictitious person, namely, a corporation, two further factors arising from the legal characteristics of a corporation have to be borne in mind. The first is that the capacity of a corporation is limited by its constitution, that is, in the case of a company incorporated under the Companies Act, by its memorandum and articles of association; the second is that a corporation cannot do any act, and that includes making a representation, except through its agent.

Under the doctrine of ultra vires the limitation of the capacity of a corporation by its constitution to do any acts is absolute. This affects the rules as to the "apparent" authority of an agent of a corporation in two ways. First, no representation can operate to estop the corporation from denying the authority of the agent to do on behalf of the corporation an act which the corporation is not permitted by its constitution to do itself. Secondly, since the conferring of actual authority upon an agent is itself an act of the corporation, the capacity to do which is regulated by its constitution, the corporation cannot be estopped from denying that it has conferred upon a particular agent authority to do acts which by its constitution, it is incapable of delegating to that particular agent.

To recognize that these are direct consequences of the doctrine of ultra vires is, I think, preferable to saying that a contractor who enters into a contract with a corporation has constructive notice of its constitution, for the expression "constructive notice" tends to disguise that constructive notice is not a positive, but a negative doctrine, like that of estoppel of which it forms a part. It operates to prevent the contractor from saying that he did not know that the constitution of the corporation rendered a particular act or a particular delegation of authority ultra vires the corporation. It does not entitle him to say that he relied upon some unusual provision in the constitution of the corporation if he did not in fact so rely.

The second characteristic of a corporation, namely, that unlike a natural person it can only make a representation through an agent, has the consequence that in order to create an estoppel between the corporation and the contractor, the representation as to the authority of the agent which creates his "apparent" authority must be made by some person or persons who have "actual" authority from the corporation to make the representation. Such "actual" authority may be conferred by the constitution of the corporation itself, as, for example, in the case of a company, upon the board of directors, or it may be conferred by those who under its constitution have the powers of management upon some other person to whom the constitution permits them to delegate authority to make representations of this kind. It follows that where the agent upon whose "apparent" authority the contractor relies has no "actual" authority from the corporation to enter into a particular kind of contract with the contractor on behalf of the corporation, the contractor cannot rely upon the agent's own representation as to his actual authority. He can rely only upon a representation by a person or persons who have actual authority to manage or conduct that part of the business of the corporation to which the contract relates.

The commonest form of representation by a principal creating an "apparent" authority of an agent is by conduct, namely, by permitting the agent to act in the management or conduct of the principal's business. Thus, if in the case of a company the board of directors who have "actual" authority under the memorandum and articles of association to manage the company's business permit the agent to act in the management or conduct of the company's business, they thereby represent to all persons dealing with such agent that he has authority to enter on behalf of the corporation into contracts of a kind which an agent authorized to do acts of the kind which he is in fact permitted to do usually enters into in the ordinary course of such business. The making of such a representation is itself an act of management of the company's business. Prima facie it falls within the "actual" authority of the board of directors, and unless the memorandum or articles of the company either make such a contract ultra vires the company or prohibit the delegation of such authority to the agent, the company is estopped from denying to anyone who has entered into a contract with the agent in reliance upon such "apparent" authority that the agent had authority to contract on behalf of the company.

If the foregoing analysis of the relevant law is correct, it can be summarized by stating four conditions which must be fulfilled to entitle a contractor to enforce against a company a contract entered into on behalf of the company by an agent who had no actual authority to do so. It must be shown:

- that a representation that the agent had authority to enter on behalf of the company into a contract of the kind sought to be enforced was made to the contractor;
- that such representation was made by a person or persons who had "actual" authority to manage the business of the company either generally or in respect of those matters to which the contract relates;
- that he (the contractor) was induced by such representation to enter into the contract, that is, that he in fact relied upon it; and
- that under its memorandum or articles of association the company was not deprived of the capacity either to enter into a contract of the kind sought to be enforced or to delegate authority to enter into a contract of that kind to the agent.

The confusion which, I venture to think, has sometimes crept into the cases is in my view due to a failure to distinguish between these four separate conditions, and in particular to keep steadfastly in mind (a) that the only "actual" authority which is relevant is that of the persons making the representation relied upon, and (b) that the memorandum and articles of association of the company are always relevant (whether they are in fact known to the contractor or not) to the questions whether Condition (2) is fulfilled, and whether Condition (4) is fulfilled, and (but only if they are in fact known to the contractor) may be relevant as part of the representation on which the contractor relied ...

In the present case the findings of fact by the county court judge are sufficient to satisfy the four conditions, and thus to establish that Kapoor had "apparent" authority to enter into contracts on behalf of the company for their services in connection with the sale of the company's property, including the obtaining of development permission with respect to its use. The judge found that the board knew that Kapoor had throughout been acting as managing director in employing agents and taking other steps to find a purchaser. They permitted him to do so, and by such conduct represented that he had authority to enter into contracts of a kind which a managing director or an executive director responsible for finding a purchaser would in the normal course be authorized to enter into on behalf of the company. Condition (1) was thus fulfilled. The articles of association conferred full powers of management on the board. Condition (2) was thus fulfilled. The plaintiffs, finding Kapoor acting in relation to the company's property as he was authorized by the board to act, were induced to believe that he was authorized by the company to enter into contracts on behalf of the company for their services in connection with the sale of the company's property, including the obtaining of development permission with respect to its use. Condition (3) was thus fulfilled. The articles of association, which contained powers for the board to delegate any of the functions of management to a managing director or to a single director, did not deprive the company of capacity to delegate authority to Kapoor, a director, to enter into contracts of that kind on behalf of the company. Condition (4) was thus fulfilled.

Case Study 2

试用英文对以下案例进行分析和讨论：

兴华百货公司与张某签订了一份委托代理合同，委托张某订购一批新款流行时装，并给了张某一些空白合同纸（盖有兴华百货公司的合同专用章），合同规定授权期限为6个月，价款不得超过50万元，张某的酬金是1万元。张某持百货公司的介绍信到苏州寻找货源，不久即与当地依棉服装制品有限责任公司签订一份买卖合同，约定总价款为10万元，约定依棉服装公司分两次供货，由兴华百货公司自提。合同订立后，张某不想在此地久留，于是委托其原来的合作伙伴李某代为订购，并将空白合同纸留给他一些，称自己去另一地考察，请李某订立合同后立即与他联系，但价款不能超过40万元。依棉服装公司通知兴华百货公司来提第一批500件服装，这批服装提回公司后，兴华百货公司认为张某购买的服装不属于新款流行，表示不承认这份合同，并通知张某撤销其委托授权，要其即日将所剩空白合同纸及介绍信送回。张某不同意百货公司的说法，认为这是百货公司授权不明造成的。张某接通知后第三日，李某给张某来电称已与七匹狼服装公司订立了价款为40万元的合同，10日后将货送至兴华百货公司，张某将此事告知兴华百货公司，兴华百货公司称张某是于代理权终止后作出的行为，应由其自己承担。10日后，七匹狼服装公司来送货，兴华百货公司拒收，与此同时，依棉服装公司再次通知提第二批货，兴华百货公司也拒绝提货。

请根据有关法律回答下列问题：

（1）张某转托李某订购服装的行为是何性质？

（2）兴华百货公司可否拒收七匹狼服装公司送来的服装？为什么？

（3）兴华百货公司能否要求张某承担赔偿责任？

（4）兴华百货公司撤销委托授权的通知是否有效？为什么？

（5）因兴华百货公司不来提货而给依棉服装制品有限责任公司造成的损失，兴华百货公司是否应承担责任？张某对此是否有责任？为什么？

（选自司法考试案例精选：http://www.zyf123.com/thread-156275-1-1.html）

Sources of Information and Further Readings

1. LS Sealy and RJA Hooley. *Commercial Law: Text, Cases and Materials.* Butterworths, 1999.
2. http://en.wikipedia.org/wiki/Apparent_authority
3. http://www.articlesbase.com/law-articles/agency-law
4. http://en.wikipedia.org/wiki/Duty_of_care
5. http://en.wikipedia.org/wiki/Fiduciary

Chapter 13

Product Liability Law[1]

Key Concepts

product liability
defects
strict liability
breach of warranty
negligence
product recall

Learning Objectives

1. Understand the rationale of strict liability.
2. Understand the essentials of the theory of negligence.
3. Be familiar with the main features of American product liability law.
4. Understand the basis of liabilities between the producer and the seller.

An Overview

Product liability law, also called "products liability", governs the liability of manufacturers, wholesalers, distributors, and vendors for damages caused by dangerous or defective products. The goal of product liability laws is to help protect consumers from dangerous products, while holding manufacturers, distributors, and retailers responsible for putting into the marketplace products that they knew or should have known were dangerous or defective. Depending upon the jurisdiction, the liability of the various parties involved as the product passes from the manufacturer to the consumer will vary.

Product liability frequently involves retail items, but can extend to pretty much anything that can be sold. It is possible, for example, for a product liability action to arise from a defect in real estate such as a leaky wall or poorly installed vapor barrier that causes mold to grow inside a wall, or from a product used in real estate, such as defective siding.

Product liability claims can be brought under a number of theories, depending upon local law.

Design Defects: Liability arises from a mistake or oversight in the design of a product, which makes it dangerous when used as intended, or when used for another reasonably foreseeable purpose.

Manufacturing Defects: Liability arises from a defect that results from the manufacturing process.

Marketing Defects: A marketing defect involves such issues as inadequate warning labels or instructions, which, for example, prevent a user from recognizing a defect in the product, or from being aware of how to safely use or apply the product.

The elements of what a plaintiff must prove to prevail in a product liability action will also vary with the jurisdiction. It may be possible for a plaintiff to pursue more than one theory of liability.

Negligence[2]: In a negligence action, the plaintiff must typically demonstrate that the parties responsible for placing the product into commerce had a duty to provide the goods fit for their foreseeable uses, would have detected the defect with the exercise of reasonable care in the design, manufacture, or inspection process, failed to meet its obligations, and that the plaintiff was injured by the product as a result of the defect while engaged in a foreseeable use of the product.

Strict Liability[3]: Under a strict liability standard, once the plaintiff establishes that a product is defective, liability results from that fact alone no matter how much care was applied during design, manufacture, marketing, distribution and sale.

Breach of Warranty[4]: A warranty is essentially a contract of fitness between a manufacturer or vendor and its customer. Under a breach of express warranty theory, the plaintiff alleges the violation of the actual written warranty associated with a product. Under a breach of implied warranty theory, the plaintiff alleges that although there is no express warranty or the defect alleged is not covered by the express warranty, a defect in the goods renders them unfit for the purpose intended.

Product Liability Law in USA

After World War II, US economy began to develop very rapidly, many new techniques, new production procedures, product composition become more and more complex. Consequently, there occurred more and more product liability accidents. In the United States, the accidents and loss of property related to product liability began to strike the consumer considerably. For example, Consumer Product Safety Commission issued some statistics in 1986, due to safety problems of product, every year, about 36 million were injured and 30 thousand were dead. The US lawyers make their earnings in positive proportion to the compensation from the defective products. The lawyers and also the jury are inclined to show partiality to the consumer. American consumers have a strong sense of claiming damages.

Theories of Liability

In the United States, the claims most commonly associated with product liability are negligence, strict liability, breach of warranty, and various consumer protection claims. The majorities of product liability laws are determined at the state level and vary widely from state to state. Each type of product liability claim requires different elements to be proven to present a successful claim.

Types of Liability

Section 2 of the *Restatement (Third) of Torts*: *Products Liability* distinguishes between three major types of product liability claims:

- manufacturing defect;
- design defect;
- a failure to warn (also known as marketing defects).

However, in most states, these are not legal claims in and of themselves, but are pleaded in terms of the theories mentioned above. For example, a plaintiff might plead negligent failure to warn or strict liability for defective design. Manufacturing defects are those that occur in the manufacturing process and usually involve poor-quality materials or shoddy workmanship. Design defects occur where the product design is inherently dangerous or useless (and hence defective) no matter how carefully manufactured; this may be demonstrated either by showing that the product fails to satisfy ordinary consumer expectations as to what constitutes a safe product, or that the risks of the product outweigh its benefits. Failure-to-warn defects arise in products that carry inherent nonobvious dangers which could be mitigated through adequate warnings to the user, and these dangers are present regardless of how well the product is manufactured and designed for its intended purpose.

Breach of Warranty

Warranties are statements by a manufacturer or seller concerning a product during a commercial transaction. Warranty claims commonly require privity between the injured party and the manufacturer or seller; in plain English, this means they must be dealing with each other directly. Breach of warranty-based product liability claims usually focus on one of three types: (1) breach of an express warranty, (2) breach of an implied warranty of merchantability, and (3) breach of an implied warranty of fitness for a particular purpose. Additionally, claims involving real estate may also take the form of an implied warranty of habitability. Express warranty claims focus on express statements by the manufacturer or the seller concerning the product (e.g., "This chainsaw is useful to cut turkeys"). The various implied warranties cover those expectations common to all products (e.g., that a tool is not unreasonably dangerous when used for its proper purpose), unless specifically disclaimed by the manufacturer or the seller.

Negligence

A basic negligence claim consists of proof of

- a duty owed,
- a breach of that duty,
- the breach was the cause in fact of the plaintiff's injury (actual cause),
- the breach proximately caused the plaintiff's injury,
- and the plaintiff suffered actual quantifiable injury (damages).

As demonstrated in cases such as Winterbottom v. Wright, the scope of the duty of care was limited to those with whom one was in privity. Later cases like MacPherson v. Buick Motor Co. broadened the duty of care to all who could be foreseeably injured by one's conduct. In common law negligence now is a tort, if the plaintiff sues the defendant in a law-court, it's not necessary to show Privity of Contract[5] between them, because this lawsuit is not made in the light of the contract. Therefore, the plaintiff may include not only the buyer, but also his relatives, friends, visitors or onlookers.

Strict Liability

Rather than focus on the behavior of the manufacturer (as in negligence), strict liability claims focus on the product itself. Under strict liability, the manufacturer is liable if the product is defective, even if the manufacturer was not negligent in making that product defective.

The difficulty with negligence is that it still requires the plaintiff to prove that the defendant's conduct fell below the relevant standard of care. However, if an entire industry tacitly settles on a somewhat careless standard of conduct, then the plaintiff may not be able to recover even though he or she is severely injured, because although the defendant's conduct caused his or her injuries, such conduct was not negligent in the legal sense. As a practical matter, with the increasing complexity of products, injuries, and medical care (which made many formerly fatal injuries survivable), it is quite a difficult and expensive task to find and retain good expert witnesses who can establish the standard of care, breach, and causation.

Therefore, in the 1940s and 1950s, many American courts departed from the MacPherson standard and decided that it was too harsh to require seriously injured consumer plaintiffs to prove negligence claims against manufacturers or retailers. To avoid having to deny such plaintiffs any relief, these courts began to look for facts in their cases which they could characterize as an express or implied warranty from the manufacturer to the consumer. The *res ipsa loquitur* (or thing speaks for itself) doctrine was also stretched to reduce the plaintiff's burden of proof. Over time, the resulting legal fictions became increasingly strained.

Of the various US states, California was the first to throw away the fiction of a warranty and to boldly assert the doctrine of strict liability in tort for defective products, in 1963 (under the guidance of then-Associate Justice Roger J. Traynor). See Greenman v. Yuba Power Products, 59 Cal. 2d 57 (1963). The importance of Greenman cannot be overstated: in 1996, the Association of Trial Lawyers of

America (now known as the American Association of Justice) celebrated its 50th anniversary by polling lawyers and law professors on the top ten developments in tort law during the past half-century, and Greenman topped the list.

In Greenman, Traynor cited to his own earlier concurrence in Escola v. Coca-Cola Bottling Co., 24 Cal. 2d 453, 462 (1944) (Traynor, J., concurring). In *Escola*, now widely recognized as a landmark case in American law, Justice Traynor laid the foundation for Greenman with these words:

Even if there is no negligence, however, public policy demands that responsibility be fixed wherever it will most effectively reduce the hazards to life and health inherent in defective products that reach the market. It is evident that the manufacturer can anticipate some hazards and guard against the recurrence of others, as the public cannot. Those who suffer injury from defective products are unprepared to meet its consequences. The cost of an injury and the loss of time or health may be an overwhelming misfortune to the person injured, and a needless one, for the risk of injury can be insured by the manufacturer and distributed among the public as a cost of doing business. It is to the public interest to discourage the marketing of products having defects that are a menace to the public. If such products nevertheless find their way into the market it is to the public interest to place the responsibility for whatever injury they may cause upon the manufacturer, who, even if he is not negligent in the manufacture of the product, is responsible for its reaching the market. However intermittently such injuries may occur and however haphazardly they may strike, the risk of their occurrence is a constant risk and a general one. Against such a risk there should be general and constant protection and the manufacturer is best situated to afford such protection.

The year after Greenman, the Supreme Court of California proceeded to extend strict liability to all parties involved in the manufacturing, distribution, and sale of defective products (including retailers) and in 1969 made it clear that such defendants were liable not only to direct customers and users, but also to any innocent bystanders randomly injured by defective products.

Since then, many jurisdictions have been swayed by Justice Traynor's strongly persuasive arguments on behalf of the strict liability rule in Escola, Greenman, and subsequent cases—including nearly all US states, the European Union, Australia, and Japan—and have adopted it either by judicial decision or by legislative act.

Notably, South Africa, New Zealand, and the US state of North Carolina have soundly rejected strict liability; Canada continues to officially reject it but under American influence has gradually adjusted certain aspects of negligence and warranty law to make them more favorable to consumers.

Oddly, although the Greenman rule was transmitted to most other states via Section 402A of the Restatement of Torts, Second (published in 1964 after Greenman), the Supreme Court of California refused to adopt Section 402A's "unreasonably dangerous" limitation upon strict liability in 1972. Thus, strict liability in California is truly strict, in that the plaintiff need not show that the defect was unreasonable or dangerous. On the other hand, in California, the defendant is allowed to introduce evidence in a strict products liability action that the plaintiff contributed to his or her own injuries.

Although the Supreme Court of California has since become more conservative, it continues to endorse and expand the doctrine. In 2002 it held that strict liability for defective products even applies to makers of component products that are installed into and sold as part of real property.

Consumer Protection

In addition to the above common law claims, many states have enacted consumer protection statutes providing for specific remedies for a variety of product defects. Statutory remedies are often provided for defects which merely render the product unusable (and hence cause economic injury) but do not cause physical injury or damage to other property; the "economic loss rule" means that strict liability is generally unavailable for products that damage only themselves. The best known examples of consumer protection laws for product defects are lemon laws, which became widespread because automobiles are often an American citizen's second-largest investment after buying a home.

Defenses

In general, the liability defenses may include:

- unforeseeability;
- state of art;
- obvious danger (also called generally known danger, the manufacturer has no duty to warn

of obvious danger);

- inherent product danger (such as knife and medicine, elimination of such danger may change the substantial characteristics of the product);
- product misuse and alteration (the manufacturer has the duty to take measures to avoid the risk in reasonably foreseeable misuse and alteration);
- plaintiff's fault (the plaintiff's conduct fails to conform to generally applicable rules establishing appropriate standard of care, the recovery of damages for harm may be reduced).

Product Liability in the European Union

Moves towards a strict liability regime in Europe began with the Council of Europe Convention on Products Liability in regard to Personal Injury and Death (the Strasbourg Convention[6]) in 1977. On July 25, 1985, the European Economic Community adopted the Product Liability Directive 85/374/EEC. In language similar to Traynor's, the Directive stated that "liability without fault on the part of the producer is the sole means of adequately solving the problem, peculiar to our age of increasing technicality, of a fair apportionment of the risks inherent in modern technological production. However, the Directive also gave each member state the option of imposing a liability cap of 70 million euros per defect.

Rationale for and Debate over Strict Liability

The fundamental rationale of strict liability is to force producers to internalize the external costs they impose on society. By placing liability for all injuries caused by a product on its manufacturer, the manufacturer is forced to take into account, when deciding whether and how much to produce the product, the harm caused by it. If this internalized harm is so great that the manufacturer cannot profit from producing the product, it will discontinue the product, or sell it only at a higher price to consumers who value it especially highly (in economic terms, modify its activity level). In this way, strict liability provides a mechanism for ensuring that the societal good of products in the marketplace outweighs their societal harm.

Moreover, proponents of strict liability for defective products argue that strict liability is sensible because between two parties who are not negligent (manufacturer and consumer), one will still have to suffer the economic cost of the injury. They argue that it is preferable to place the economic costs on the manufacturer because it can better absorb them and pass them on to other consumers by the way of higher prices. As such, the manufacturer becomes the insurer of consumers that are injured by its defective products, with premiums paid by other consumers.

A related argument arises from the fact that the distribution of information about any given product is highly asymmetrical; the manufacturer of any given product is in a better position than the consumer to know of its particular dangers. Therefore, in order to fulfill the public policy of minimizing injury, it is more reasonable to impose the burden of finding and correcting such dangers upon the manufacturer as opposed to imposing the burden of finding and avoiding unsafe products upon the consumer. These arguments are often mentioned in cases of design and warning defects and less so in the case of manufacturing defects, since the latter are thought to be less preventable by the manufacturer because he is already acting with due care.

Critics charge that strict liability incentivizes product misuse (particularly in jurisdictions where this may not be a defense) and creates a moral hazard problem on the part of potential buyers. Reasoning that consumers will recover regardless of the amount of care they take in using the product, critics assert that consumers will underinvest in care even when they are the least-cost avoiders, thus leading to a lower aggregate level of care than under a negligence standard.

While proponents assert that the producer can build the cost into the price as insurance, critics argue that this assertion is ignorant of economics and only holds true in inelastic regions of the demand curve. As a result of strict liability for their products, manufacturers may not produce the socially optimal level of goods. Particularly with elastic regions of the demand curve, where consumers are very price-sensitive, the manufacturer by definition cannot pass on the economic costs to the consumers as a form of insurance without pricing many of those consumers out of the market for that good. However, because consumers are not willing to pay for this insurance, proponents of strict liability would argue that this is evidence of a product whose harm outweighs its good, in which case it should be removed from the market.

Critics also argue that applying strict liability to products results in substantially higher transaction costs. One example of these transaction costs is the creation of maintenance of legal disclaimers on products that would be unnecessary to the reasonable person such as the improperly algorithmic "lather, rinse, repeat" instructions on shampoos and the ubiquitous "not for human consumption" labelling on an inordinate number of non-food items. This results in a waste of time and resources for the producers who have to create these warnings, decreasing the producer surplus from trade. This also lowers the consumer surplus from these transactions, as all reasonably diligent consumers will read the unnecessary instructions, whereas the consumers likely to misuse the product are unlikely to be sufficiently diligent to read the instructions.

On the other hand, strict liability likely reduces litigation costs, because a plaintiff need only prove causation, not imprudence. When it is clear that the product caused the plaintiff's harm, parties under a strict liability regime are prone to settle out of court, because only damages are in dispute.

A product recall[7] is a request to return to the maker a batch or an entire production run of a product, usually due to the discovery of safety issues. The recall is an effort to limit liability for corporate negligence (which can cause costly legal penalties) and to improve or avoid damage to publicity. Recalls are costly to a company because they often entail replacing the recalled product or paying for damage caused by use, although possibly less costly than consequential costs caused by damage to brand name and reduced trust in the manufacturer.

A country's consumer protection laws will have specific requirements in regard to product recalls. Such regulations may include how much of the cost the maker will have to bear, situations in which a recall is compulsory (usually because the risk is big enough), or penalties for failure to recall. The firm may also initiate a recall voluntarily, perhaps subject to the same regulations as if the recall were compulsory. In the case of a compulsory recall, consumers who fail to dispose of it or return it to the manufacturer for replacement or refund could be fined for as much as $5,000.

Product Liability Law in Japan

Introduction of the Product Liability System

Through the rapid development of science and technology and aggressive innovation in economic activities, Japan has attained a society of mass production and mass consumption. On the other hand, because consumers use and consume high-tech and complicated products daily, their safety primarily depends on product manufacturers.

Therefore, in order to change the principle of liability for damages in product-related accidents from "negligence" to "defect", and relieve the injured persons in a swift and appropriate manner, the Product Liability Law shall come into force from July 1, 1995. With the introduction of the Product Liability system, it is expected that the way of thinking and the approach concerning product safety of both the industry business segment and the consumer segment will change and improve.

Definition of Product Liability

Product Liability shall be defined as liability for damages in such case as follows: In the case where due to a defect in the delivered product, a life, a body or property of another person (including a third party not using or consuming the product directly, and a legal person as well as a natural person) is injured, the person who manufactured, processed, imported or put his name, etc on the product as business is liable for damages of the injured person.

Significance of Introduction of the Product Liability Law

Previously in Japan, claims for damages have usually been made based on the Civil Code Article No. 709 in case the injury is caused by a defect in the product. The Civil Code Article No. 709 employs the "fault-based liability (negligence) principle", and requires the "intention or fault" of the manufacturer, etc as a condition for liability.

The Product Liability Law takes the "defect in the product" as a condition for liability instead of the "intention or fault" of the manufacturer, etc. Therefore, after introduction of the Product Liability Law, the injured has only to verify the "defect in the product" for claiming damages.

Civil Code Article No. 709	Product Liability Law
• The damage • The intention or fault of the accused • The causal relationship between the damage and the intention or fault	• The damage • The defect in the product (at the time distribution commences) • The causal relationship between the damage and the defect

The Product Liability Law can be said to employ the "liability without fault principle"[8], that is, the manufacturer, etc is liable for damages if the injury is caused by a defect in the product regardless of whether it was his intention or fault. However, the manufacturer, etc is not liable when there is no defect in the product. As the Product Liability Law is a means for claiming damages, the plaintiff side bears the burden of proof. The enactment of the Product Liability Law means a change in the liability rule from fault-based liability principle to defect-based liability principle.

Points of the Product Liability Law

Scope of the Product

By definition, "product" means movable property manufactured or processed. Therefore, incorporeal property such as services, information, software, electricity, etc, and immovables are not the object of the Law. Moreover, agricultural, forestal, marine and mineral products which are not processed artificially are not the object of the Law.

Parties Subject to Liability

Parties subject to liability are as follows: Any person who puts his name, etc on the product with such titles as "manufacturer" or "importer", or any person who puts his name, etc on the product in a manner mistakable for its manufacturer or importer (For instance, any person selling OEM[9] products using his company brand name). Any person who, by putting his name, etc on the product, may be recognized as its manufacturer-in-fact, in the light of a manner concerning manufacturing, processing, importation or sales, and other circumstances. (For instance, any person, even though he puts his name, etc on the product with such titles as "seller" or "sales agency", who is socially recognized as its manufacturer-in-fact or is a sole distributor of the product.)

Concept of the Term "Defect"

A "defect" does not mean mere lack of quality of the product, but means lack of safety in the product which may cause the injury to life, body, or property. In the law, the term "defect" is defined as "lack of safety that the product ordinarily should provide", taking into account "the nature of the product", "the ordinarily foreseeable manner of use of the product", "the time when the manufacturer, etc delivered the product", and other circumstances concerning the product. These three above-mentioned circumstances include such respective factors, as are presented below. In the actual trial, while the weight of each factor is different depending on individual cases, these factors are comprehensively taken into account in judging whether the product is defective or not. "The nature of the product" means the circumstances of the product itself, including factors such as the following: representation of the product (instructions, warnings, etc to prevent accidents), effectiveness and usefulness of the product (compared to its danger), cost vs. effect (the safety standard of products in the same price range), probability of occurrence of accident and its extent ordinary use period and durable period of the product. "The ordinarily foreseeable manner of use of the product" means the circumstances concerning use of the product, including factors such as the following reasonably foreseeable use of the product possibility of preventing damage from occurring by the product user. "The time when the manufacturer, etc delivered the product" means the circumstances when the manufacturer, etc delivered the product, including factors such as the following: situation at the time the product was delivered (the safety level required in society at the time the product was delivered) technological capabilities (the prior state of safety regulations and possibility of alternative design).

Exemptions

The Product Liability Law admits "Development Risk Defense" as an exemption. This means the manufacturer, etc shall not be liable for damages, if the manufacturer, etc proves that the state of "scientific or technical knowledge" at the time when the manufacturer, etc delivered the product was not such as to enable the existence of the defect in the product to be discovered. "Scientific or technical knowledge" means all the established knowledge that could influence the decision on the existence of the defect, and not the knowledge held by a peculiar person but the total knowledge that objectively exists in society. Component or Raw Material Manufacturer's Defense Insofar as components or raw materials are "products" movable property manufactured or processed, their manufacturers are also subject to liability in the Law. However, if the manufacturer, etc of a component or raw material proves that the defect is substantially attributable to compliance with the instructions concerning the specifications given by the assembling manufacturer who incorporates the component or raw material into another product, and that the manufacturer, etc is not negligent on occurrence of the defect, the manufacturer of the component or raw material shall not be liable for damages.

Time Limitations

The right for damages provided in the Law shall be extinguished by prescription if the injured person or his legal representative does not exercise their rights within the following period: A period of three years from the time when the injured person or his legal representative becomes aware of the damage and the liable party for the damage (short-term negative prescription). A period of ten years from the time when the manufacturer, etc delivered the product (long-term liable period).

Concerning introduction of the Product Liability Law, the cooperation of all divisions of a company is indispensable. Namely, not only development, design, manufacturing and quality control divisions, but also general affairs, law and consumer divisions, etc are recommended to cooperate with each other on product safety measures.

In case injury to life, body or property is caused by a defect in the product, all product-related manufacturers as well as the assembling manufacturer of the finished product shall be liable jointly and severally for the damages described in the Law.

Comparison of Japan's Product Liability Law with Product Liability System of EU and USA

	Japan	European Union	USA
	The P L Law	EC Product Liability Directive (Council Directive of 25 July 1985)	Judicial Precedents
Principle Liability for Damages	Liability without Fault Principle (Defect-based Liability Principle)		

(Continued)

Burden of Proof[10] (Adoption of Presumption Rule)	The plaintiff side bears the burden of proof of damage, defect and causal relationship between defect and damage.		
	No	No	No
	(flexible application of empirical rules and inference)		Preponderance of the Evidence Discovery
Adoption of Development Risk Defense	Yes	Yes	Yes
		(option: adopted by 12 of 14 countries)	(state of the art defense)
Liable Period	10 years from the delivery of the product (10 years from the time the damage arises in case such damage as caused by accumulation of substances or others)	10 years from the delivery of the product	10 years from the delivery of the product (in many states)

Product Liability Law in China

Brief Introduction

In 1986, the General Principles of the Civil Law was passed by the NPC (National People's Congress), in which there is one article (Article 122) governing the product liability, which is taken as a formal beginning of the legislation on product liability of China, saying that "if a substandard product causes property damage or physical injury to others, the manufacturer or seller shall bear civil liability according to law."

In 1993, the Product Quality Law of PRC (amended in 2000), the amendment strengthens the product quality supervision system and enlarges the categories of the damages for personal injury.

Liability Basis

The producer shall undertake the strict liability for the damages or injuries caused by the defective products, whereas the seller undertakes fault-based liability. The producer and the seller shall undertake joint and several liability. If the liability falls on the producer, but the seller has made compensation, the seller shall have the right to recover the loss from the producer, and vice versa.

Defenses

The producer may exempt himself from the liability if he can prove the existence of any of the following circumstances:

- The product has not been put in circulation;
- The defect causing the damage did not exist at the time when the product was put in circulation;
- The science and technology at the time the product was put into circulation was at a level incapable of detecting the defect.

Limitation Period

The limitation period to bring an action of product liability is 2 years from the date when the plaintiff knew or should have known the infringement of his rights and interests; 10 years from the date when the product was delivered to the first user or consumer.

Notes

1. Product Liability Law 《产品责任法》

产品责任是指产品生产者、销售者因生产、销售有缺陷产品致使他人遭受人身伤害、财产损失所应承担的赔偿责任。《产品责任法》是确定生产者、销售者承担此种民事责任的法律规范的总称,旨在保护广大用户、消费者的合法权益。《产品责任法》主要包括产品责任含义、产品缺陷(瑕疵)、责任主体、归责原则、举证责任、赔偿范围、诉讼时效、抗辩事由等内容。

2. Negligence 疏忽

疏忽是指产品的生产者或销售者未尽到相应的注意义务(duty of care),致使产品有缺陷,由于这种缺陷使消费者的人身或财产遭到损害,对此,产品生产者或销售者应承担责任。这是建立在过失责任理论之上的,这种疏忽在英美法中是一种侵权行为。

3. Strict Liability 严格责任

严格责任是一种不以过错为要件的责任形态，只要某种行为客观上造成危害后果，不论行为人主观上有无过错，就应承担责任。在产品责任法中，只要产品存在缺陷，对使用者或消费者具有不合理的危险并因此造成人身或财产伤害，该产品的生产者或销售者就应承担赔偿责任。严格责任为英美法系中的一个概念，大陆法系通常采用无过错责任（liability without fault）。

4. Warranty 担保

担保分为明示担保（express warranty）与默示担保（implied warranty），前者是指产品的生产者对其产品所做的明示说明，包括对其性能、质量、用途等的介绍。产品制造者应保证其产品质量达到其所明示说明的质量标准，如果达不到这一标准而给他人造成损害，则认为是违反明示担保，应当承担相应的法律责任。默示担保具有两层含义：对产品商销性（merchantability）的默示担保与产品适合特定用途（fitness of particular purpose）的默示担保。产品制造者虽然没有作出明示的说明，也应担保其产品一般的效用、具有平均的品质且不含有隐蔽缺陷；还应担保其产品适合某一特定用途。否则，因产品缺陷造成买受人损害，则认为产品制造人违反默示担保，应当承担赔偿责任。担保理论的局限性主要是受害人应与产品的生产、销售者之间存在合同关系，否则难以援引该理论提供法律救济。

5. Privity of Contract 直接合同关系原则，合同关系不涉及第三人原则

直接合同关系原则是指消费者只有同生产者、销售者之间存在直接合同关系（主要指买卖合同关系），才能依合同就缺陷产品对自己造成的人身、财产损害要求生产者、销售者承担民事责任，即“无合同则无责任”规则。

6. Strasbourg Convention 《斯特拉斯堡公约》

《斯特拉斯堡公约》全称为《关于人身伤亡产品责任欧洲公约》（European Convention on Products Liability in Regard to Personal Injury and Death），欧洲理事会于 1977 年 1 月 27 日在法国斯特拉斯堡通过该公约。

7. product recall 产品召回

产品召回是指生产商将已经送到批发商、零售商或最终用户手上的产品收回。产品召回的典型原因是所售出的产品被发现存在缺陷。产品召回制度则是针对厂家原因造成的批量性问题而出现的处理办法。

8. liability without fault principle 无过错责任原则

无过错责任原则是指没有过错造成他人损害的，依法律规定应由与造成损害原因有关的人承担民事责任的原则。英美法称之为“严格责任”。我国民法通则规定的典型的适用无过错责任的案件有：产品缺陷致人损害、高度危险作业致人损害、环境污染致人损害、地面施工致人损害、饲养的动物致人损害等损害赔偿案件。

9. OEM 原始设备制造商，原厂委托制造商

OEM 全称为 Original Equipment Manufacturer，按原单位（品牌单位）委托合同进行产品开发和制造，用原单位商标，由原单位销售或经营的合作经营生产方式，又称为“代工生产”

或“贴牌生产”。相关用语如 ODM (Original Design Manufacturer,原始设计制造商、原厂委托设计制造商)以及 OBM (Original Brand Manufacturer,原始品牌制造商)。

10. Burden of Proof 举证责任

举证责任的一般原则是指“谁主张,谁举证”,而“举证责任倒置”是这一原则的例外。

Study Questions

1. What are the main theories involved in the product liability law?
2. What are the differences of the product liability law of Japan, USA and EU?
3. What are the definifions of strict liability, absolute liability, liability without fault, fault-based liability and joint and several liability?
4. What are the liability defenses involved in the product liability law?

Case Study

Greenman v. Yuba Power Products, Inc. (1963) 59 C2d 57

WILLIAM B. GREENMAN, Plaintiff and Appellant, v. YUBA POWER PRODUCTS, INC., Defendant and Appellant; THE HAYSEED, Defendant and Respondent.

COUNSEL

No appearance for Defendant and Respondent.

Holt, Macomber, Graham & Baugh and William H. Macomber for Defendant and Appellant.

Reed, Brockway & Ruffin and William F. Reed for Plaintiff and Appellant.

OPINION

TRAYNOR, J.

Plaintiff brought this action for damages against the retailer and the manufacturer of a Shopsmith, a combination power tool that could be used as a saw, drill, and wood lathe. He saw a Shopsmith demonstrated by the retailer and studied a brochure prepared by the manufacturer. He decided he wanted a Shopsmith for his home workshop, and his wife bought and gave him one for Christmas in 1955. In 1957 he bought the necessary attachments to use the Shopsmith as a lathe for turning a large piece of wood he wished to make into a chalice. After he had worked on the piece of wood several times without difficulty, it suddenly flew out of the machine and struck him on the forehead, inflicting serious injuries. About ten and a half months later, he gave the retailer and the manufacturer written notice of claimed breaches of warranties and filed a complaint against them alleging such breaches and negligence.

After a trial before a jury, the court ruled that there was no evidence that the retailer was negligent or had breached any express warranty and that the manufacturer was not liable for the breach of any implied warranty. Accordingly, it submitted to the jury only the cause of action alleging breach of implied warranties against the retailer and the causes of action alleging negligence and breach of express warranties against the manufacturer. The jury returned a verdict for the retailer against plaintiff and for plaintiff against the manufacturer in the amount of $65,000. The trial court denied the manufacturer's motion for a new trial and entered judgment on the verdict. The manufacturer and plaintiff appeal. plaintiff seeks a reversal of the part of the judgment in favor of the retailer, however, only in the event that the part of the judgment against the manufacturer is reversed.

Plaintiff introduced substantial evidence that his injuries were caused by defective design and construction of the Shopsmith. His expert witnesses testified that inadequate set screws were used to hold parts of the machine together so that normal vibration caused the tailstock of the lathe to move away from the piece of wood being turned permitting it to fly out of the lathe. They also testified that there were other more positive ways of fastening the parts of the machine together, the use of which would have prevented the accident. The jury could therefore reasonably have concluded that the manufacturer negligently constructed the Shopsmith. The jury could also reasonably have concluded that statements in the manufacturer's brochure were untrue, that they constituted express warranties, fn. 1 and that plaintiff's injuries were caused by their breach.

The manufacturer contends, however, that plaintiff did not give it notice of breach of warranty within a reasonable time and that therefore his cause of action for breach of warranty is barred by Section 1769 of the Civil Code. Since it cannot be determined whether the verdict against it was based on the negligence or warranty cause of action or both, the manufacturer concludes that the error in presenting the warranty cause of action to the jury was prejudicial.

Section 1769 of the Civil Code provides: "In the absence of express or implied agreement of the parties, acceptance of the goods by the buyer shall not discharge the seller from liability in damages or other legal remedy for breach of any promise or warranty in the contract to sell or the sale. But, if, after acceptance of the goods, the buyer fails to give notice to the seller of the breach of any promise or warranty within a reasonable time after the buyer knows, or ought to know of such breach, the seller shall not be liable therefor."

Like other provisions of the Uniform Sales Act (Civ. Code, Ë 1721 – 1800), Section 1769 deals with the rights of the parties to a contract of sale or a sale. It does not provide that notice must be given of the breach of a warranty that arises independently of a contract of sale between the parties.

Such warranties are not imposed by the sales act, but are the product of common-law decisions that have recognized them in a variety of situations. (See Gagne v. Bertran, 43 Cal. 2d 481, 486 – 487 〔275 P. 2d 15〕, and authorities cited; Peterson v. Lamb Rubber Co, 54 Cal. 2d 339, 348 〔5 Cal. Rptr. 863, 353 P. 2d 575〕; Klein v. Duchess Sandwich Co, Ltd. , 14 Cal. 2d 272, 276-283 〔93 P. 2d 799〕; Burr v. Sherwin Williams Co. , 42 Cal. 2d 682, 695 – 696 〔268 P. 2d 1041〕; Souza & McCue Constr. Co, Inc. v. Superior Court, 57 Cal. 2d 508, 510 – 511 〔20 Cal. Rptr. 634, 370 P. 2d 338〕.) It is true that in many of these situations the court has invoked the sales act definitions of warranties (Civ. Code, Ë 1732, 1735) in defining the defendant's liability, but it has done so, not because the statutes so required, but because they provided appropriate standards for the court to adopt under the circumstances presented. (See Clinkscales v. Carver, 22 Cal. 2d 72, 75 〔136 P. 2d 777〕; Dana v. Sutton Motor Sales, 56 Cal. 2d 284, 287 〔14 Cal. Rptr. 649, 363 P. 2d 881〕.)

The notice requirement of Section 1769, however, is not an appropriate one for the court to adopt in actions by injured consumers against manufacturers with whom they have not dealt. (La Hue v. Coca-Cola Bottling, Inc. , 50 Wn. 2d 645 〔314 P. 2d 421, 422〕; Chapman v. Brown, 198 F. Supp. 78, 85, affd. Brown v. Chapman, 304 F. 2d 149.)

"As between the immediate parties to the sale 〔the notice requirement〕 is a sound commercial rule, designed to protect the seller against unduly delayed claims for damages. As applied to personal injuries, and notice to a remote seller, it becomes a booby-trap for the unwary. The injured consumer is seldom ' steeped in the business practice which justifies the rule', 〔James, Product Liability, 34 Texas L. Rev. 44, 192, 197〕 and at least until he has had legal advice it will not occur to him to give notice to one with whom he has had no dealings. " (Prosser, Strict Liability to the Consumer, 69 Yale L. J. 1099, 1130, footnotes omitted.) It is true that in Jones v. Burgermeister Brewing Corp. , 198 Cal. App. 2d 198, 202 –203 〔18 Cal. Rptr. 311〕; Perry v. Thrifty Drug Co. , 186 Cal. App. 2d 410, 411 〔9 Cal. Rptr. 50〕, Arata v. Tonegato, 152 Cal. App. 2d 837, 841 〔314 P. 2d 130〕, and Maecherlein v. {Page 59 Cal. 2d 62} Sealy Mattress Co, 145 Cal. App. 2d 275, 278 〔302 P. 2d 331〕, the court assumed that notice of breach of warranty must be given in an action by a consumer against a manufacturer. Since in those cases, however, the court did not consider the question whether a distinction exists between a warranty based on a contract between the parties and one imposed on a manufacturer not in privity with the consumer, the decisions are not authority for rejecting the rule of the La Hue and Chapman cases, supra. (Peterson v. Lamb Rubber Co., 54 Cal. 2d 339, 343 [5 Cal. Rptr. 863, 353 P. 2d 575]; People v. Banks, 53 Cal. 2d 370, 389 [1 Cal. Rptr. 669, 348 P. 2d 102].)

We conclude, therefore, that even if plaintiff did not give timely notice of breach of warranty to the manufacturer, his cause of action based on the representations contained in the brochure was not barred.

Moreover, to impose strict liability on the manufacturer under the circumstances of this case, it was not necessary for plaintiff to establish an express warranty as defined in Section 1732 of the Civil Code.

A manufacturer is strictly liable in tort when an article he places on the market, knowing that it is to be used without inspection for defects, proves to have a defect that causes injury to a human being. Recognized first in the case of unwholesome food products, such liability has now been extended to a variety of other products that create as great or greater hazards if defective. (Peterson v. Lamb Rubber Co., 54 Cal. 2d 339, 347 [5 Cal. Rptr. 863, 353 P. 2d 575] [grinding wheel]; Vallis v. Canada Dry Ginger Ale, Inc., 190 Cal. App. 2d 35, 42 – 44 [11 Cal. Rptr. 823] [bottle]; Jones v. Burgermeister Brewing Corp., 198 Cal. App. 2d 198, 204 [18 Cal. Rptr. 311] [bottle]; Gottsdanker v. Cutter Laboratories, 182 Cal. App. 2d 602, 607 [6 Cal. Rptr. 320] [vaccine]; McQuaide v. Bridgeport Brass Co, 190 F. Supp. 252, 254 [insect spray]; Bowles v. Zimmer Manufacturing Co, 277 F. 2d 868, 875 [surgical pin]; Thompson v. Reedman, 199 F. Supp. 120, 121 [automobile]; Chapman v. Brown, 198 F. Supp. 78, 118, 119, affd. Brown v. Chapman, 304 F. 2d 149 [skirt]; B. F. Goodrich Co. v. Hammond, 269 F. 2d 501, 504 [automobile tire]; Markovich v. McKesson & Robbins, Inc., 106 Ohio App. 265 [149 N. E. 2d 181, 186 – 188] {Page 59 Cal. 2d 63} [home permanent]; Graham v. Bottenfield's, Inc., 176 Kan. 68 [269 P. 2d 413, 418] [hair dye]; General Motors Corp. v. Dodson, 47 Tenn. App. 438 [338 S. W. 2d 655, 661] [automobile]; Henningsen v. Bloomfield Motors, Inc., 32 N. J. 358 [161 A. 2d 69, 76-84, 75 A. L. R. 2d 1] [automobile]; Hinton v. Republic Aviation Corp., 180 F. Supp. 31, 33 [airplane].)

Although in these cases strict liability has usually been based on the theory of an express or implied warranty running from the manufacturer to the plaintiff, the abandonment of the requirement of a contract between them, the recognition that the liability is not assumed by agreement but imposed by law (See e. g., Graham v. Bottenfield's, Inc., 176 Kan. 68 [269 P. 2d 413, 418]; Rogers v. Toni Home Permanent Co, 167 Ohio St. 244 [147 N. E. 2d 612, 614, 75 A. L. R. 2d 103]; Decker & Sons v. Capps, 139 Tex. 609, 617 [164 S. W. 2d 828, 142 A. L. R. 1479]), and the refusal to permit the manufacturer to define the scope of its own responsibility for defective products (Henningsen v. Bloomfield Motors,

Inc. , 32 N. J. 358 〔161 A. 2d 69, 84-96, 75 A. L. R. 2d 1〕; General Motors Corp. v. Dodson, 47 Tenn. App. 438 〔338 S. W. 2d 655, 658-661〕; State Farm Mut. Auto Ins. Co. v. Anderson-Weber, Inc. , 252 Iowa 1289 〔110 N. W. 2d 449, 455-456〕; Pabon v. Hackensack Auto Sales, Inc. , 63 N. J. Super. 476 〔164 A. 2d 773, 778〕; Linn v. Radio Center Delicatessen, 169 Misc. 879 〔6 N. Y. S. 2d 110, 112〕) make clear that the liability is not one governed by the law of contract warranties but by the law of strict liability in tort.

Accordingly, rules defining and governing warranties that were developed to meet the needs of commercial transactions cannot properly be invoked to govern the manufacturer's liability to those injured by its defective products unless those rules also serve the purposes for which such liability is imposed.

We need not recanvass the reasons for imposing strict liability on the manufacturer. They have been fully articulated in the cases cited above. (See also 2 Harper and James, Torts, Ë 28.15-28.16, pp. 1569－1574; Prosser, Strict Liability to the Consumer, 69 Yale L. J. 1099; Escola v. Coca Cola Bottling Co. , 24 Cal. 2d 453, 461 〔150 P. 2d 436〕, concurring opinion.)

The purpose of such liability is to insure that the costs of injuries resulting from defective products are borne by the manufacturers that put such products on the market rather than by the injured persons who are powerless to protect themselves. Sales warranties serve this purpose fitfully at best. (See Prosser, Strict Liability to the Consumer, 69 Yale L. J. 1099, 1124－1134.)

In the present case, for example, plaintiff was able to plead and prove an express warranty only because he read and relied on the representations of the Shopsmith's ruggedness contained in the manufacturer's brochure. Implicit in the machine's presence on the market, however, was a representation that it would safely do the jobs for which it was built. Under these circumstances, it should not be controlling whether plaintiff selected the machine because of the statements in the brochure, or because of the machine's own appearance of excellence that belied the defect lurking beneath the surface, or because he merely assumed that it would safely do the jobs it was built to do. It should not be controlling whether the details of the sales from manufacturer to retailer and from retailer to plaintiff's wife were such that one or more of the implied warranties of the sales act arose. (Civ. Code, 1735.) "The remedies of injured consumers ought not to be made to depend upon the intricacies of the law of sales. " (Ketterer v. Armour & Co, 200 F. 322, 323; Klein v. Duchess Sandwich Co, Ltd. , 14 Cal. 2d 272, 282 〔93 P. 2d 799〕.)

To establish the manufacturer's liability it was sufficient that plaintiff proved that he was injured while using the Shopsmith in a way it was intended to be used as a result of a defect in design and manufacture of which plaintiff was not aware that made the Shopsmith unsafe for its intended use.

The manufacturer contends that the trial court erred in refusing to give three instructions requested by it. It appears from the record, however, that the substance of two of the requested instructions was adequately covered by the instructions given and that the third instruction was not supported by the evidence.

The judgment is affirmed.

Gibson, C. J., Schauer, J., McComb, J., Peters, J., Tobriner, J., and Peek, J., concurred.

FN 1 In this respect the trial court limited the jury to a consideration of two statements in the manufacturer's brochure. (1) "When Shopsmith is in Horizontal Position-Rugged construction of frame provides rigid support from end to end. Heavy centerless-ground steel tubing insures perfect alignment of components." (2) "Shopsmith maintains its accuracy because every component has positive locks that hold adjustments through rough or precision work."

FN 2 Any affirmation of fact or any promise by the seller relating to the goods is an express warranty if the natural tendency of such affirmation or promise is to induce the buyer to purchase the goods, and if the buyer purchases the goods relying thereon. No affirmation of the value of the goods, nor any statement purporting to be a statement of the seller's opinion only shall be construed as a warranty.

Sources of Information and Further Readings

1. http://en.wikipedia.org/wiki/Product_liability
2. The European Convention on Products Liability in regard to Personal Injury and Death, Council of Europe, 1977.
3. Section 2 of the Restatement (Third) of Torts: Products Liability
4. The Product Liability Directive 85/374/EEC
5. Japanese Civil Code Article No. 709
6. Japanese Product Liability Law
7. Product Liability Forum-British Institute of International and Comparative Law
8. http://en.wikipedia.org/wiki/Tort

Chapter 14

Legal Forms of Foreign Direct Investment in China[1]

Key Concepts

equity joint venture
contractual joint venture
solely foreign funded enterprise
limited liability company
franchise agreement
BOT

Learning Objectives

1. Understand the types of foreign direct investment in China.
2. Understand the differences between equity joint venture and contractual joint venture.
3. Understand the impact of BOT.

Equity Joint Venture[2]

In China, the Chinese-foreign equity joint venture is established in accordance with the provisions of the relevant laws of China. The foreign participants may be foreign companies, enterprises, other economic entities or individuals while the Chinese participants shall be Chinese companies, enterprises or other economic entities other than individuals. The duly established Chinese-foreign joint venture enjoys the status as Chinese legal person, and the lawful rights and interests of the parties are under the protection of the law of China.

All activities of an equity joint venture shall comply with the provisions of the law, decrees, and pertinent regulations of China. The state shall not nationalize or requisition any equity joint venture. Under special circumstances, when public interest requires, equity joint venture may be requisitioned by the legal procedure and appropriate compensation shall be made.

An equity joint venture shall take the form of a limited liability company.

The proportion of the joint venture participant's investment shall be not less than 25% of its registered capital. The parties to the venture shall share profits, risks and losses in proportion to their contributions to the registered capital. If any party wishes to assign its shares in the registered capital, it shall obtain the consent of the other party to the venture. The latter shall enjoy the priority to purchase it if the conditions are the same. The parties to the venture may make their contributions in form of cash, industrial property rights, equipments and so on. The technology and equipments contributed by the foreign party as its investment shall be state-of-the-art, and suit China's needs. If the right to the use of the site is not taken as a part of the Chinese Party's investment, the equity joint venture shall pay the government for its use.

The above-mentioned investments shall be specified in the contract and articles of association of the venture, and their value shall be assessed by the parties to the venture.

The net profit of the venture shall be distributed among the parties to the venture in proportion to their respective contributions to the registered capital, after the payment of the tax, and the deduction of a reserve fund, a bonus and welfare fund and the expansion fund.

In case heavy losses, failure of a party to perform its obligations under the contract and the articles of association, or force majeure, etc, the parties to the venture may terminate the contract through their consultation and agreement, subject to the approval by the competent authority. In case of losses caused by a breach of the contract, the liabilities shall be borne by the party that has breached the contract.

Contractual Joint Venture

The Chinese-foreign contractual joint venture is established in China by and between foreign enterprises and other economic entities or individuals and Chinese enterprises or other economic entities in accordance with the provisions of the relevant law of China.

A contractual joint venture which meets the required conditions may acquire the status as a Chinese legal person. The lawful rights and interests shall be under the protection of the law of China.

In establishing a contractual joint venture, the Chinese and foreign parties shall, in accordance with the law of china, prescribe in their joint venture contract such matters as the investment or conditions for cooperation, the distribution of earnings or products, the sharing of risks and losses, the manner of cooperation, and management and the ownership of the property at the termination of the venture.

The parties to the venture shall share earnings or products, bear risks and losses in accordance with the stipulations in the agreement. The contractual joint venture shall abide by the Chinese laws and regulations and shall not injure the public interests of China. The state shall encourage the establishment of productive contractual joint venture that are export-oriented or technologically advanced.

Any disputes between the Chinese and foreign parties arising from the execution of the contract or the articles of association shall be settled through consultation or mediation. In case of a dispute which the Chinese or the foreign party is unwilling to settle through consultation or mediation, or of a dispute which they have failed to reach an agreement, they may submit the dispute case to a Chinese arbitration agency or any arbitration agency for arbitration in accordance with the arbitration clause in the joint venture contract or a written arbitration agreement concluded afterwards. In case of no arbitration clauses or arbitration agreement[3], the Chinese party may bring a suit in a Chinese court.

Solely Foreign Funded Enterprise

With a view to expanding economic cooperation and technical exchange with foreign countries and promoting the development of the national economy, the Chinese government permits foreign enterprises, other economic entities or individuals to establish the solely foreign funded enterprises in the territory of China.

A solely foreign funded enterprise duly established in accordance with the law of China enjoys the status as a Chinese legal person. It shall be established in such a manner as to help the development of China's national economy, they shall use advanced technology or market all or most of their products outside China. The investments of the foreign investors in China, the profits they earn and their lawful rights and interests shall be under the protection of the law of China.

The solely foreign funded enterprise shall abide by the laws and regulations of China and shall not engage in any activities detrimental to China's public interests. The state shall not nationalize or requisition any enterprise with foreign capitals. Under special circumstances, when the public interest requires, a solely foreign funded enterprise may be nationalized or requisitioned by legal procedures and appropriate compensation shall be made.

Cooperative Development

Cooperative Exploitation of On-Shore Petroleum Resources with Foreign Enterprises

The Chinese government encourages the cooperative exploitation activities with foreign enterprises. The investments, profits and other lawful rights and interests of foreign enterprises in the cooperative exploitation of on-shore petroleum resources shall be under the protection of the law of China.

The activities involving the cooperative exploitation of on-shore petroleum resources must comply with relevant laws, rules and regulations of China, and shall be subject to supervision and control by the relevant authorities.

A department or unit authorized by the state council shall be responsible for demarcating cooperation blocks, determining the forms of cooperation, arranging for formulation of relevant plans and policies, and examining and approving overall development programs for oil (gas) fields in cooperation with foreign enterprises, for the cooperation areas approved by the state council. The China National Petroleum and Natural Gas Corporation shall be responsible for business matters in respect of the exploitation of on-shore petroleum resources in cooperation with foreign enterprises, and for negotiating, entering into and implementing contracts for cooperation with foreign enterprises.

Following the invitations to bid or negotiations, the China National Petroleum and Natural Gas Corporation shall enter into contracts with foreign enterprises for cooperative exploitation of on-shore petroleum resources in the cooperation blocks demarcated in the areas approved by the state council. Such contracts shall become effective only after the approval by the Ministry of Foreign Trade and Economic Cooperation. In the exploitation of such resources, the principle of taking both the central and local interests shall be observed. Appropriate consideration shall be given to the local interests.

The relevant local governments shall protect the normal production and business activities carried out in cooperation areas according to the law and shall render effective assistance in respect of land use, road access and living amenities, etc.

Cooperative Development of Continental Petroleum Resources with Foreign Enterprises

The cooperative development of continental oil resources by the Chinese and foreign partners within the territory of China shall abide by the laws and regulations of China. The Chinese government protects the activities, investments, profits and other legitimate rights and interests of the foreign enterprises.

According to the relevant stipulations of the state, the China National Oil and Gas Exploration and Development Corporation is responsible for the operations of the cooperative development of continental oil resources, including holding talks, signing and executing contracts on cooperative development of the oil resources with foreign enterprises. It has exclusive right in exploration, development and production of oil resources in cooperation with foreign enterprises within the regions for cooperative development of oil resources approved by the state council.

BOT[4]

According to the relevant stipulations of China, "BOT projects" as used here shall refer to the infrastructure projects built, operated and transferred (BOT) by foreign investors. A government authority may, through a franchise agreement[5] and within a specified period, authorize a BOT project to a project company established by a foreign investor particularly for such BOT project, and have the project company responsible for its financing, construction, operation and maintenance.

After the expiration of the franchise period, the project company shall transfer the entire facilities of such BOT project to the government authority in good condition and without any claim.

Within the franchise period, the project company shall operate lawfully and independently, and recover and obtain returns on its investment through payments received from the users of the facilities.

The form of the project company shall be a limited liability company. The registered capital shall not be less than 25% of its total investment. The project company shall be entitled to the ownership and management rights of such facilities during the franchise period. In principle, the franchise period shall not exceed 30 years.

"BOT projects" may include: coal-fired power stations and hydro-power stations under 250MW (giving consideration to flood control and water supply), high grade roads, local railways, bridges, tunnels, city water supply sources, water purification plants and sewage treatment plants. BOT project should be included in the State and local five-year plans. The above range of BOT projects may, on the basis of specific conditions, be subject to expansion.

A proposed BOT project shall be subject to the examination and approval by the competent authorities of China.

Notes

1. Legal Forms of Foreign Direct Investment in China 中国外商直接投资的法律形式

本单元主要介绍中国外商直接投资的法律形式，主要包括合资经营企业、合作经营企业、外商独资企业、合作开发自然资源、BOT项目等形式。

2. Equity Joint Venture 合资经营企业

合资经营企业通常指的是“股权式”(equity)经营企业。合营企业包括合资经营企业和合作经营企业，两者的法律性质不同，前者是“股权式”(股份式)的，即合资企业各方按其出资比例分享盈亏、分担风险；而后者则为“契约式”的，即合营各方在企业中的权利和义务取决于合营契约的约定。

3. arbitration clauses or arbitration agreement 仲裁条款或仲裁协议

仲裁条款通常只是合同中的一个条款而已，而仲裁协议则是有关争端解决的一份独立的书面约定，它可以在争端发生之前或之后订立。

4. BOT （built-operate-transfer 的缩略词）建设—经营—转让

建设—经营—转让是指政府通过契约授予外国企业以一定期限的特许专营权，许可其融资建设和经营特定的公用设施，并准许其通过向用户收取费用以清偿贷款、回收投资并赚取利润；而经营期满时，则将该基础设施无偿转移给政府。

5. franchise agreement　特许协议

特许协议是由东道国政府部门与外国投资者之间签订的协议，因此这种协议又称为“国家合同”，它不同于一般当事人之间订立的协议。

Study Questions

1. What are the differences between the equity joint venture and the contractual joint venture?
2. What are the main legal forms of foreign direct investment?
3. How does the direct investment differ from the indirect investment?
4. Are there any limitations upon the establishment of solely foreign funded enterprise? Briefly explain the reasons.
5. Why do some developing countries show great interest in BOT?
6. Try to know the essentials of the following Joint Venture Agreement：

Joint Venture Agreement

本协议于××××年××月××日签订。

签约第一方：ABC 公司，该公司系中国公司，在中国××注册（以下简称“甲方”）；签约第二方：XYZ 公司，系美国公司，在美国××注册（以下简称“乙方”）。

This Agreement made this ________ day of ________, 19 by ABC Corporation (hereinafter called “Party A”), a Chinese corporation having its registered office at ________, China, and XYZ Company (hereinafter called “Party B”), an American company having its registered office at ________, USA.

兹证明 WITNESSES：

甲方在中国生产和销售××产品；乙方生产和销售××产品（以下称“许可产品”），拥有许可产品的美国专利（以下称“专利”）和×号注册商标；WHEREAS Party A is engaged in manufacturing and selling in China; and WHEREAS Party B is engaged in manufacturing and selling (hereinafter called “Licensed Product”) and has American patent rights to Licensed Product (hereinafter called “Patents”) and registered Trademark No. ________ (hereinafter called “Trademark”); and

甲乙双方认为按照中华人民共和国的法律成立共同所有的公司（以下称“合营公司”），

在××地从事生产、销售和开发许可产品，对双方都是有利的；WHEREAS the Parties consider it mutually advantageous to organize a jointly owned corporation (hereinafter called "Joint Venture") under the laws of the People's Republic of China to engage in the manufacture, sale and development of Licensed Product in ______.

为此，鉴于本协议所述的前提与约定，特此立约如下：NOW THEREFORE, in consideration of the premises and convenance described hereinafter Party A and Party B agree as follows:

第一条 定义 Article 1 Definitions

在本协议中，除非文中另有明确规定，下列短语具有以下意思：1.“合营企业”，系指根据本协议建立的公司。2.“许可产品”，系指××××。3.“专利”，系指××××。4.“商标”，系指××××……

In this Agreement, the following terms have the following meanings unless the context clearly dictates otherwise. 1. "Joint Venture" means the corporation to be organized pursuant to the provisions of Article 2 hereto. 2. "Licensed Product" means ______. 3. "Patents" means ______. 4. "Trademark" means ______...

第二条 建立合营企业 Article 2 Formation of Joint Venture

1. 甲方和乙方按照中华人民共和国的法律建立合营企业。

2. 合营企业称为××××，地址为××××。

3. 合营企业的一切活动必须遵守中华人民共和国的法律、法令和有关条例规定。

4. 合营企业的组织形式为有限责任公司。甲乙双方以各自认缴的出资额对合营公司的债务承担责任。各方按其出资额在注册资本中的比例分享利润和分担风险及亏损。

5. 合营企业的组建费用由甲乙双方平均分担。

1. Party A and Party B shall spare no efforts for the organization of Joint Venture under the laws of the People's Republic of China. 2. The name of Joint Venture is ______ with its legal address: ______. 3. All activities of Joint Venture shall comply with the provisions of the laws, decrees and pertinent regulations of the People's Republic of China. 4. Joint Venture shall take the form of a limited liability company. The profits, risks and losses of Joint Venture shall be shared by both Party A and Party B in proportion to the contributions to the registered capital. 5. The expenses of organizing Joint Venture shall be equally borne by Party A and Party B.

第三条 生产经营的目的、范围和规模 Article 3 Purpose, Scope and Size of Business

1. 甲、乙双方合资经营的目的是：本着加强经济合作和扩大技术交流的愿望，采用先进而适用的技术和科学的经营管理方法，提高产品质量，开发新产品，并在质量、价格等方面具有国际市场上的竞争能力，提高经济效益，使投资各方获得满意的经济利益。

2. 合营企业生产××××(许可产品),生产能力为每年××××。合营企业将努力改进许可产品,改善管理,以适应国际竞争。

3. 合营企业尽可能开发许可产品的新品种,以满足国内外市场的发展需要。

1. In line with the spirit of strengthening economic cooperation and expanding technical exchange, Joint Venture is to use state-of-the-art and appropriate technology and equipment, with efficient management systems, to produce Licensed Product which shall be of top quality and competitive in the world markets, so as to achieve satisfactory economic returns. 2. Joint Venture is to product ________(Licensed Product) with a production capacity of ________ per year. Joint Venture shall do its best to improve Licensed Product and management so as to be able to meet competition worldwide. 3. Joint Venture shall, if possible, develop new varieties of Licensed Product in order to keep up with market developments both in the host country and in the world.

第四条　资本结构　Article 4　Capital Structure

1. 合营企业的注册资本为××××,其中甲、乙双方各出资××××,即各占50%。

2. 甲方出资(1)厂房:××××;(2)国产设备:××××;(3)现金:××××;(4)合资企业厂地:××××。

3. 乙方出资(1)现金:××××;(2)先进设备:××××;(3)工业产权:××××。乙方向甲方提供工业产权的技术资料包括影印本的专利证书和注册商标证书、有效期说明、技术特点、实际价值、价格计算依据等。

4. 合营企业各方必须在19××年×月×日前交付其出资。迟交必须交纳利息或赔偿因此而造成的损失。

5. 甲乙双方中任何一方转让其出资额,须经另一方同意和其政府批准,该方享有优先购买权。

1. The registered capital of Joint Venture shall be (amount of capital), of which half (50%) will be contributed by each Party.

2. Party A's contributions include (1) Buildings and premises: ________(value); (2) Domestically-made equipment: ________(value); (3) Cash: ________; (4) The site of Joint Venture: ________(value).

3. Party B's contributions include (1) Cash: ________; (2) Sophisticated equipment: ________(value); (3) Industrial property ________(value). Party B shall present to Party A the relevant documentation on the industrial property including photocopies of the patent certificates and trademark registration certificates, statements of validity, their technical characteristics, practical value, the basis for calculating the price, etc.

4. Each Party to Joint Venture shall pay in its contributions before ________(time limit). Any delay in payment will be subject to a payment of interest or a compensation for

the loss occurred therein.

5. The transfer of one Party's share in the registered capital shall be effected with the prior consent of the other Party and approval of its government and the latter shall enjoy priority to purchase it.

第五条 专利许可 Article 5 Patent Licensing Arrangement

1. 乙方同意向合营企业转让下列独家许可：

(1) 专利独占许可——依据本协议的专利许可协议，用乙方专利生产、使用和销售许可产品。

(2) 商标独占许可——依据本协议的专利许可协议，用乙方商标销售许可产品。

(3) 专有技术独占许可——根据本协议的技术援助协议，用乙方专有技术生产和销售专利产品。

2. 甲乙双方同意，在执行本协议的同时，将全面贯彻执行上述 3 个协议：专利许可协议、商标许可协议和技术援助协议。

1. Party B agrees to grant Joint Venture the following exclusive licences: (1) An exclusive license to manufacture, use and sell Licensed Product under Party B's Patents according to the terms and conditions of the Patent License Agreement attached hereto. (2) An exclusive license to use Trademark in marketing Licensed Product according to the terms and conditions of the Trademark License Agreement attached hereto. (3) An exclusive license to practise Party B's know-how for manufacturing and marketing Licensed Product according to the terms and conditions of the Technical Asistance Agreement attached hereto. 2. Party A and Party B agree that simultaneously with the execution of this Agreement, they shall carry out, the above three agreements—the Patent License Agreement, the Trademark License Agreement and the Technical Assistance Agreement.

第六条 产品销售 Article 6 Marketing Arrangements

1. 甲乙双方共同负责销售许可产品。

2. 通过乙方世界销售系统销售的产品初期销售量为总产量的××%。同时，甲方将协助合营企业通过中国的外贸公司出口许可产品。

3. 许可产品也可以在中国市场出售。

4. 中营企业所需购买的原材料、半成品、燃料、配套件等，在条件相同的情况下，应首先在中国购买。当然，也可使用自己的外汇直接从世界市场购进。

1. Party A and Party B shall be responsible for the sales of Licensed Product. 2. The initial amount of Licensed Product to be sold on the foreign markets is ________% of the total production through Party B's marketing system worldwide. Meanwhile Party A shall help Joint Venture to export Licensed Product through China's trade establishments. 3. Licensed Product may also be distributed on the Chinese market. 4. In purchase of the

required raw materials and semiprocessed products, fuels, auxiliary equipment etc, Joint Venture shall give first priority to Chinese sources where conditions are the same, but may also acquire them directly from the world market with its own foreign exchange funds.

第七条 董事会 Article 7 Board of Directors

1. 董事会是合营企业的最高领导机构,负责合营企业的主要事宜。

2. 董事会由××名董事组成,其中××名(包括董事长)由甲方指定;××名(包括副董事长)由乙方指定。董事的任期为4年,若双方同意,任期可以延长。

3. 董事会每年召开一次,原则上在合营企业的法定地址举行。出席会议的法定人数不得少于董事人数的2/3。若董事不能出席会议,应授权代表出席会议,代表他投票。

若在任期内,因死亡、退休或因其他原因,董事在任期届满前不能履行职责者,双方同意充分合作,并由因其指定的董事死亡、退休或其他原因造成空位的一方给予更换。

4. 对于下列问题,必须经出席会议的董事一致通过,方可作出决定:(1) 修改合营企业章程;(2) 终止和解散合营企业;(3) 增加或转让合营企业的注册资本;(4) 合营企业同其他经济组织合并。

其他问题的决定,以出席会议董事人数的微弱多数票作出。

1. The Board of Directors is the top leadership of Joint Venture. It is responsible for all major issues concerning Joint Venture. 2. The Board of Directors consists of ________ (number) directors, of whom ________ (number) including the chairman shall be appointed by Party A, and ________ (number) including the deputy chairman shall be appointed by Party B. The office term for the directors is 4 years, which may be renewed with the consent of the Parties to Joint Venture. 3. Board meetings shall generally be held at the location of Joint Venture's legal address, once each year. A quorum for a meeting shall consist of not fewer than two-thirds (2/3) of the directors. Should any director be unable to attend the meeting, he shall authorize a representative to be present at the meeting and vote for him. In case a director dies, resigns, or is otherwise unable to fulfil his duties prior to the fulfilment of his term, the Parties agree to cooperate fully to have as his replacement a director nominated by the Party that nominated the director whose death, resignation or other conditions created the vacancy. 4. Decisions on the following items shall be made only when unanimously agreed upon by the directors present at the Board meeting. (1) Amendment to the articles of incorporation of Joint Venture; (2) Termination and dissolution of Joint Venture; (3) Increase or assignmnet of the registered capital of Joint Venture; (4) Merger of Joint Venture with another economic organization. Decisions on other items shall be made by a simple majority vote of the directors present at the meeting.

第八条 管理 Article 8 Management

1. 合营企业设经营管理机构,负责企业的日常经营管理工作。

2．经营管理机构设经理1人、副经理2人，任期4年。总经理由甲方指定，负责执行董事会的决议和日常管理工作。副总经理由双方各指定1人，协助总经理工作。

3．管理机构设若干部门，在总经理和副总经理的领导下，负责企业各部门的工作。

1．Joint Venture shall establish a management office which shall be responsible for daily management of Joint Venture. 2．The management office shall have a general manager and two deputy general managers, whose term is 4 years. The general manager nominated by Party A is responsible for the implementation of the decisions of the Board of Directors and daily operation. The deputy managers, one of whom is nominated by each Party, shall assist the general manager in his duties. 3. The management office may have its subdivisions, the duties of which are to manage different business departments under the leadership of the general manager or deputy general managers.

第九条　劳动管理　Article 9　Labour management

1．合营企业的中方专家、技术人员、工人和其他人员由甲方招聘；合营企业的外方专家由乙方招聘。

2．合营企业的专家、职员或工人的雇用、辞退、工资、劳动保险、生活福利和奖惩等项，由董事会按照《中华人民共和国中外合资经营企业法实施条例》决定。

1．Party A agrees to help Joint Venture to invite and recruit Chinese experts, technicians, workers and other personnel and Party B agree to help Joint Venture to invite and recruit foreign experts. 2．The employment and dismissal, wages, insurance, welfare, awards, and fines of its experts, staff members and workers shall be decided by the Board of Directors according to Regulations for the Implementation of the Law of the People's Republic of China on Chinese Foreign Joint Venture。

条十条　财务与会计　Article 10　Financial Affairs and Accounting

1．协议双方充分认识到，为了他们自己和合营企业的最大利益，必须尽一切可能增加生产。因此，双方同意合营企业应保留足够的收益，用于扩大生产的其他需要，如奖金和福利基金。合营企业的年留用奖金比率由董事会决定。

2．合营企业雇用合格的财务人员和审计员，设立会计账目，合营各方可随时查看有关帐目。

3．合营企业的财政年度自1月1日至12月31日。合营企业的净收入，在扣除储备金、奖金和企业发展奖金以后，根据各方出资在注册证中占的比例进行分配。红利以××（货币）支付。

1．The parties hereto are fully aware that the best interests of their own and Joint Venture will be served by taking all reasonable measures to ensure increase in production and in order to achieve this goal, the Parties agree to retain sufficient earnings in Joint Venture for the expansion of production and other requirements, such as bonus and welfare funds. The annual proportion of the earnings to be retained shall be decided by the Board of Directors. 2. Joint Venture shall employ competent treasurers and auditors to keep all books of accounts, which are accessible at any time to each Party hereto. 3. The fiscal year of Joint Venture shall begin on January 1st and end on December 31st. The net profit of Joint Venture shall be distributed between the Parties to Joint Venture in proportion to their respective shares in the registered capital after the deduction therefrom of the reserve funds, the bonus and the expansion funds of Joint Venture. Dividends shall be paid in (currency)。

第十一条　税费　Article 11　Tax

1. 合营企业必须按照中华人民共和国的法律纳税。

2. 合营公司的职员和工人必须按照《中华人民共和国个人所得税》纳税。

3. 合营企业进出口货物根据中华人民共和国的法律缴纳或减免关税。

1. Joint Venture shall pay taxes in accordance with the relevant laws of the People's Republic of China. 2. The staff members and workers employed by Joint Venture shall pay individual income tax according to the Individual Income Tax Law of the People's Republic of China. 3. Joint Venture shall pay or exempt from customs duty and industrial and commercial consolidated tax on goods imported or exported in accordance with the relevant laws of the People's Republic of China.

第十二条　合营期限　Article 12　Duration of Joint Venture

1. 合营期限为××年。合营企业的成立日期为合营公司营业执照签发之日。

2. 若双方同意延期,合营企业必须在期满前6个月向中国政府的主管部门提出延长期限的申请。

1. The duration of Joint Venture is ________ years, which begins on the date when Joint Venture is issued the business license. 2. When both Parties to Joint Venture agree to extend the duration, Joint Venture shall file an application for extending the duration to the relevant authority of the Chinese governmnent 6 months befor its expiration date.

第十三条　解散与清算　Article 13　Dissolution and Liquidation

董事会宣布解散合营企业,必须制定清算程序和原则,并成立清算委会。

合营企业解散和清算的一切事宜均按中华人民共和国法律办理。

Upon announcement of the dissolution of Joint Venture, its Board of Directors shall work out procedures and principles for the liquidation and set up a liquidation committee. All matters concerning the dissolution and liquidation of Joint Venture shall be dealt with in accordance with the relevant laws of the People's Republic of China.

第十四条　保险　Article 14　Insurance

合营企业的各项保险均在中保财产保险公司投保。

Insurance against various risks shall be effected by Joint Venture with the People's

Insurance Company of China.

第十五条 仲裁 Article 15 Arbitration

有关本协议的一切分歧与争议,若董事会不能通过协商解决,则提交中国国际贸易促进委员会对外贸易仲裁委员会,根据该会仲裁程序暂行规则进行仲裁。该委员会的裁决是终局的,对双方均具有约束力。

All disputes, controversies or differences which may arise between the Parties hereto, out of or in relation to this Agreement and which the Board of Directors fails to settle through consultation, shall finaly be submitted to arbitration which shall be conducted by the Foreign Trade Arbitration Commission of the China Council for the Promotion of International Trade in accordance with the Provisional Rules of Procedure of Arbitration of the said commission, the decision of which shall be final and binding upon both parties.

第十六条 协议的修改 Article 16 Amendment

本协议的修改,必须经甲乙双主同意,签署书面协议,并报中华人民共和国主管部门批准。

This Agreement may be amended during the duration of this Agreement by the Parties, provided that such amendment shall be in writing and signed by both Parties and shall be approved by the competent agency of the governmnet of the People's Republic of China.

第十七条 不可抗力 Article 17 Force Majeure

1. 本协议任何一方因地震、火灾、洪水、爆炸、风暴、事故、战争等不可抗力事件,未能履行协议,不构成违约或索赔之缘由。

2. 遭受不可抗力事件一方必须立即电报通知另一方,并在发报后××天内提交当地主管部门出具的证明文件,供双方据以友好合理地解决有关问题。

1. Any failure or delay in the performance by either Party hereto of its obligations under this Agreement shall not constitute a breach hereof or give rise to any claims for damages if it is caused by the following occurrences beyond the control of the Party: earthquake, fire, floods, explosions, storms, accidents, war. 2. The Party affected by force majeure event shall immediately cable the other Party about the event, and submit within ______ days after the cable the certified documents issued by a public competent organization at the place where the force majeure event has taken place, with which the two Parties hereto shall settle the problem in a friendly and reasonable way.

第十八条 通知 Article 18 Notice

一切有关本协议的通知必须采用书面形式,其地址如下:ABC 公司地址:XYZ 公司地址:合营企业地址:通知日期以通知发出日为准,但改变地址的通知以通知收到日为准。时间按通知方所在的时区计算。

Any notice required or permitted under the provisions of this Agreement shall be in writing and addressed as follows: To ABC Corporation: at ________. To XYZ Company: at ________. To Joint Venture: at ________. Notice shall be deemed to have been given on the date of mailing except the notice of change of address which shall be deemed to have been given when received. The time shall be calculated according to that of the time zone of the addresser or sender.

第十九条　唯一协议　Article 19　Sole Agreement

本协议是当事人的唯一协议，并取代当事人双方以前明确表示和暗示方式所达成的一切协议和承诺。

This Agreement consititutes the entire and only Agreement between the Parties hereto and supersedes and nullifies all prior agreements, commitments, expressed or implied, between the Parties hereto.

第二十条　适用法律　Article 20　Governing Law

本协议的形式、有效期、解释和履行均以中华人民共和国法律为准。

The formation, validation, interpretation and performance of this Agreement are governed by the laws of the People's Republic of China.

第二十一条　文字　Article 21　Language

本协议以中、英文书写，两种文本对双方均具有约束力，但在产生分歧时，以中文本为准。

兹证明，双方委派各自代表，在以下开首语中书明的日期签署盖章。本协议一式两份。

This Agreement shall be executed by the Parties hereto in both Chinese version and English version, each of which shall be binding upon both Parties. But the Chinese version shall prevail in the event of any discrepancy between the two said versions. IN WITNESS WHEREOF, the Parties hereto have executed this Agreement in duplicate by their duly authorized representatives as of the date first above written.

ABC 公司：________　　　　XYZ 公司：________

Sources of Information and Further Readings

1. The Law of the People's Republic of China on Chinese-Foreign Equity Joint Ventures
2. The Law of the People's Republic of China on Chinese-Foreign Contractual Joint Ventures
3. The Law of the People's Republic of China on Wholly Foreign-Owned Enterprises
4. http://www.chinalawedu.com/new/23223a23226a2010/20101221guopei 132248.shtml

Chapter 15

Trade Related Investment Measures Agreement[1]

Key Concepts

TRIMs national treatment general elimination of quantitative restrictions transparency requirements of local contents requirements of balance of trade

Learning Objectives

1. Be familiar with main contents of TRIMs.
2. Understand TRIMs elimination and transitional period.
3. Understand WTO members' commitment to their obligations.
4. Understand the principle of transparency.

An Overview

In the late 1980s, there was a significant increase in foreign direct investment throughout the world. However, some of the countries receiving foreign investment imposed numerous restrictions on that investment designed to protect and foster domestic industries, and to prevent the outflow of foreign exchange reserves. Examples of these restrictions include local content requirements (which require that locally-produced goods be purchased or used), manufacturing requirements (which require the domestic manufacturing of certain components), trade balancing requirements, domestic sales requirements, technology transfer requirements, export performance requirements (which require the export of a specified percentage of production volume), local equity restrictions, foreign exchange restrictions, remittance restrictions, licensing requirements, and employment restrictions. These measures can also be used in connection with fiscal incentives as opposed to requirement. Some of these investment measures distort trade in violation of GATT Article III and XI, and are therefore prohibited. Until the completion of the Uruguay Round negotiations, which produced a well-rounded Agreement on Trade-Related Investment Measures (hereinafter the "TRIMs Agreement"), the few international agreements providing disciplines for measures restricting foreign investment provided only limited guidance in terms of content and country coverage. The OECD Code on Liberalization of Capital Movements, for example, requires members to liberalize restrictions on direct investment in a broad range of areas. The OECD Code's efficacy, however, is limited by the numerous reservations made by each of the members. In addition, there are other international treaties, bilateral and multilateral, under which signatories extend most-favoured-nation treatment to direct investment. Only a few such treaties, however, provide national treatment for direct investment. Moreover, although the APEC Investment Principles adopted in November 1994 provide rules for investment as a whole, including non-discrimination and national treatment, they have no binding force.

GATT 1947 prohibited investment measures that violated the principles of national treatment[2] and the general elimination of quantitative restrictions, but the extent of the prohibitions was never clear. The TRIMs Agreement, however, contains statements prohibiting any TRIMs that are inconsistent with the provisions of Articles III or XI of GATT 1994. In addition, it provides an illustrative list that explicitly prohibits local content requirements, trade balancing requirements, foreign exchange restrictions and export restrictions (domestic sales requirements) that would violate Article III: 4 or XI: 1 of GATT 1994. TRIMs prohibited by the Agreement include those that are mandatory or enforceable under domestic law or administrative rulings, or those with which compliance is necessary to obtain an advantage (such as subsidies or tax breaks). Indeed, the TRIMs Agreement is not intended to impose new obligations, but to clarify the pre-existing GATT 1947 obligations. Under the WTO TRIMs Agreement, countries are required to rectify any measures inconsistent with the Agreement, within a set period of time, with a few exceptions.

What Is a TRIM?

The Agreement did not define TRIMs, but provided an illustrative list as follows:

TRIMs that are inconsistent with the obligation of national treatment provided for in Paragraph 4 of Article III of GATT 1994 include those which are mandatory or enforceable under domestic law or under administrative rulings, or compliance with which is necessary to obtain an advantage[3], and which require: a) the purchase or use by an enterprise of products of domestic origin or from any domestic source, whether specified in terms of particular products, in terms of volume or value of products, or in terms of a proportion of volume or value of its local production[4]; or b) that an enterprise's purchases or use of imported products be limited to an amount related to the volume or value of local products that it exports[5].

TRIMS that are inconsistent with the obligation of general elimination of quantitative restrictions provided for in Paragraph 1 of Article XI of GATT 1994 include those which are mandatory or enforceable under domestic law or under administrative rulings, or compliance with which is necessary to obtain an advantage, and which restrict: a) the importation by an enterprise of products used in or related to its local production, generally or to an amount related to the volume or value of local production that it exports[6]; b) the importation by an enterprise of products used in or related to its local production by restricting its access to foreign exchange to an amount related to the foreign exchange inflows attributable to the enterprise[7]; or c) the exportation or sale for export by an enterprise of products, whether specified in terms of particular products, in terms of volume or value of products, or in terms of a proportion of volume or value of its local production[8]. The lack of a precise definition means that the issue is not always clear-cut and there has been considerable disagreement as to whether or not certain measures are covered by the Agreement.

Examples of TRIMs Explicitly Prohibited by the TRIMs Agreement

Local Content Requirement

Measures requiring the purchase or use by an enterprise of domestic products, whether specified in terms of particular products, in terms of volume or value of products, or in terms of a proportion of volume or value of its local production. (Violation of GATT Article Ⅲ: 4)

Trade Balancing Requirements

Measures requiring that an enterprise's purchases or use of imported products be limited to an amount related to the volume or value of local products that it exports. (Violation of GATT Article Ⅲ: 4)

Measures restricting the importation by an enterprise of products used in or related to its local production, generally or to an amount related to the volume or value of local production that it exports. (Violation of GATT Article XI: 1)

Foreign Exchange Restrictions

Measures restricting the importation by an enterprise of products (parts and other goods) used in or related to its local Production by restricting its access to foreign exchange to an amount related to the foreign exchange inflows attributable to the enterprise. (Violation of GATT Article XI: 1)

Export Restrictions (Domestic Sales Requirements)

Measures restricting the exportation or sale for export by an enterprise of products, whether specified in terms of particular products, in terms of volume or value of products, or in terms of a proportion of volume or value of its local production. (Violation of GATT Article XI: 1)

TRIMs Elimination and Transition Periods

Under the Agreement member states were given 90 days to notify the WTO of any existing TRIMs. There were 43 notifications by 24 developing countries (19 related to the auto industry and 10 to the agri-food industry). Member states were then given a "transition period" during which their notified TRIMs were to be eliminated. The length of time was based on a state's level of development, i. e., developed countries were given 2 years; developing countries were given 5 years; and least-developed countries were given 7 years. Therefore, all developing countries should have implemented the TRIMs Agreement and eliminated their regulations by 1 January 2000.

However, Article 5.3 of the Agreement permits developing and least-developed countries to apply for an extension of the transition period. 10 WTO members have so far submitted transitional period extension requests (Annex 2). It is likely that a number of other countries will seek extended transitional periods, but are waiting to see what happens with the "first batch". The requests range from Chile 1 year to Pakistan 7 years.

Since 1995 the TRIMs obligations that new members face on accession to the WTO depend on the terms of their accession. So far all acceding countries have agreed to implement the TRIMs agreement upon accession regardless of whether they are developing countries or not.

Exceptions for Developing Countries

Developing countries are permitted to retain TRIMs that constitute a violation of GATT Article III or XI, provided the measures meet the conditions of GATT Article XVIII which allows specified derogation from the GATT provisions, by virtue of the economic development needs of developing countries.

Transparency[9]

Members reaffirm, with respect to TRIMs, their commitment to obligations on transparency and notification in Article X of GATT 1994, in the undertaking on "Notification" contained in the Understanding Regarding Notification, Consultation, Dispute Settlement and Surveillance adopted on 28 November 1979 and in the Ministerial Decision on Notification Procedures adopted on 15 April 1994.

Each Member shall notify the Secretariat of the publications in which TRIMs may be found, including those applied by regional and local governments and authorities within their territories. Each Member shall accord sympathetic consideration to requests for information, and afford adequate opportunity for consultation, on any matter arising from this Agreement raised by another Member. In conformity with Article X of GATT 1994 no Member is required to disclose information the disclosure of which would impede law enforcement or otherwise be contrary to the public interest or would prejudice the legitimate commercial interests of particular enterprises, public or private.

Extension Request Negotiations

Discussions about extension requests take place within the WTO Council for Trade in Goods (CTG). The countries submit an extension request to the CTG and then have to justify the request in the face of detailed questioning from other members—the US, EC and Japan have usually been the most active.

The first round of extension requests have now been largely settled. Argentina, Colombia, Malaysia, Mexico, Pakistan, the Philippines, Romania and Thailand have accepted the Chair of the CTG's "two by two" proposal in November 2000. This involves automatic 2-year extensions until the end of 2001 with requests for additional extensions for a maximum period of two years to be submitted by 31 August 2001 (though requests arriving after this date will be considered). These further extensions would need to be accompanied by a reasonable phase out plan for the remaining TRIMs. The extensions are not guaranteed and will be dealt with on a case by case basis. Chile's request for an extension until 31 December 2001 had already been agreed.

The only country yet to come to an agreement is Egypt, whose application for an extension was made after 31 December 1999. If this is not accepted by the CTG the request would have to be treated as a waiver under GATT Article IX (see Annex 3).

TRIMs Review

There will be a joint WTO/UNCTAD study on TRIMs. This will be an examination of how governments have used TRIMs as policy tools for industrial development and their effect on international trade, investment flows, economic growth, etc.

Notes

1. Trade Related Investment Measures Agreement (TRIMs) 与贸易有关的投资措施协议

一般来说,投资与贸易是相互促进的,但有时东道国的一些投资措施会对货物贸易产生限制、扭曲作用,从而对国际贸易的自由发展带来负面影响。因此,为了禁止那些限制、扭曲贸易的投资措施，自1986年开始的乌拉圭回合谈判，投资措施被列入多边贸易谈判的议题，TRIMs协议是其所取得的成果之一，并成为WTO法律体制的有机组成部分。

2. national treatment 国民待遇

国民待遇即外国投资者应享有与东道国国民同等的待遇。

3. those which are mandatory or enforceable under domestic law or under administrative rulings, or compliance with which is necessary to obtain an advantage 依照国内法律或行政法规规定的那些强制性或可予强制执行的措施，或者为了取得一项利益而需遵循的那些措施

4. the purchase or use by an enterprise of products of domestic origin or from any domestic source, whether specified in terms of particular products, in terms of volume or value of products, or in terms of a proportion of volume or value of its local production （要求）企业购买或使用国内产的或源于国内渠道的产品，而不论按其具体产品、具体产品的数量或价值进行规定，还是按当地产品的数量或价值的比例进行规定（此条规定的是当地成份要求）

5. that an enterprise's purchases or use of imported products be limited to an amount related to the volume or value of local products that it exports （要求）企业购买或使用的进口产品限定在其当地产品出口数量或价值的一定范围内（此条规定的是贸易平衡要求）

6. restrict the importation by an enterprise of products used in or related to its local production, generally or to an amount related to the volume or value of local production that it exports 一般性地限制企业进口用于当地生产或与其有关的产品，或按企业出口产品的数量或价值对其进口产品进行限制

7. restrict the importation by an enterprise of products used in or related to its local production by restricting its access to foreign exchange to an amount related to the foreign exchange inflows attributable to the enterprise 通过将企业用汇限制在其创汇的一定额度内以限制其进口用于当地生产或与此有关的产品

8. restrict the exportation or sale for export by an enterprise of products, whether specified in terms of particular products, in terms of volume or value of products, or in terms of a proportion of volume or value of its local production 限制企业出口或销售其出口的产品，而不论按其具体产品、具体产品的数量或价值进行限制，还是按当地产品的数量或价值的比例进行限制（此条实际上规定的是国内销售要求）

9. Transparency 透明度

透明度即信息公开和披露要求，每一成员方应遵守其在透明度和通知方面所承诺的义务。

Study Questions

1. What is the quantitative restriction?

2. What is the national treatment?
3. With respect to investment issues, what are the main differences between TRIMs Agreement and GATS?
4. What are the main exceptional provisions in TRIMs Agreement?
5. What is the principle of transparency?

Sources of Information and Further Readings

1. http://en.wikipedia.org/wiki/Agreement_on_Trade_Related_Investment_Measures
2. http://www.wto.org/english/tratop_e/invest_e/invest_e.htm
3. The General Agreement on Tariffs and Trade ("GATT 1947")
4. http://en.wikipedia.org/wiki/General_Agreement_on_Tariffs_and_Trade

Chapter 16

Multilateral Investment Guarantee Agency[1]

Key Concepts

eligibility non-commercial risks currency transfer risk MIGA
expropriation breach of contract risk subrogation

Learning Objectives

1. Understand the mission of MIGA.
2. Be familiar with the scope of covered risks.
3. Understand the eligibility of investments under MIGA.
4. Understand the mission of MIGA.
5. Understand the principle of subrogation.

Background for Establishment of MIGA

Considerable attention has been focused in recent years on the need to remove barriers impeding the growth of foreign investment in developing countries. Many countries have enacted new laws to promote foreign investment and entered into bilateral investment treaties with capital-exporting countries for this purpose.

The concept of providing foreign investors with financial guarantees against noncommercial risks in developing countries has emerged as a means of improving the investment climate in these countries and, hence, of stimulating investment flows to them. Almost all developed countries and two developing countries have established official schemes to provide guarantees against noncommercial risks to their nations for investments into developing countries. In addition, the InterArab Investment Guarantee Corporation provides guarantees on a regional basis. A private political risk insurance market has also been operating internationally for over a decade. The activities of these entities are subject to several limitations and the perception of political risk remains a significant barrier to investment in developing countries. There is need for a multilateral investment guarantee agency to complement these schemes and improve the investment climate by issuing guarantees and engaging in other investment promotion activities.

Status, Establishment and Purpose

The Multilateral Investment Guarantee Agency (MIGA) is a member organization of the World Bank Group that offers political risk insurance. It was established to promote foreign direct investment into developing countries. MIGA was founded in 1988 with a capital base of $1 billion and is headquartered in Washington, DC 175 member countries comprise MIGA's shareholders.

MIGA promotes foreign direct investment into developing countries by insuring investors against political risk, advising governments on attracting investment, sharing information through on-line investment information services, and mediating disputes between investors and governments. MIGA's membership in the World Bank Group enables the organization to intervene with host governments to resolve claims before they are filed.

The Multilateral Investment Guarantee Agency (referred to the Agency) is an autonomous international organization with "full juridical personality" under international law and the domestic laws of its members with the main objective of encouraging the flow of investments for productive purposes among its member countries and in particular to its developing member countries. The reference to "investments for productive purposes" emphasizes the Agency's concentration on concrete projects and programs in all sectors of the economy. It does not imply a restriction of its operations to the manufacturing sector. In addition to guaranteeing investments in these member countries against non-commercial risks, the Agency is to carry out complementary activities to promote investment flows of the Conventions sets out the promotional activities the Agency will provide.

Scope of Covered Risks

The Convention provides for coverage of the three generally accepted categories of non-commercial risks: the currency transfer risk[2] resulting from host government restrictions and delays in converting and transferring local currency earned by an investor, expropriation[3], and the risk of war and civil disturbance. The Convention adds to these traditionally covered risks the risk of breach or repudiation of a contractual commitment by the host government towards an investor.

The currency transfer risk is broadly defined in Article 11 (a)(i) of the convention. It is intended to encompass all forms of new direct restrictions, including additions to existing restrictions, as well as indirect or disguised restrictions, whether such restrictions are imposed by law or in fact. The restriction must be "attributable to the host government", restrictions imposed by public agencies and other public organs of the host country are intended to be covered by this language. The provision is also intended to include the failure of the host government to act within "a reasonable period of time" on a transfer application. The provision does not define the specific period but it is expected that this will be accomplished in the rules and regulations to be issued by the Board and specifically in the contracts of guarantee. In determining what constitutes a "reasonable period", the Agency will need to reconcile the investors' interest in a speedy transfer with the fact that certain delays in the processing of applications by governments may be justified.

The expropriation risk would encompass measures attributable to the host government such as nationalization, confiscation, sequestration, seizure, attachment and freezing of assets. The phrase "any legislative or administration action" in the provision includes measures by the executive, but not measures taken by judicial bodies in the exercise of their functions. Measures normally taken by governments to regulate their economic activities such as taxation, environmental and labor legislation as well as normal measures for the maintenance of public safety, are not intended to be covered by this provision unless they discriminate against the holder of the guarantee. In defining these measures, the Agency's practice would not be meant to prejudice the rights of a member country or of investors under bilateral investment treaties, other treaties and international law.

The breach of contract risk[4] is contained in Article 11 (a)(iii). Indemnification is available only when an investor has no forum to pursue the contractual claim against the government or when recourse to such a forum is hampered by an unreasonable delay as defined in the guarantee contract or when, after obtaining a final decision in his favor, the investor is unable to enforce it.

The risk of war and civil disturbance[5] is contained in Article 11 (a)(iv). It is intended to include revolutions, insurrections, coups d'état and similar political events which are typically outside the control of the host government. Acts of terrorists and similar activities which are specifically directed against the holder of the guarantee are, however, not intended to be covered by this provision but may be covered under Article 11 (b).

The Convention provides additional flexibility by allowing the coverage of other specific non-commercial risks, but only at the joint request of the investor and the host country and with approval of the Board by special majority. Such approval may be issued on a case by case basis or in the form of regulations specifying the cases to be covered under this provision.

Eligibility[6]

It is envisaged that the Agency will focus on guaranteeing investments eligible under Article 12 (a), i. e., equity investment, different forms of direct investment, and medium- to long-term loans made or guaranteed by owners of equity in the enterprise concerned (so-called equity-type or sponsored loans). The term "direct investment" is a generic term whose precise scope will have to be determined by the Board. The Board is expected to be guided by the International Monetary Fund's definition of foreign direct investment as an "investment that is made to acquire a lasting interest in an enterprise operating in an economy other than that of the investor, the investor's purpose being to have an effective voice in the management of the enterprise". The Board may consider as direct investment such new forms of investment as service and management contracts as well as franchising, licensing, leasing, and production-sharing agreements where the investor's return depends on the performance of the enterprise. In any case, it is immaterial whether the investment is made in monetary form or in kind such as the contribution of machinery, service, technical processes and technology.

To conserve the Agency's scarce resources, the Agency would not guarantee or reinsure any export credit, regardless of its form, which is provided, guaranteed or reinsured by a government or an official export credit agency. Because the coverage of the Agency is restricted to investments, exports will be covered (within the limits of the preceding sentence) only to the extent that they represent a contribution to a specific investment. An agency or distributorship arrangement, which is designed primarily to promote exports, and in which an investor has an inconsequential equity interest, would not be covered by the Agency. The Agency would function as an investment guarantee agency, and would not function as an export credit agency which could compete with official export credit agencies.

To serve its objective without undermining its financial viability, the Agency will limit its guarantees to sound investments. It should satisfy itself that the investment concerned will contribute to the economic and social development of the host country, comply with the laws and regulations of that country, and be consistent with the country's declared development objectives. It should also be satisfied that appropriate investment conditions, including the availability of fair and equitable treatment and legal protection, will apply to the investment concerned. In case no such protection is assured under the laws of the host country or under bilateral investment treaties, the Agency will issue the guarantee only after it reaches agreement with the host country pursuant to Article 23 (b)(ii) or otherwise on the treatment to be extended to the investments covered by the Agency. Investments guaranteed by the Agency should also be new, that is implemented subsequent to the registration of the application for the guarantee by the Agency. The exclusion of pre-existing investments would not bar the Agency from covering investments made to develop an existing investment or from covering the reinvestment earnings which could otherwise be transferred outside the host country. The term "earnings" in Article 12 (c)(ii) is intended to include royalties and license fees.

Host Country Approval and Subrogation[7]

The Agency will not conclude any contract of guarantee before "the host government has approved the issuance of the guarantee by the Agency against the risks designated for cover". Any host government may withhold its approval. This enables the host country to evaluate a proposed investment before giving its consent.

The Agency is expected to establish procedures for obtaining consents under this provision. These may include requesting approvals on a no objection basis. Although the approval of the home country of the investor is not required, it would not be appropriate for the Agency to cover an investment if informed by the investor's home country that it would be financed with funds transferred outside such country in violation of laws.

Article 18 (a) provides that where the Agency compensates or agrees to compensate an investor under a contract of guarantee, it assumes the rights that the investor acquired against the host country as a result of the event giving rise to the claim against the Agency. Subrogation is an accepted principle of insurance law. It provides for the assignment of an existing claim from the guaranteed investor to the Agency and the Agency as subrogee acquires the same rights as the investor had. The contracts of guarantee will define the terms and conditions of subrogation. These terms and conditions are of special significance for the investor in view of the fact that the Agency will compensate investors only for part of their losses. Article 18 (b) provides for the recognition of the Agency's right of subrogation by all members.

Notes

1. **Multilateral Investment Guarantee Agency　多边投资担保机构**

   多边投资担保机构于1985年在汉城召开的世界银行年会正式通过，又称《汉城公约》，中国于1988年批准该公约，成为其会员国。该机构具有完全法律人格的国际组织，其主要职责是对会员国内来自其他会员国的投资的非商业性风险提供担保。

2. **currency transfer risk　货币汇兑转移险**

   货币汇兑转移险，即东道国政府采取措施，限制投资者将其货币兑换成可自由使用的货币或投保人可接受的另一种货币，并转移到东道国境外。

3. **expropriation　征用(风险)**

   征用(风险)，即东道国政府采取立法或行政措施，剥夺投资者对其投资及收益的所有权或控制权而导致损失的风险。

4. **breach of contract risk　违约险**

   违约险，即东道国撕毁或违反它与投资者签定的投资合同的风险。

5. **risk of war and civil disturbance　战争与内乱险**

   战争与内乱险，即东道国境内发生军事行动或内乱导致投资者的损失。

6. **Eligibility　适格性**

   适格性，即合格的投资。MIGA对其承保的投资必须具备一定的条件，即所谓合格的投资。例如,其承保的投资必须为直接投资,必须在合格的东道国(发展中国家的会员国)的投资等。

7. Subrogation 代位权

代位权,即当 MIGA 对投资者支付或同意支付赔偿金时,代位取得向东道国索赔的权利。

Study Questions

1. What is the mission of MIGA?
2. What is the impact of MIGA?
3. How do you understand the qualified investments?
4. What kind of investors may be eligible?
5. What are the non-commercial risks?

Sources of Information and Further Readings

1. http://en.wikipedia.org/wiki/Multilateral_Investment_Guarantee_Agency
2. http://www.miga.org/
3. http://www.worldbank.org/

Chapter 17

Paris Convention for the Protection of Industrial Property[1]

Key Concepts

Industrial property | national treatment | compulsory license | right of priority
well-known marks | unfair competition | independence of patent

Learning Objectives

1. Understand the scope of industrial property.
2. Understand the implications of national treatment.
3. Understand the independence of patent.
4. Be familiar with well-known marks and their protection.

This Convention was first passed on March 20, 1883, in Paris. It was revised at Brussels, Belgium, on December 14, 1900, at Washington, United States, on June 2, 1911, at The Hague, Netherlands, on November 6, 1925, at London, United Kingdom, on June 2, 1934, at Lisbon, Portugal, on October 31, 1958, and at Stockholm, Sweden, on July 14, 1967, and was amended on September 28, 1979.

The Convention now has 173 contracting member countries, which makes it one of the most widely adopted treaties worldwide. China has acceded to this Convention in 1985. The Paris Convention is administered by the World Intellectual Property Organization (WIPO), based in Geneva, Switzerland.

Scope of Industrial Property[2]

The protection of industrial property has as its object patents, utility models, industrial designs, trademarks, service marks, trade names, indications of source or appellations of origin, and the repression of unfair competition. Industrial property shall be understood in the broadest sense and shall apply not only to industry and commerce proper, but likewise to agricultural and extractive industries and to all manufactured or natural products, for example, wines, grain, tobacco leaf, fruit, cattle, minerals, mineral waters, beer, flowers, and flour. Patents shall include the various kinds of industrial patents recognized by the laws of the countries of the Union, such as patents of importation, patents of improvement, patents and certificates of addition, etc.

National Treatment

Nationals of any country of the Union shall, as regards the protection of industrial property, enjoy in all the other countries of the Union the advantages that their respective laws now grant, or may hereafter grant, to nationals; all without prejudice to the rights specially provided for by this Convention. Consequently, they shall have the same protection as the latter, and the same legal remedy against any infringement of their rights, provided that the conditions and formalities imposed upon nationals are complied with.

Nationals of countries outside the Union who are domiciled or who have real and effective industrial or commercial establishments in the territory of one of the countries of the Union shall be treated in the same manner as nationals of the countries of the Union.

Right of Priority[3]

Any person who has duly filed an application for a patent, or for the registration of a utility model, or of an industrial design, or of a trademark, in one of the countries of the Union, or his successor in title, shall enjoy, for the purpose of filing in the other countries, a right of priority. Any filing that is equivalent to a regular national filing under the domestic legislation of any country of the Union or under bilateral or multilateral treaties concluded between countries of the Union shall be recognized as giving rise to the right of priority. The periods of priority referred to above shall be twelve months for patents and utility models, and six months for industrial designs and trademarks.

If the last day of the period is an official holiday, or a day when the Office is not open for the filing of applications in the country where protection is claimed, the period shall be extended until the first following working day.

Any person desiring to take advantage of the priority of a previous filing shall be required to make a declaration indicating the date of such filing and the country in which it was made. Each country shall determine the latest date on which such declaration must be made.

The countries of the Union may require any person making a declaration of priority to produce a copy of the application (description, drawings, etc.) previously filed. The copy, certified as correct by the authority which received such application, shall not require any authentication, and may in any case be filed, without fee, at any time within three months of the filing of the subsequent application. They may require it to be accompanied by a certificate from the same authority showing the date of filing, and by a translation.

Independence of Patents

Patents applied for in the various countries of the Union by nationals of countries of the Union shall be independent of patents obtained for the same invention in other countries, whether members of the Union or not.

The foregoing provision is to be understood in an unrestricted sense, in particular, in the sense that patents applied for during the period of priority are independent, both as regards the grounds for nullity and forfeiture, and as regards their normal duration.

Patents obtained with the benefit of priority shall, in the various countries of the Union, have a duration equal to that which they would have, had they been applied for or granted without the benefit of priority.

Compulsory Licenses[4]

Each country of the Union shall have the right to take legislative measures providing for the grant of compulsory licenses to prevent the abuses which might result from the exercise of the exclusive rights conferred by the patent, for example, failure to work.

Forfeiture of the patent shall not be provided for except in cases where the grant of compulsory licenses would not have been sufficient to prevent the said abuses. No proceedings for the forfeiture or revocation of a patent may be instituted before the expiration of two years from the grant of the first compulsory license.

A compulsory license may not be applied for on the ground of failure to work or insufficient working before the expiration of a period of four years from the date of filing of the patent application or three years from the date of the grant of the patent, whichever period expires last; it shall be refused if the patentee justifies his inaction by legitimate reasons. Such a compulsory license shall be non-exclusive and shall not be transferable, even in the form of the grant of a sub-license, except with that part of the enterprise or goodwill which exploits such license.

The protection of industrial designs shall not, under any circumstance, be subject to any forfeiture, either by reason of failure to work or by reason of the importation of articles corresponding to those which are protected.

If, in any country, use of the registered mark is compulsory, the registration may be cancelled only after a reasonable period, and then only if the person concerned does not justify his inaction.

Concurrent use of the same mark on identical or similar goods by industrial or commercial establishments considered as co-proprietors of the mark according to the provisions of the domestic law of the country where protection is claimed shall not prevent registration or diminish in any way the protection granted to the said mark in any country of the Union, provided that such use does not result in misleading the public and is not contrary to the public interest.

Period of Grace for the Payment of Fees for the Maintenance of Rights

A period of grace of not less than six months shall be allowed for the payment of the fees prescribed for the maintenance of industrial property rights, subject, if the domestic legislation so provides, to the payment of a surcharge.

The countries of the Union shall have the right to provide for the restoration of patents which have lapsed by reason of non-payment of fees.

Conditions of Registration; Independence of Protection of Same Mark in Different Countries

The conditions for the filing and registration of trademarks shall be determined in each country of the Union by its domestic legislation. However, an application for the registration of a mark filed by a national of a country of the Union in any country of the Union may not be refused, nor may a registration be invalidated, on the ground that filing, registration, or renewal, has not been effected in the country of origin. A mark duly registered in a country of the Union shall be regarded as independent of marks registered in the other countries of the Union, including the country of origin.

Well-Known Marks

The countries of the Union undertake, ex officio if their legislation so permits, or at the request of an interested party, to refuse or to cancel the registration, and to prohibit the use, of a trademark which constitutes a reproduction, an imitation, or a translation, liable to create confusion, of a mark considered by the competent authority of the country of registration or use to be well known in that country as being already the mark of a person entitled to the benefits of this Convention and used for identical or similar goods. These provisions shall also apply when the essential part of the mark constitutes a reproduction of any such well-known mark or an imitation liable to create confusion therewith.

Assignment of Marks

When, in accordance with the law of a country of the Union, the assignment of a mark is valid only if it takes place at the same time as the transfer of the business or goodwill to which the mark belongs, it shall suffice for the recognition of such validity that the portion of the business or goodwill located in that country be transferred to the assignee, together with the exclusive right to manufacture in the said country, or to sell therein, the goods bearing the mark assigned.

The foregoing provision does not impose upon the countries of the Union any obligation to regard as valid the assignment of any mark the use of which by the assignee would, in fact, be of such a nature as to mislead the public, particularly as regards the origin, nature, or essential qualities, of the goods to which the mark is applied.

Protection of Marks

Every trademark duly registered in the country of origin shall be accepted for filing and protected as is in the other countries of the Union, subject to the reservations indicated in this Article. Such countries may, before proceeding to final registration, require the production of a certificate of registration in the country of origin, issued by the competent authority. No authentication shall be required for this certificate.

Shall be considered the country of origin the country of the Union where the applicant has a real and effective industrial or commercial establishment, or, if he has no such establishment within the Union, the country of the Union where he has his domicile, or, if he has no domicile within the Union but is a national of a country of the Union, the country of which he is a national.

In determining whether a mark is eligible for protection, all the factual circumstances must be taken into consideration, particularly the length of time the mark has been in use.

No trademark shall be refused in the other countries of the Union for the sole reason that it differs from the mark protected in the country of origin only in respect of elements that do not alter its distinctive character and do not affect its identity in the form in which it has been registered in the said country of origin.

Unfair Competition[5]

The countries of the Union are bound to assure to nationals of such countries effective protection against unfair competition. Any act of competition contrary to honest practices in industrial or commercial matters constitutes an act of unfair competition. The following in particular shall be prohibited: (1) all acts of such a nature as to create confusion by any means whatever with the establishment, the goods, or the industrial or commercial activities, of a competitor; (2) false allegations in the course of trade of such a nature as to discredit the establishment, the goods, or the industrial or commercial activities, of a competitor; (3) indications or allegations, the use of which in the course of trade is liable to mislead the public as to the nature, the manufacturing process, the characteristics, the suitability for their purpose, or the quantity, of the goods.

Notes

1. **Paris Convention for the Protection of Industrial Property** 《保护工业产权巴黎公约》

   《保护工业产权巴黎公约》简称《巴黎公约》，该公约于1883年在巴黎通过，目前，多数成员国采用1967年斯德哥尔摩修订的版本。我国于1985年成为该公约的成员国。巴黎公约旨在保护工业产权，包括专利、实用新型、外观设计、商标、服务标记、厂商名称、货源标记(indications of source)和原产地标记(appellation of origin)、制止不正当竞争(repression of unfair competition)。而国民待遇原则、优先权原则和专利独立性原则为《巴黎公约》的3个基本原则。该公约历经100多年，至今仍发挥着重要作用。

2. **Scope of Industrial Property** 工业产权范围

   《巴黎公约》对工业产权作了广义的解释。

3. **Right of Priority** 优先权

   优先权，即指特定的申请人在某一成员国提出工业产权申请的基础上，如在一定期限内就同一申请也在其他成员国提出时，第一次的申请日则被视为其后的申请日。换言之，在申请时间方面，后面的申请享有等同于第一次申请日的优先地位。

4. **Compulsory Licenses** 强制许可

   强制许可旨在防止专利权人在行使专利权时有可能产生的滥用独占权(abuses of exclusive right)现象，如不实施专利(failure to work)。

5. **Unfair Competition** 不正当竞争

   《巴黎公约》对不正当竞争作了原则性的规定，即在商业活动中的一切违背诚信的行为均属不正当竞争行为。例如，在商业活动制造混淆、诋毁商誉及误导公众的行为为不正当竞争。

Study Questions

1. What is industrial property?
2. What are the principles of Paris Convention?
3. What is the role of Paris Convention?
4. What do you think of the principle of the national treatment which the developing

countries shall follow?

5. What are the other international treaties on intellectual property?

Sources of Information and Further Readings

1. Paris Convention for the Protection of Industrial Property of 1883
2. http://en.wikipedia.org/wiki/Paris_Convention_for_the_Protection_of_Industrial_Property
3. http://www.wipo.int/portal/index.html.en
4. http://en.wikipedia.org/wiki/World_Intellectual_Property_Organization

Chapter 18

Patent Law in China[1]

Key Concepts

practical applicability	inventiveness	novelty
patent for invention	utility model	design

Learning Objectives

1. Be familiar with the types of patent.
2. Be familiar with the requirements for grant of patent right in China.
3. Be familiar with the application for patent in China.
4. Understand the compulsory license for exploitation of patent in China.

In legal sense, patent means the exclusive or monopolized right granted by the state in accordance with the law. In perspective of the technology, patent is also a kind of new invention and creation, being an important part of the scientific technology as the first productivity. In general, patent refers to inventions, utility models and designs. After the grant of the patent right for an invention, utility model or design, no entity or individual may, without the authorization of the patentee, exploit the patent, that is, make, sell or import the patented products, or use the patented process or design for production or business purposes. Any entity or individual exploiting the patent of another shall conclude with the patentee a written license contract for exploitation and pay the patentee a fee for the exploitation of the patent. The licensee has no right to authorize any entity or individual to exploit the patent, other than that referred to in the contract.

Requirements for Grant of Patent Right

Any invention or utility model for which patent right may be granted must possess novelty, inventiveness and practical applicability[2]. Novelty means that, before the date of filing, no identical invention or utility model has been publicly disclosed in publication in the country or abroad or has been publicly used or made known to the public by any other means in the country, nor has any other person filed previously with the patent administration department an application which described the identical invention or utility model and was published after the said date of filing. Inventiveness means that, as compared with the technology existing before the date of filing, the invention has prominent substantive features and represents a notable progress and that the utility model has substantive features and represents progress. Practical applicability means that the invention or utility model can be made or used and can produce effective results.

Any design for which patent right may be granted must not be identical with and similar to any design which, before the date of filing, has been publicly disclosed in publication in the country or abroad or has been publicly used in the country, and must not be in conflict with any prior right of any other person.

Any invention-creation for which a patent is applied for does not lose its novelty where, within six months before the date of filing, one of the following events occurred:

- where it was first exhibited at an international exhibition sponsored or recognized by the Chinese government;
- where it was first made public at a prescribed academic or technological meeting;
- where it was disclosed by any person without the consent of the applicant.

For any of the following, no patent right shall be granted:

- scientific discoveries;
- rules and methods for mental activities;
- animal and plant varieties;
- substances obtained by means of nuclear transformation.

Application for Patent

Where an application for a patent for invention or utility model is filed, a request, a description and its abstract, and claims shall be submitted. The request shall state the title of the invention or utility model, the name of the inventor or creator, the name and the address of the applicant and other related matters. The description shall set forth the invention or utility model in a manner sufficiently clear and complete so as to enable a person skilled in the relevant field of technology to carry it out; where necessary, drawings are required. The abstract shall state briefly the main technical points of the invention or utility model. The claims shall be supported by the description and shall state the extent of the patent protection asked for. In accordance with bilateral agreement between China and the foreign country, or in accordance with the relevant international treaty, or on the basis of the principle of mutual recognition of the right of priority[3], where, within twelve months from the date on which any applicant first filed in a foreign country an application for a patent for invention or utility model, or within six months for a patent for a design, he files in China an application for a patent for the same subject matter, he may enjoy right of priority. An applicant who claims the right of priority shall make a written declaration, and a copy of the application document which was first filed.

Examination for and Approval of Application for Patent

Upon receipt of an application for a patent for invention, the patent administration shall have preliminary examination[4]. If the application is in conformity with the requirements of the law, it shall be published. If it is not in conformity with the provisions of the law, the patent administration department shall notify the applicant and request him to submit his observations or to amend the application. The application shall be rejected if it is still not in line with the provisions of the law. Where it is found after examination that there is no cause for rejection of application for a patent for invention, the patent administration department shall make a decision to grant the patent right for invention, issue the certificate of patent for invention, and register and announce it. The patent right for invention shall take effect as of the date of the announcement. For an application for invention that has been already filed in a foreign country, the patent administration department may ask the applicant to furnish within a specified time limit documents concerning any search made for the purpose of examining that application, or concerning the results of any examination made in that country. If, at the expiration of the specified time limit, without any justified reason, the said documents are not furnished, the application shall be deemed to have been withdrawn. If the applicant is not satisfied with the decision of the said department rejecting the application, the applicant may, within three months from the date of receipt of notification, request the patent reexamination board[5] to make a reexamination. Where the applicant for patent is not satisfied with the decision of the patent reexamination board, he may, within three months from the date of receipt of the notification, institute legal proceedings in the people's court.

Duration, Cessation and Invalidation of Patent Right

The duration of patent right for invention shall be twenty years, and ten years for utility models and designs, counted from the date if filing. The patentee shall pay an annual fee beginning with the year in which the patent right was granted. The patent right shall cease before the expiration of its duration if annual fee is not paid as prescribed, or the patentee abandons his patent right by written declaration. Any cessation of the patent right shall be registered and announced by the patent administration department. Any entity or individual considers that the grant of the said patent right is not in conformity with the relevant provisions of this law, he or it may request the patent reexamination board to declare the patent right invalid. Any patent right which has been declared invalid shall be deemed to be non-existent from the beginning. The decision declaring the patent right invalid shall have no retroactive effect on any judgment or ruling of patent infringement which has been pronounced and enforced by the court, on any decision concerning the handling of a dispute over patent infringement which has been complied with or compulsorily executed, or on any contract of patent license or of assignment of patent right which has been performed prior to the declaration of the patent right invalid; however, the damage caused to other persons in bad faith on the part of the patentee shall be compensated. If the patentee or assignor of patent right makes no payment to the licensee or the assignee of the patent right of the fee for the exploitation of patent or of the price for the assignment of the patent right, which is obviously contrary to the principle of equity, the patentee or the assignor shall refund the whole or part of the fee for the exploitation of the patent or of the price for the assignment of the patent right to the licensee or the assignee of the patent right.

Compulsory License[6] for Exploitation of Patent

Where a national emergency or any extraordinary state of affairs occurs, or where the public interests so requires, the patent administration department may grant a compulsory license to exploit the patent for invention or utility model. Where the invention or utility model for which the patent right has been granted involves important technical advance of considerable economic significance in relation to another invention or utility model for which a patent right has been granted earlier and the exploitation of the later invention or utility model depends on the exploitation of the earlier invention or utility model, the patent administration department may, upon the request of the later patentee, grant a compulsory license to exploit the earlier invention or utility model. Where any entity which is qualified to exploit the invention or utility model has made requests for authorization from the patentee of an invention or utility model to exploit its or his patent on reasonable terms and conditions and such efforts have not been successful within a reasonable period of time, the patent administration department may, upon the request of that entity, grant a compulsory license to exploit the patent for invention or utility model. In the decision granting the compulsory license for exploitation, the scope and duration of the exploitation shall be specified on the basis of the reasons justifying the grant. Any entity or individual that is granted to a compulsory license for exploitation shall not have an exclusive right to exploit and shall not have the right to authorize others to exploit. The entity or individual that is granted to a compulsory license for exploitation shall pay to the patentee a reasonable exploitation fee, to be fixed by both parties through consultations.

The administrative authority for patent affairs shall not take part in recommending any patented product for sale to the public or any such commercial activities. Otherwise, it shall be ordered by the authority at the next higher level or the supervisory authority to correct its mistakes and eliminate the bad effects. The illegal earnings, if any, shall be confiscated. Where the circumstances are serious, the persons who are directly in charge and the other persons who are directly responsible shall be given disciplinary sanction in accordance with law. Where any state functionary working for patent administration or any other state functionary concerned neglects his duty, abuses his power, or engages in malpractice for personal gain, which constitutes a crime, shall be prosecuted for his criminal liability in accordance with law.

Notes

1. Patent Law in China 《中国专利法》

《中国专利法》于1984正式通过,1985年4月1日起实施。1992年我国对《中国专利法》作了修订,使其与国际标准接轨。我国专利法规定了3种专利,即明、实用新型和外观设计。此外,专利法还采用先申请制度和《巴黎公约》中的优先权制度,并对外国人实行国民待遇。

2. novelty, inventiveness and practical applicability 新颖性、创造性和实用性

新颖性主要从一项技术是否被公开来判定;创造性是指同申请日以前已有的技术相比,是否具有突出的实质性特点和显著的进步;实用性则注重能在产业上进行制造或使用,并能产生积极的效果。

3. right of priority 优先权

专利优先权可分为国内优先权和国际优先权。国内优先权,又称为"本国优先权",是指专利申请人就相同主题的发明或者实用新型在中国第一次提出专利申请之日起12个月内,又向我国国家知识产权局专利局提出专利申请的,可以享有优先权。在我国优先权制度中不包括外观设计专利。国际优先权,又称"外国优先权",其内容是:专利申请人就同一发明或者实用新型在外国第一次提出专利申请之日起12个月内,或者就同一外观设计在外国第一次提出专利申请之日起6个月内,又在中国提出专利申请的,中国应当以其在外国第一次提出专利申请之日为申请日,该申请日即为优先权日。

4. preliminary examination 初步审查

初步审查也称为"形式审查"或"格式审查",是国务院专利行政部门对发明、实用新型和外观设计专利申请是否具备形式条件进行的审查。初步审查的主要目的是查明申请专利的发明是否符合《中国专利法》关于形式要求的规定,为以后的公开和实质审查做准备;查明申请专利的实用新型和外观设计是否符合《中国专利法》关于授予专利权的规定,对符合授权条件的实用新型和外观设计依法授予专利权。而实质审查是指专利局在对申请案进行审查时,不仅要对申请案的形式要件进行审查,还要对申请案中的发明创造是否符合新颖性、创造性、实用性等实质性要件进行审查。根据《中国专利法》,对发明专利实行实质审查制,而对实用新型专利和外观设计专利实行形式审查制。

5. patent reexamination board 专利复审委员会

国家知识产权局专利复审委员会成立于1984年11月,专利复审委员会负责对复审请求的审查、初审驳回的复审、实审驳回的复审、专利权无效宣告请求的审查以及出庭应诉。

6. compulsory license 强制许可

强制许可是指国务院专利行政部门依照专利法规定，不经专利权人同意，直接允许其他单位或个人实施其发明创造的一种许可方式，又称"非自愿许可"。在国家出现紧急状态或者非常情况时，或者为了公共利益的目的，国务院专利行政部门可以给予实施发明专利或者实用新型专利的强制许可。

Study Questions

1. What are the requirements for grant of patent right?
2. What is the novelty of an invention?
3. Why may the patent administrative grant the compulsory license for the exploitation of a patent?
4. According to the patent law of China, what is the duration of the patent right?
5. What do you think of the license of the patent right?

Case Study

试用英文对以下案例进行分析和讨论：

公民张某于2000年4月完成了一项"水变油"方法的发明，5月利用A企业提供的物质技术条件对该方法进行了验证和测试，并向A企业支付了100万元的测试费用。在测试过程中，A企业的职工王某窃取了张某的技术秘密后，于2000年6月将该技术秘密转让给李某，李某不知道王某的技术秘密系窃取所得，并向王某支付了200万元的转让费。张某得知李某使用自己的技术秘密后，要求李某向其支付合理的使用费、承担保密义务，李某向张某支付使用费后，张某要求李某停止使用该技术秘密。

2001年12月，张某将该项技术的专利申请权以300万元的价格转让给甲公司，2002年1月1日，甲公司向国家知识产权局提出发明专利的书面申请。国家知识产权局经初步审查认为该方法发明符合专利法的规定要求，于2003年7月1日即行公布。2004年10月1日，国家知识产权局根据甲公司的请求，对该方法发明进行实质审查后，于2005年1月1日作出授予甲公司发明专利权的决定，并于同日予以登记和公告。2005年4月，甲公司对乙公司、丙公司、丁公司分别提起专利侵权诉讼，人民法院在审理过程中，查明以下情况：

（1）乙公司于2004年1月1日开始，多次使用甲公司的该项方法发明。2004年12月15日甲公司得知后要求乙公司支付使用费时，遭到乙公司的拒绝。

（2）2005年4月1日，甲公司得知丙公司在未经许可的情况下，于2005年2月1日在与某公司的买卖合同中使用甲公司的专利号，非法获利20万元。

（3）丁公司在2002年1月1日前已经使用相同的方法，甲公司于2005年1月1日取得发明专利权后，丁公司在原有范围内继续使用该方法。

2005 年 6 月 1 日，人民法院经审理，判决丙公司的侵权行为成立。丙公司于 2005 年 6 月 10 日向甲公司支付了赔偿金 20 万元。

2005 年 8 月 1 日，甲公司的发明专利被国家知识产权局宣告无效，于是丙公司向甲公司要求退还 20 万元的专利侵权赔偿金。

根据上述内容，分别回答以下问题：

（1）张某的发明是否属于 A 企业的职务发明？并说明理由。

（2）张某要求李某停止使用该技术秘密的主张是否成立？并说明理由。

（3）甲公司的发明专利权自何日起生效？其 20 年的保护期限从何日起计算？

（4）指出甲公司对乙公司提起诉讼的具体诉讼时效期间，并说明理由。

（5）指出甲公司对丙公司提起诉讼的具体诉讼时效期间，并说明理由。

（6）丙公司的行为属于何种性质的违法行为？丙公司及直接责任人员应承担何种刑事责任？

（7）在甲公司对丙公司的专利侵权诉讼中，举证责任在甲公司还是丙公司？并说明理由。

（8）丁公司的行为是否属于专利侵权？并说明理由。

（9）丙公司向甲公司要求退还 20 万元的专利侵权赔偿金的主张是否成立？并说明理由。

（选自司法考试案例分析题：http://www.yuloo.com/news/1011/515242.shtml）

Sources of Information and Further Readings

1. Patent Law of the People's Republic of China of 1984 (as revised in 1992)
2. John Shijian Mo. *International Commercial Law.* Lexis Nexis, 2003.
3. http://www.lawinfochina.com/display.aspx? lib=law&id=7289
4. http://www.china.org.cn/government/laws/2007-04/21/content_1207499.htm
5. http://www.most.gov.cn/eng/policies/regulations/200501/t20050107_18490.htm
6. http://en.wikipedia.org/wiki/Patent

Chapter 19

Trademark Law in China[1]

Key Concepts

registered trademark
goods trademark
service trademark
collective trademark
principle of reciprocity
certification trademark
well-known trademark

Learning Objectives

1. Be familiar with the types of trademark.
2. Understand the principle of reciprocity.
3. Be familiar with the determination of well-known trademark.
4. Understand the application for trademark registration.

Introduction

Trademark law is designed to reinforce the administration of trademarks, protect the exclusive rights to use registered trademarks, and encourage manufacturers and sellers to ensure the quality of their goods and services and keep the prestige of their trademarks, with a view to protecting the legitimate interests of the consumers, manufacturers and sellers.

A registered trademark[2] means a trademark that has been approved and registered by the trademark office. It may fall into a goods trademark, a service trademark, a collective trademark, or a certification trademark[3]. The trademark registrant shall enjoy an exclusive right to use the trademark, which shall be protected by law.

Collective trademark means any mark registered in the name of an entity, association or other organization for being used by the members of this organization in their commercial activities to indicate the users' qualifications in this organization.

Certification trademark means any mark controlled by an organization in charge of the supervision over certain goods or services and used by the entity or individual outside this organization in respect of its goods or services to certify its origin, raw material, manufacturing method, quality or other specific qualities of the said goods and services.

Where the natural person, legal person or other organization intends to acquire the exclusive right to use a trademark for the goods he or it produces, manufactures, processes, selects or markets, or for service he or it provides, an application should be filed with the trademark office for registration of a goods trademark or a service trademark.

As for any of the goods, as prescribed by the state, that must bear a registered trademark, a trademark registration shall be applied for. Where no trademark registration has been granted, such goods shall not be sold on the market.

Any visual mark, consists of words, devices, letters, numbers, three-dimensional marks, combined colors, or the combination of said factors, that can distinguish the goods of a natural person, legal person or other organization from those goods of others, can be applied as a trademark for registration.

Any trademark applied for registration shall be distinctive as to be distinguishable and shall not be in conflict with other people's prior acquired legitimate rights. The following things shall not be used as a trademark:

- those identical with or similar to the state name, national flag, national emblem, military flag or medals of PRC, and those identical with the name of specific place where the central organization of the state or the party are located or the name, device of any symbolic building of the place;
- those identical with or similar to the state name, national flag, national emblem or military flag of any foreign countries, except those approved by the government of the country

concerned;

- those identical with or similar to the name, flag or emblem of any international intergovernmental organizations, except those unlikely to mislead the public;
- those identical with or similar to the official sign or inspection mark indicating under control and guarantee, except those with official authorization;
- those identical with or similar to the symbols, or names of the Red Cross;
- those having the nature of discrimination against any nationality;
- those having the nature of exaggeration and fraud in advertising goods;
- those detrimental to socialist morals or customs, or having unhealthy influences.

In addition, the geographical names as the administrative divisions at or above the county level and the foreign geographical names well-known to the public shall not be used as trademarks.

Any of the following marks shall not be registered as a trademark:

- those only having the generic names, designs or models of the goods in respect of the trademark is used;
- those only having direct reference to the quality, main raw materials, function, use, weight, quantity or other features of the goods in respect of which the trademark is used;
- those lacking the distinctive features;

The following factors shall be taken into account in identification of a well-known trademark:

- extent of the relevant public's awareness of the target trademark;
- duration of the use of the target trademark;
- duration, extent and geographical scope of any publicizing work for the target trademark;
- protection records of the target trademark as a well-known trademark[4].

Where any foreign citizen or enterprises applies for registration of a trademark in China, the application shall be handled in accordance with any agreement concluded between its or his country and China, or any international treaty to which both countries are members, or on the basis of the principle of reciprocity[5].

Where any foreign citizen or enterprise applies for registration of a trademark or has other trademark affairs to attend to in China, he or it shall entrust a state-designated trademark agency with qualifications for foreign-related trademark affairs to act on his or its behalf.

Application of Trademark Registration

An applicant for the registration of a trademark shall indicate the class of the goods and the designation of the goods to use the trademark in the application form in accordance with the prescribed classification of the goods. Where any sign of a registered trademark is to be altered, a new application for registration shall be filed. After the registration of a trademark, the name, address or other registered matters concerning the registrant change, an application for the change shall be filed.

Within six months from the date when any trademark applicant first filed a trademark application in the foreign country, he or it files an application in China for registration of the same trademark in respect of the goods in the same class, he or it may enjoy the right of priority in accordance with the agreement concluded between his or its country and China, or in accordance with any international treaty to which both countries are members, or on the basis of the principle of mutual recognition of the right of priority. Where any trademark which is used for the first time on the goods exhibited at an international exhibition sponsored or recognized by the Chinese government, the applicant for registering this trademark may enjoy the right of priority within six months from the date of exhibition. The trademark applicant claiming the right of priority shall make a written statement and other relevant supporting documents within the time limit, otherwise, the claim to the right of priority shall be deemed to have not been made. The items applied for trademark registration and the materials provided should be authentic, accurate and complete.

Examination for and Approval of Trademark Rsegistration

Where a trademark is in conformity with the relevant provisions of the law, the trademark office shall, after examination of its application for registration, preliminarily approve the trademark and publish the same. Where two or more applicants apply for the registration of identical or similar trademarks for the same or similar goods, the preliminary approval, after examination, and the publication shall be made for the trademark which was first filed. Any person, within three months from the date of the publication, file an opposition against the trademark that has, after examination, been preliminarily approved. Where no opposition has been filed at the expiration of the publication period, the registration shall be approved, a certificate of trademark registration shall be issued and the trademark shall be published. Where the application for registration of a trademark is refused, the applicant may, within fifteen days from the receipt of the notification, apply for a review in the Trademark Review and Adjudication Board. Any party who is dissatisfied with the decision made by the Board, he may, within thirty days from the receipt of the notification, institute legal proceedings in the court. The application for the trademark registration, and for trademark review should be examined in a timely manner.

Renewal, Assignment and Licensing of Registered Trademark[6]

The period of validity of a registered trademark shall be ten years, counted from the date of approval of the registration. Where the registrant intends to continue to use the registered trademark beyond the expiration of the period of validity, an application for renewal of the registration shall be made within six months before the said expiration. A grace period of six months may be allowed if no application is filed within the said period. The period of validity of each renewal of registration shall be ten years. Any renewal of registration shall be published after it has been approved.

Where a registered trademark is assigned , both the assignor and assignee shall sign a contract of assignment and jointly file an application with trademark office. The assignee shall guarantee the quality of the goods in respect of which the registered trademark is used.

Any trademark registrant may, by signing a trademark license contract, authorize other persons to use his registered trademark. The licensor shall supervise the quality of the goods in respect of which the licensee uses his registered trademark. In addition, the name of the licensee and the origin of the goods must be indicated on the goods that bear the registered trademark. The trademark license contract shall be submitted to the trademark office for record.

Administration of the Utilization of Trademark

In case a registered trademark is altered unilaterally, or the name, address or other registered matters concerning the registrant of a registered trademark are changed unilaterally, or the registered trademark is assigned unilaterally, or the registered trademark has ceased to be used for three consecutive years, the trademark office shall order the registrant to rectify the situation within a specified period or cancel the registered trademark. Where a registered trademark is used in respect of the goods that have been roughly or poorly manufactured, or whose superior quality has been replaced by interior quality, so that consumers are deceived, the administrative authorities for industry and commerce at different levels shall, according to circumstances, order rectification of the situation within a specified period, and may, in addition, circulate a notice of criticism or impose a fine, and the trademark office may even cancel the registered trademark.

Any person who uses an unregistered trademark shall not falsely represent its trademark as a registered one, otherwise the administrative authority for industry and commerce may stop the use of the trademark, order him to rectify the situation within a specified period, and may, in addition, circulate a notice of criticism or impose a fine.

Protection of the Exclusive Right to Use Registered Trademark

The exclusive right to use a registered trademark shall be limited to the trademark which has been approved for registration and to the goods in respect of which the use of the trademark has been approved. Any of the following acts constitute infringement of the exclusive right to use a registered trademark:

- to use a trademark that is identical with or similar to a registered trademark in respect of the same or similar goods without authorization of the proprietor of the registered trademark;
- to sell the goods that infringe the exclusive right to use a registered trademark;
- to counterfeit, or to make without authorization, representations of a registered trademark of another person, or to sell such representations of a registered trademark as were counterfeited, or made without authorization;
- to replace, without authorization, a registered trademark and put the goods bearing the replaced trademark on the market.

Where the case is so serious as to constitute a crime, he shall be prosecuted, according to the law, for his criminal liabilities in addition to his compensation for the damages suffered by the infringed.

The amount of compensation for the infringement of the exclusive right to use a registered trademark shall be the profit that the infringer has earned through the infringement or damages that the infringed has suffered through the infringement, including the rational expenses paid by the infringed for stopping the infringing act. If it is difficult to determine the amount of the infringer's profit from the infringing act or the amount of loss suffered by the infringed, the court may make a ruling on the amount of compensation below RMB ¥500,000.00, taking into account the seriousness of the infringement. The seller shall not bear the liability to make compensation if he does not know that the goods have infringed other people's exclusive right to use a registered trademark or he has evidence to prove that he obtained the goods though the legal channels and indicate the name of supplier.

Before instituting the legal proceedings, the trademark registrant or the interested party may request the people's court to order the infringer to stop the infringing act and adopt measures for property preservation, or request the court to take measure for preserving evidence.

The functionaries of the state engaged in the matters of trademark registration, management and review shall be fair and honest in enforcement of the law and shall be devoted to their official duties and civilized services. The administrative authority for industry and commerce shall establish a complete and sound system of internal supervision for inspecting the functionaries of the state checking up performance of the law and administrative regulations and their observation of disciplines. In case any functionaries of the state has committed such acts as dereliction of duty, misfeasance or favoritism, or accept article of property from the interest party or seeking illegal profit, the offender shall be prosecuted for his criminal liabilities if the case is so serious as to constitute a crime, or shall be punished with a disciplinary sanction if the case is not so serious as to constitute a crime.

Notes

1. Trademark Law in China 《中国商标法》

商标法主要调整因商标注册、使用、管理和保护商标专用权而发生的各种社会关系。《中国商标法》于1982年通过,1993年进行了修订,它是商标所有人享有商标专用权的依据,也是生产者、经营使用商标应遵守的法律,也是国家机关进行商标管理的依据。商标法的基本原则主要有:保护商标专用权和保护消费者利益原则、注册原则、优先权原则、先申请原则、自愿注册原则等。

2. registered trademark 注册商标

我国商标法保护的主要是注册商标。

3. goods trademark, service trademark, collective trademark, or certification trademark 商品商标、服务商标、集体商标或证明商标。

从商标使用者角度可将商标分为制造商标、销售商标、服务商标和集体商标,而从商标的功能、用途角度可将其分为证明商标、联合商标、防御商标等。

4. well-known trademark 驰名商标

驰名商标是指在中国为相关公众广为知晓并享有较高声誉的商标。驰名商标是中国国家工商行政管理局商标局,根据企业的申请,进行官方认定的一种商标类型。对驰名商标的保护不仅仅局限于相同或者类似商品或服务,就不相同或者不相类似的商品申请注册或者使用时,都将不予注册并禁止使用,因此驰名商标被赋予了比较广泛的排他性权利。而且“驰名商标”持有企业的公司名以及网址域名都会受到不同于普通商标的格外法律保护。目前获得中国“驰名商标”认定的商标共有1624个,其中外资品牌占98个。

5. principle of reciprocity 对等原则(互惠原则)

对等原则是指两个国家之间就某一事项的交往相互给予对方彼此同等的待遇。

6. Renewal, assignment and licensing of registered trademark 注册商标的续展、转让和(使用)许可

注册商标的续展,是指注册商标所有人在商标注册有效期届满前后的一定时间内,依法办理一定的手续,延长其注册商标有效期的制度。简言之,就是注册商标有效期限的延续。注册商标的转让,是指商标注册人将其注册商标专用权,依照法定程序转移给他人的法律行为。注册商标转让的实质是商标信誉的转让。注册商标的使用许可,是指注册商标所有人通过订立许可使用合同,许可他人使用其注册商标的法律行为。注册商标使用许可的形式主要有三种:普通许可、排他许可和独占许可。在排他许可中,被许可人虽然取得了注册商标的使用权,但许可人仍然保留使用该注册商标的权利,所以只是排除了其他第三人对注册商标的使用。在独占许可中,只能由被许可人使用该注册商标,即使许可人也不能使用该注册商标,否则即构成违约。

Study Questions

1. What are the differences between a brand and a trademark?
2. What are the principles of trademark registration?
3. What are the major advantages and disadvantages of the license of registered trademark?
4. How do you think of the protection of trademark right?
5. Why is the acquisition of trademark right subject to the registration in some countries?

Case Study

试用英文对以下案例进行分析和讨论：

河南省洛阳市举行洛阳牡丹节，某纺织厂设计了一种款式新颖的短衫，在牡丹节期间投放市场，销路很好，后来许多厂家相继仿制，对该纺织厂的产品销路影响很大。为了维护工厂的利益和把握市场前景，该厂于1994年6月10日向国家商标局提出"洛阳"牌商标的注册申请。在其申请注册期间，某服装厂仍继续生产与纺织厂样式完全相同的短衫，并使用了"洛阳"商标（仅文字相同，图案、字形均不相同）。纺织厂即向工商行政管理部门提出保护其商标专用权的申请。1994年7月2日，商标局驳回纺织厂的商标注册申请。纺织厂收到驳回通知后，很不服气，欲申请复议。同时，服装厂看到纺织厂没有取得商标注册，更无顾忌，继续进行生产。

现问：

（1）商标局驳回纺织厂的商标注册申请是否正确，理由是什么？

（2）纺织厂收到驳回申请通知后，可否申请复议？

（3）纺织厂向工商行政管理机关提出的保护权益请求是否应予受理？理由是什么？

（4）工商行政管理机关对纺织厂的商标使用行为是否有权管理？应如何管理和规范？

（5）服装厂在纺织厂的商标注册申请被驳回后是否可以继续生产带有该种商标的产品？为什么？

（选自张海峡的商标法案例：http://www.edu1488.com/article/2010-4/42394422.shtml）

Sources of Information and Further Readings

1. Trademark Law of the People's Republic of China of 1982 (as revised in 1993, 2001)
2. http://en.wikipedia.org/wiki/Trademark_Law_of_the_People's_Republic_of_China
3. http://www.china.org.cn/government/laws/2007-04/21/content_1207502.htm
4. http://www.saic.gov.cn/english/LawsRegulations/Regulations/200602/t20060227_55262.html
5. http://www.kd325.com/ShowArticle.shtml?ID=201051016174886123.htm
6. http://en.wikipedia.org/wiki/Trademark

Chapter 20

Copyright Law in China[1]

Key Concepts

works copyright copyright licensing contract
copyright transfer contract neighboring rights

Learning Objectives

1. Understand the concept of "works".
2. Understand the features of copyright law in China.
3. Understand limitations on copyright rights.
4. Be familiar with neighboring rights.

Introduction

Works of Chinese citizens, legal entities or other bodies, whether published or not, shall enjoy copyright. The copyright in any work of a foreigner or stateless person enjoying under an agreement concluded between China and the country to which the author belongs or in which the author has his habitual residence, or under an international treaty to which both countries are parties, shall be protected. Works of foreigners or stateless persons first published in the territory of the People's Republic of China shall enjoy copyright. Any work of a foreigner or stateless person first published in a member country of a international treaty to which China is a party, or simultaneously published in a member country of the treaty and in a non-member country, shall be protected, even if the country to which the author belongs or in which the author has his habitual residence has not concluded any copyright agreement with China, nor is it a member country of any international copyright treaty to which China is a party.

The term "works"[2] includes works of literature, art, natural science, social science, engineering technology and the like which are expressed in the following forms:

- written works;
- oral works;
- musical, dramatic, *quyi*, choreographic and acrobatic works[3];
- works of fine art and architecture;
- photographic works;
- cinematographic works to which are assimilated works expressed by a process analogous to cinematography;
- graphic works such as drawings of engineering designs and product designs, maps and sketches, and model works;
- computer software;
- other works as provided for in laws and administrative regulations.

Works of which the publication or dissemination is prohibited by law shall not be protected. Copyright owners, in exercising their copyright, shall not violate the Constitution or laws, nor shall they prejudice the public interests.

This Law shall not be applicable to:

- laws; regulations; resolutions, decisions and orders of State organs; other documents of a legislative, administrative or judicial nature; and their official translations;
- news on current affairs;
- calendars, numerical tables and forms of general use, and formulas.

Copyright owners or owners of rights related to copyright may authorize copyright collective administration organizations[4] to exercise their copyright or rights related to copyright. With the authorization of a right owner, a copyright collective administration organization may exercise the copyright in its own name for the right owner and other obligees related to copyright and participate as a party in legal or arbitration proceedings concerning copyright or rights related to copyright.

Copyright collective administration organizations shall be of non-profit nature, and the way of their establishment, their rights and obligations, the collection and the distribution of copyright licensing remuneration, and the supervision and the administration of such organizations shall established separately by the State Council.

Copyright Owners and Their Rights

The term "copyright owners" shall include authors, and other citizens, legal entities and other bodies enjoying copyright in accordance with the Law.

The term "copyright" shall include the following personality rights and property rights:

- the right of publication, that is, the right to decide whether to make the work available to the public;
- the right of authorship, that is, the right to claim authorship in respect of, and to have the author's name mentioned in connection with, the work;
- the right of alteration, that is, the right to alter or authorize others to alter the work;
- the right of integrity, that is, the right to protect the work against distortion and mutilation;
- the right of reproduction, that is, the right to produce one or more copies of the work by printing, photocopying, lithographing, making a sound recording or video recording, duplicating a recording, or duplicating a photographic work, or by other means;
- the right of distribution, that is, the right to provide the original copy or reproductions of the work to the public by selling or donating;
- the right of rental, that is, the right to authorize others to use temporarily and onerously the original copy or reproductions of the cinematographic work to which are assimilated works expressed by a process analogous to cinematography, or of the computer software, except where the software itself is not the essential object of the rental;
- the right of exhibition, that is the right to publicly display the original copy or reproductions of the work of fine art or of the photographic work;
- the right of performance, that is, the right to publicly perform the work, and to publicly communicate the performance of the work by any means or process;
- the right of presentation, that is, the right to publicly present the work of art, the photographic work, the cinematographic work to which are assimilated works expressed by a process analogous to cinematography, or other works, by projector, slide projector or any other analogous instrument;
- the right of broadcasting, that is, the right to broadcast the work or communicate it to the public by any wireless means, to communicate the broadcast of the work to the public by wire or by rebroadcasting, and to publicly communicate the broadcast of the work by

loudspeaker or any other analogous instrument transmitting signs, sounds or images;

- the right of communication through information network, that is, the right to make the work available to the public in such a way that members of the public may access the work from a place and at a time individually chosen by them;
- the right of cinematography, that is, the right to fix an adaptation of the work in a medium by cinematography or a process analogous to cinematography;
- the right of adaptation, that is, the right to change the work in an original manner for creating a new work;
- the right of translation, that is, the right to converse the language in which the work is written into another language;
- the right of compilation, that is, the right to compile the preexisting works or passages therefrom by selection or arrangement for creating a new work;
- other rights which shall be enjoyed by copyright owners.

Copyright owners may authorize others' exercising the rights provided for in (5) to (17) of the preceding paragraph and receive remuneration in accordance with the terms of the contracts or the relevant provisions in the Law. Copyright owners may transfer, wholly or in part, the rights provided for in (5) to (17), and receive transfer fees in accordance with the terms of the contracts or the relevant provisions in the Law.

Ownership of Copyright

The copyright in a work shall belong to its author. The author of a work is the citizen who has created the work. Where a work is created according to the intention, and under the supervision and the responsibility, of a legal entity or other body, such legal entity or other body shall be deemed to be the author of the work. The citizen, legal entity or other body whose name is mentioned in connection with a work shall, in the absence of proof to the contrary, be deemed to be the author of the work.

The copyright in a cinematographic work and the works expressed by a process analogous to cinematography shall be enjoyed by the producer of the work, while its scriptwriter, director, cameraman, lyricist, composer and other authors shall enjoy the right of authorship therein, and shall be entitled to receive remuneration in accordance with the terms of the contracts concluded between them and the producer.

A work created by a citizen in the fulfillment of tasks assigned to him by a legal entity or other body is a work created in the course of employment. The copyright in such work shall be enjoyed by the author; however, the legal entity or other body shall have a priority right to exploit the work within the scope of its professional activities. Within the two years after the completion of the work, the author shall not, without the consent of the legal entity or other body, authorize a third party to exploit the work in the same way as the legal entity or other body does.

In case of drawings of engineering designs and product designs, maps, computer software and other works created in the course of employment mainly with the material and technical resources of the legal entity or other body and under its responsibility, the author of a work created in the course of employment shall enjoy the right of authorship, while the legal entity or other body shall enjoy the other rights included in the copyright and may reward the author.

The ownership of the copyright in a commissioned work[5] shall be agreed upon in a contract between the commissioning and the commissioned parties. In the absence of a contract or of an explicit agreement in the contract, the copyright in such a work shall belong to the commissioned party.

The transfer of ownership of the original copy of a work of fine art or other works shall not be deemed to include the transfer of the copyright in such work; however, the right to exhibit the original copy of the work of fine art shall be enjoyed by the owner of the original copy.

Duration of Protection

The rights of authorship, alteration and integrity of an author shall be unlimited in time. In respect of a work of a citizen, the term of protection of the right of publication and the rights as above provided for in (5) to (17) shall be the lifetime of the author and fifty years after his death, expiring on December 31 of the fiftieth year after his death. In the case of a work of joint authorship[6], such term shall expire on December 31 of the fiftieth year after the death of the last surviving author.

In respect of a work of a legal entity or other body or a work created in the course of employment in which a legal entity or other body enjoys the copyright (except the right of authorship), the term of protection of such rights shall be fifty years, expiring on December 31 of the fiftieth year after the first publication of such work; however, such work shall be no longer protected under this Law if it fails to be published within fifty years after the completion of its creation.

In respect of a cinematographic work to which are assimilated works expressed by a process analogous to cinematography or a photographic work, the term of protection of the right of publication and other relevant rights as provided for in (5) to (17), shall be fifty years, expiring on December 31 of the fiftieth year after the first publication of such work; however, such work shall be no longer protected under this Law if it fails to be published within fifty years after the completion of its creation.

Limitations on Rights

In the following cases, a work may be used without permission from, and without payment of remuneration to, the copyright owner, provided that the name of the author and the title of the work are mentioned, and the other rights enjoyed by the copyright owner in accordance with this Law are not prejudiced:

- use of a published work for the purposes of the user's own personal study, research or self-entertainment;
- appropriate quotation from a published work in one's own work for the purposes of introduction to, or comments on, a work, or of demonstration of a point;
- unavoidable inclusion or quotation of a published work in a newspaper, periodical, or broadcast, etc for the purpose of reporting current events;
- reproduction or broadcasting by a newspaper or periodical publisher, radio station or television station, etc of an article published by another newspaper or periodical publisher, radio station or television station, etc on current political, economic or religious topics, except where the author has declared that reproduction or broadcasting is not permitted;
- publication or broadcasting by a newspaper or periodical publisher, radio station or television station, etc of a speech delivered at a public gathering, except where the author has declared that publication or broadcasting is not permitted;
- translation, or reproduction in a small quantity of copies, of a published work by teachers or scientific researchers for use in classroom teaching or scientific research, provided that the translation or the reproductions are not published;
- use of a published work by a State organ to a justifiable extent for the purpose of fulfilling its official duties;
- reproduction of a work in its collections by a library, archive, memorial hall, museum, art gallery or similar institution, for the purposes of the display, or preservation of a copy, of

the work;

- free-of-charge live performance of a published work, where fees are not charged on the public, and nor are payments made to the performers;
- copying, drawing, photographing or video recording of an artistic work located or on display in an outdoor public place;
- translation of a published work of a Chinese citizen, legal entity or other body from Han language into minority nationality languages for publication in the country;
- transliteration of a published work into Braille and publication of the work so transliterated.

Copyright Licensing and Transfer Contracts[7]

Anyone who exploits a work created by another shall conclude a copyright licensing contract with the copyright owner, except where no permission need be obtained under the Law.

A copyright licensing contract shall include the following basic contents:

- the category of the right to exploit the work covered by the license;
- the exclusive or non-exclusive nature of the right to exploit the work covered by the license;
- the territory and the term covered by the license;
- the amount of the remuneration and the method of its payment;
- the liabilities in the case of breach of the contract;
- other matters that the parties consider as necessary.

Anyone who transfers any of the rights provided for in (5) to (17) should conclude a written contract. A copyright transfer contract shall include the following basic contents:

- the title of the work;
- the category of the right transferred and the territory covered by the transfer;
- the amount of the transfer fee;
- the date and the method of paying the transfer fee;
- the liabilities in the case of breach of the contract;
- other matters that the parties consider as necessary.

The remuneration for the exploitation of works may be paid in accordance with the tariffs agreed between the parties or the tariffs established by the copyright administration department under the State Council in collaboration with other departments concerned. In the absence of an explicit agreement in the contract, the remuneration shall be paid in accordance with the tariffs established by the copyright administration department under the State Council in collaboration with other departments concerned.

Neighboring Rights[8]

Neighboring rights refer to the rights enjoyed by the concerned parties during the communications of the works to the public. Neighboring rights may involve the rights of performers, producers of phonograms and broadcasting organizations.

Publication of Books, Newspapers and Periodicals

A book publisher who publishes a book shall conclude a publishing contract with, and pay remuneration to, the copyright owner. The book publisher shall notify, and pay remuneration to, the copyright owner when the work is to be reprinted or republished. If the publisher refuses to reprint or republish the work when stocks of the book are exhausted, the copyright owner shall have the right to terminate the contract.

The publisher shall enjoy the right to authorize or prohibit others to exploit the typographical design of the book or the periodical which he has published. The term of protection of the right shall be ten years, expiring on December 31 of the tenth year after the first publication of the book or the periodical in which the typographical designs is used.

Performance

A performer (an individual performer or a performing group) who exploits, for a performance, a work created by another shall obtain permission from and pay remuneration to the copyright owner. Where a performance takes place under a person's organization, it is the person organizing the performance that shall obtain from, and pay remuneration to, the copyright owner. Anyone who exploits, for a performance, a work created by adaptation, translation, annotation or arrangement of a preexisting work shall obtain permission both from and pay remuneration both to the owner of the copyright in the work created by adaptation, translation, annotation or arrangement and the owner of the copyright in the preexisting work.

A performer shall, in respect of his performance, enjoy the right:

- to claim performership;
- to protect the image inherent in his performance from distortion;

- to authorize others' broadcasting or communicating to the public of his live performance, and receive remuneration therefor;
- to authorize others' making sound recordings and video recordings of his performance, and receive remuneration therefor;
- to authorize others' reproduction and distribution of the sound recordings and video recordings of his performance, and receive remuneration therefor;
- to authorize others' making available to the public of his performance through information network, and receive remuneration therefor.

Sound Recording and Video Recording

A producer of sound recordings or video recordings who exploits, for making a sound recording or video recording, a work created by another shall obtain permission from and pay remuneration to the copyright owner.

A producer of sound recordings or video recordings who exploits a work created by adaptation, translation, annotation or arrangement of a preexisting work shall obtain permission both from and pay remuneration both to the owner of the copyright in the work created by adaptation, translation, annotation or arrangement and the owner of the copyright in the preexisting work. When making a sound recording or video recording of a performance, the producer shall conclude a contract with and pay remuneration to the performer.

Broadcasting by a Radio Station or Television Station

A radio station or television station which broadcasts an unpublished work created by another shall obtain permission from, and pay remuneration to, the copyright owner.

A radio station or television station which broadcasts a published work created by another need not obtain permission from, but shall pay remuneration to, the copyright owner.

A radio station or television station shall enjoy the right to prohibit the following acts performed without its permission:

- to rebroadcast its broadcasts;
- to make a sound recording or video recording of its broadcasts and to reproduce the recording.

The term of protection of the right as provided for in the preceding paragraph shall be fifty years, expiring on December 31 of the fiftieth year after the first broadcasting of the broadcast.

A television station which broadcasts a cinematographic works to which are assimilated works expressed by a process analogous to cinematography or a video recording produced by another shall obtain permission from, and pay remuneration to, the producer; in case of a video recording, the television station shall also obtain permission from, and pay remuneration to, the copyright owner.

Legal Liabilities and Enforcement Measures

Anyone who commits any of the following acts of infringement shall bear civil liabilities such as ceasing the infringing act, eliminating the effects of the act, making an apology, or/and paying compensation for damages, depending on the circumstances:

- to publish a work without the consent of the copyright owner;
- to publish a work of joint authorship as a work created solely by oneself, without the consent of the other co-author;
- to have one's name mentioned in connection with a work created by another, in order to seek personal fame and gain, where one has not taken part in the creation of the work;
- to distort or to mutilate a work created by another; to plagiarize a work created by another;
- to exploit a work by exhibition, distribution, cinematography or a process analogous to cinematography, adaptation, translation, annotation or by other means, without the consent of the copyright owner, except where otherwise provided in this Law;
- to exploit a work created by another without paying remuneration where remuneration shall be paid under this Law;
- to rent a cinematographic work to which are assimilated works expressed by a process analogous to cinematography, computer software, sound recording or video recording, without the consent of the copyright owner or the owner of the right related to copyright, except where otherwise provided in this Law;
- to exploit the typographical design of a published book or periodical, without the consent of the publisher;
- to broadcast, communicate to the public, or to record a live performance, without the consent of the performer;
- to commit other acts infringing copyright and rights related to copyright.

Anyone who commits any of the following acts of infringement shall bear a civil liability for such remedies as ceasing the infringing act, eliminating the effects of the act, making an apology, or/and paying compensation for damages, depending on the circumstances; where any of the acts also prejudices the public interests, the copyright administration department may order the infringing act to be ceased, confiscate unlawful income, confiscate or destroy the infringing copies, and impose a fine; where the circumstance is serious, the copyright administration department may also confiscate the material, tools and instrument mainly used to produce infringing copies; and where any of the acts constitutes a crime, the person who commits the act shall be investigated criminal liabilities:

- to reproduce, distribute, perform, present, broadcast, compile or make available to the public through information network a work, without the consent of the copyright owner, except where otherwise provided in this Law;
- to publish a book in which the exclusive right of publication is enjoyed by another;
- to reproduce or distribute a sound recording or video recording of a performance, or to make a performance available to the public through information network, without the consent of the performer, except where otherwise provided in this Law;
- to reproduce, distribute or make available to the public through information network a sound recording or video recording, without the consent of the producer, except where otherwise provided in this Law;
- to rebroadcast a broadcast or to reproduce a sound recording or video recording of a broadcast, without the consent of the radio station or television station, except where otherwise provided in this Law;
- to knowingly circumvent or sabotage technological measures used by a copyright owner or an owner of right related to copyright for protecting the copyright in his work or the right related to copyright in his sound recording or video recording, without his consent, except where otherwise provided in laws or administrative regulations;
- to knowingly remove or alter any electronic rights management information attached to a copy of a work, sound recording or video recording, etc, without the consent of the copyright owner or the owner of a right related to copyright, except where otherwise provided in this Law;
- to produce or sell a work of which the authorship is counterfeited.

Where the actual loss of the right owner or the unlawful income of the infringer can not be determined, the people's court shall decide a compensation not more than 500,000 *yuan* in RMB, depending on the infringement circumstances. A copyright owner or an owner of right related to copyright who can present evidence to prove that another is committing, or is about to commit, an infringement which, if not being prevented promptly, is likely to cause irreparable harm to him, may, before instituting proceedings, apply to a people's court for an order of desisting the relevant act and for measures of property preservation. In order to prevent infringement, a copyright owner or an owner of right related to copyright may, before instituting proceedings, apply to a people's court for evidence preservation where the evidence is likely to be missing, or to be difficult to obtain later. The people's court, having accepted the application, shall make a ruling within forty-eight hours. Where the people's court rules to adopt a preservation measure, it shall be enforced immediately. The people's court may order the applicant to provide assurance, and shall reject the application where the applicant fails to do so. The people's court shall release the preservation measure in the case where the applicant fails to institute proceedings within fifteen days after the people's court adopted the said measure.

Notes

1. Copyright Law in China 《中国著作权法》

著作权是文学、艺术及科学作品的创作者对作品所享有的权利。就著作权和版权而言，欧洲大陆法系国家强调著作权(author's right)，即著作者的权利，尤其是作者的精神权利；而英美法系国家则强调版权(copyright)，即作品的出版、利用及作品的经济权利。我国在立法中则已规定，著作权法与版权法具有同样意义。通过对本单元的学习，应基本了解作品的概念、特征和应受法律保护的几类作品、著作权的内容(经济权利和精神权利)、邻接权(neighboring rights)(如表演权、录制权、广播组织权及出版者权)、著作权的归属与转移等相关法律知识。

2. works 作品

作品是指文学、艺术和科学领域内具有独创性并能以某种有形形式复制的智力创作成果。我国著作权法保护八类作品。

3. musical, dramatic, *quyi*, choreographic and acrobatic works 音乐、戏剧、曲艺、舞蹈和杂技作品

音乐作品是指能够演唱或演奏的带词或不带词的乐曲，而无论其是否以乐谱形式写出；戏剧作品指供舞台演出的剧本，如话剧、歌剧、地方戏剧的剧目；曲艺作品是指以说唱形式表演的作品，如相声、快板、评书等的底本；舞蹈作品是指通过连续的动作、姿势、表情表现的艺术编排设计，它可以用文字或其他方式来记载；杂技作品是指杂技、魔术、马戏等通过形体动作和技巧表现的作品。

4. copyright collective administration organizations 版权集体管理组织

版权集体管理组织实际上是著作权人和作品使用人各自组织的管理团体，是一种民间的著作权收费组织。目前,通过著作权集体管理组织行使著作权主要是音乐作品,例如,我国现有中国音乐著作权协会。

5. commissioned work 委托作品

委托作品,是指作者接受他人委托而创作的作品。受托人应当按照约定将委托作品提供给委托人使用,受托人行使著作权应当遵循诚实信用原则,不得妨碍委托人的正当使用。

6. work of joint authorship 合作作品

合作作品,是指两个以上的自然人,或者自然人与法人、其他组织,或者两个以上的法人、其他组织共同创作的作品。

7. copyright licensing and transfer contracts 版权(著作权)许可、转让合同

许可合同主要包括许可使用的权利种类、许可使用的权利是专有使用权或者非专有使用权、许可使用的地域范围、期间、付酬标准和办法、违约责任等内容;而转让合同主要包括作品的名称、转让的权利种类、地域范围、转让价金、交付转让价金的日期和方式、违约责任等内容。

8. neighboring rights 邻接权

邻接权是指作品的传播者在传播过程中享有的权利,通常包括表演权、录制权、广播组织权,我国又加上出版者权。

Study Questions

1. What is the liabilities infringement of copyright?
2. What is the neighboring right?
3. Why shall copyright be subject to certain restrictions?
4. What are the differences between copyright licensing contract and copyright transfer contract?
5. List the works under the protection of copyright law of China.

Case Study

试用英文对以下案例进行分析和讨论:

甲、乙两人共同创作一部长篇小说。初稿完工后,两人都不满意,打算抽时间再作修改。乙几次与甲商量尽早修改,甲一直抽不出时间。过了一段时间,甲再未问过此事。于是,乙请丙帮助共同修改完稿,期间丁曾帮助收集过一些资料。稿件在未经重大修改基础上进行了润色和文字性修改,后予以发表,署名乙、丙,出书后受到社会各界的好评。某剧作家A根据某制片人王某的要求将其改编成电影剧本,但未征得小说作者的同意。王某拿到剧本后聘请著名导演张某将其拍成电影,放映后引起轰动,其中片头曲和主题歌分别由李某和吴某创作。陈某和周某随即将作品译成朝鲜文,在国内出版,但事后也未征得原著作者的同意。其录像制作公司看到电影这样受欢迎，又将其拍成录像带准备向海外发行。在此期间，因这部小说获得如此大的成功，某报社发表了一篇评论员文章，称其为“新世纪”开山之作，这篇文章被许多家报刊和杂志转载。与此同时，某音像出版社看到电影主题歌这样流行，就将其收录进一盘言情歌曲磁带中出版发行，并将其作为主题歌曲。小说原著也被多家图书馆收藏，某大学中文系从该校图书馆中复制了15本作为教学之用。

现问：

（1）若甲认为其也参加了创作，而且小说也确实和初稿绝大部分相同，因此也要求享有著作权，其要求是否合法？

（2）若丁也要求享有著作权，丁的要求是否合法？

（3）剧作家A是否侵权？

（4）假设王某（制片人）征求了原著作者同意后将其摄制成影片，请问王某享有著作权吗？若有，是什么样的权利？

（5）导演张某认为其也应享有著作权，因此对电影发行后获得的利润其也有份，张某的看法是否正确？

（6）陈某和吴某各享有哪一部分作品的著作权？

（7）陈某和周某是否侵犯了原著作者的著作权？

（8）假设录像制作公司根据原著拍成录像，虽征求了原著者的同意，但称该作品已经发表，可以不支付报酬，对吗？

（9）报刊和杂志转载某报的评论员文章，是否须事先征得该报同意并支付报酬？

（10）音像出版社发行包含影片片头曲的磁带是否侵犯他人著作权？

（11）某大学图书馆复制原著是否侵权？为什么？

（选自司法考试案例分析题：http://www.yuloo.com/news/1011/515242.shtml）

Sources of Information and Further Readings

1. Copyright Law of the People's Republic of China of 1990
2. http://www.lawinfochina.com/display.aspx? lib=law&id=2108
3. http://en.wikipedia.org/wiki/Intellectual_property_in_the_People's_Republic_of_China
4. http://www.ccpit-patent.com.cn/references/Copyright_Law_China.htm
5. http://www.iolaw.org.cn/showArticle.asp? id=60
6. http://en.wikipedia.org/wiki/Copyright

Chapter 21

International Commercial Arbitration[1]

Key Concepts

arbitration	alternative dispute resolution	arbitral awards
mediation	New York Convention 1958	arbitration agreement

Learning Objectives

1. Understand the features and advantages of arbitration.
2. Understand the forms of alternative dispute resolution and their differences.
3. Be familiar with arbitration agreement (clauses).
4. Understand international commercial arbitration.

Arbitration

Arbitration, a form of alternative dispute resolution (ADR)[2], is a legal technique for the resolution of disputes outside the courts, where the parties to a dispute refer it to one or more persons (the "arbitrators", "arbiters" or "arbitral tribunal"[3]), by whose decision (the "award") they agree to be bound. It is a settlement technique in which a third party reviews the case and imposes a decision that is legally binding for both sides. Other forms of ADR include mediation (a form of settlement negotiation facilitated by a neutral third party) and non-binding resolution by experts. Arbitration is often used for the resolution of commercial disputes, particularly in the context of international commercial transactions.

Arbitration is a proceeding in which a dispute is resolved by an impartial adjudicator whose decision the parties to the dispute have agreed, or legislation has decreed, will be final and binding. Arbitration is not the same as:

- judicial proceedings, although in some jurisdictions, court proceedings are sometimes referred as arbitrations;
- alternative dispute resolution (or ADR);
- expert determination;
- mediation.

Advantages of Arbitration

Parties often seek to resolve their disputes through arbitration because of a number of perceived potential advantages over judicial proceedings:

- when the subject matter of the dispute is highly technical, arbitrators with an appropriate degree of expertise can be appointed (as one cannot "choose the judge" in litigation);
- arbitration is often faster than litigation in court;
- arbitration can be cheaper and more flexible for businesses;
- arbitral proceedings and an arbitral award are generally non-public, and can be made confidential;
- in arbitral proceedings the language of arbitration may be chosen, whereas in judicial proceedings the official language of the country of the competent court will be automatically applied;
- because of the provisions of the New York Convention 1958[4], arbitration awards are generally easier to enforce in other nations than court judgments;
- in most legal systems there are very limited avenues for appeal of an arbitral award, which is sometimes an advantage because it limits the duration of the dispute and any associated liability.

Arbitration Agreement[5]

In theory, arbitration is a consensual process; a party cannot be forced to arbitrate a dispute unless he agrees to do so. In practice, however, many fine-print arbitration agreements are inserted in situations in which consumers and employees have no bargaining power. Moreover, arbitration clauses are frequently placed within sealed users' manuals within products, within lengthy click-through agreements on websites, and in other contexts in which meaningful consent is not realistic. Such agreements are generally divided into two types:

- agreements which provide that, if a dispute should arise, it will be resolved by arbitration. These will generally be normal contracts, but they contain an arbitration clause;
- agreements which are signed after a dispute has arisen, agreeing that the dispute should be resolved by arbitration (sometimes called a "submission agreement").

Agreements to refer disputes to arbitration generally have a special status in the eyes of the law. For example, in disputes on a contract, a common defence is to plead the contract is void and thus any claim based upon it fails. It follows that if a party successfully claims that a contract is void, then each clause contained within the contract, including the arbitration clause, would be void. However, in most countries, the courts have accepted that:

- a contract can only be declared void by a court or other tribunal; and
- if the contract (valid or otherwise) contains an arbitration clause, then the proper forum to determine whether the contract is void or not, is the arbitration tribunal.

Arguably, either position is potentially unfair; if a person is made to sign a contract under duress, and the contract contains an arbitration clause highly favourable to the other party, the dispute may still referred to that arbitration tribunal. Conversely a court may be persuaded that the arbitration agreement itself is void having been signed under duress. However, most courts will be reluctant to interfere with the general rule which does allow for commercial expediency; any other solution (where one first had to go to court to decide whether one had to go to arbitration) would be self defeating.

Sources of Law

States regulate arbitration through a variety of laws. The main body of law applicable to arbitration is normally contained either in the national Private International Law Act (as is the case in Switzerland) or in a separate law on arbitration (as is the case in England). In addition to this, a number of national procedural laws may also contain provisions relating to arbitration.

By far the most important international instrument on arbitration law is the 1958 New York Convention on Recognition and Enforcement of Foreign Arbitral Awards. Some other relevant international instruments are:

- The Geneva Protocol of 1923

- The Geneva Convention of 1927
- The European Convention of 1961
- The Washington Convention of 1965 (governing settlement of international investment disputes)
- The UNCITRAL Model Law (providing a model for a national law of arbitration)
- The UNCITRAL Arbitration Rules[6] (providing a set of rules for an ad hoc arbitration)

Arbitral Tribunal

The term *arbitral tribunal* is used to denote the arbitrator or arbitrators sitting to determine the dispute. The composition of the arbitral tribunal can vary enormously, with either a sole arbitrator sitting, two or more arbitrators, with or without a chairman or umpire, and various other combinations.

In most jurisdictions, an arbitrator enjoys immunity from liability for anything done or omitted whilst acting as arbitrator unless the arbitrator acts in bad faith.

Arbitrations are usually divided into two types: *ad hoc* arbitrations and administered arbitrations.

In *ad hoc* arbitrations, the arbitral tribunals are appointed by the parties or by an appointing authority chosen by the parties. After the tribunal has been formed, the appointing authority will normally have no other role and the arbitation will be managed by the tribunal.

In administered arbitration, the arbitration will be administered by a professional arbitration institution providing arbitration services, such as the LCIA in London, or the ICC in Paris, or the American Arbitration Association in the United States. Normally the arbitration institution also will be the appointing authority.

Arbitration institutions tend to have their own rules and procedures, and may be more formal. They also tend to be more expensive, and, for procedural reasons, slower.

Duties of the Tribunal

The duties of a tribunal will be determined by a combination of the provisions of the arbitration agreement and by the procedural laws which apply in the seat of the arbitration. The extent to which the laws of the seat of the arbitration permit "party autonomy" (the ability of the parties to set out their own procedures and regulations) determines the interplay between the two.

However, in almost all countries the tribunal owes several non-derogable duties. These will normally be:

- to act fairly and impartially between the parties, and to allow each party a reasonable opportunity to put their case and to deal with the case of their opponent (sometimes shortened to: complying with the rules of "natural justice"); and
- to adopt procedures suitable to the circumstances of the particular case, so as to provide a fair means for resolution of the dispute.

Arbitral Awards[7]

Although arbitration awards are characteristically an award of damages against a party, in many jurisdictions tribunals have a range of remedies that can form a part of the award. These may include:

1. payment of a sum of money (conventional damages)
2. the making of a "declaration" as to any matter to be determined in the proceedings
3. In some jurisdictions, the tribunal may have the same power as a court to:

(1) order a party to do or refrain from doing something ("injunctive relief");

(2) to order specific performance of a contract;

(3) to order the rectification, setting aside or cancellation of a deed or other document.

4. In other jurisdictions, however, unless the parties have expressly granted the arbitrators the right to decide such matters, the tribunal's powers may be limited to deciding whether a party is entitled to damages. It may not have the legal authority to order injunctive relief, issue a declaration, or rectify a contract, such powers being reserved to the exclusive jurisdiction of the courts.

Enforcement of Arbitration Awards

One of the reasons that arbitration is so popular in international trade as a means of dispute resolution, is that it is often easier to enforce an arbitration award in a foreign country than it is to enforce a judgment of the court.

Under the New York Convention 1958, an award issued a contracting state can generally be freely enforced in any other contracting state, only subject to certain, limited defenses.

Only foreign arbitration awards can be subject to recognition and enforcement pursuant to the New York Convention. An arbitral decision is foreign where the award was made in a state other than the state of recognition or where foreign procedural law was used.

Virtually every significant commercial country in the world is a party to the Convention, but relatively few countries have a comprehensive network for cross-border enforcement of judgments of the court.

The other characteristic of cross-border enforcement of arbitration awards that makes them appealing to commercial parties is that they are not limited to awards of damages. Whereas in most countries only monetary judgments are enforceable in the cross-border context, no such restrictions are imposed on arbitration awards and so it is theoretically possible (although unusual in practice) to obtain an injunction or an order for specific performance in an arbitration proceeding which could then be enforced in another New York Convention contracting state.

The New York Convention is not actually the only treaty dealing with cross-border enforcement of arbitration awards. The earlier Geneva Convention on the Execution of Foreign Arbitral Awards 1927 remains in force, but the success of the New York Convention means that the Geneva Convention is rarely utilized in practice.

Article V of the New York Convention provides an exhaustive list of grounds on which enforcement can be challenged. These are generally narrowly construed by the courts in arbitration centres to uphold the pro-enforcement bias of the Convention.

Costs

In many legal systems—both common law and civil law—it is normal practice for the courts to award legal costs against a losing party, with the winner becoming entitled to recover an approximation of what it spent in pursuing its claim (or in defense of a claim). The United States is a notable exception to this rule, as except for certain extreme cases, a prevailing party in a US legal proceeding does not become entitled to recoup its legal fees from the losing party.

Like the courts, arbitral tribunals generally have the same power to award costs in relation to the determination of the dispute. In international arbitration as well as domestic arbitrations governed by the laws of countries in which courts may award costs against a losing party, the arbitral tribunal will also determine the portion of the arbitrators' fees that the losing party is required to bear.

International Arbitration

International arbitration is a leading method for resolving disputes arising from international commercial agreements and other international relationships. As with arbitration generally, international arbitration is a creature of contract, i. e., the parties' decision to submit disputes to binding resolution by one or more arbitrators selected by or on behalf of the parties and applying adjudicatory procedures, usually by including a provision for the arbitration of future disputes in their contract. The practice of international arbitration has developed so as to allow parties from different legal and cultural backgrounds to resolve their disputes, generally without the formalities of their respective legal systems.

International Commercial Arbitration

The resolution of disputes under international commercial contracts is widely conducted under the auspices of several major international institutions and rule making bodies. The most significant are the International Chamber of Commerce (ICC), the International Centre for Dispute Resolution (ICDR), the international branch of the American Arbitration Association), the London Court of International Arbitration (LCIA), the Hong Kong International Arbitration Centre, and the Singapore International Arbitration Centre (SIAC). Specialist ADR bodies also exist, such as the World Intellectual Property Organisation (WIPO), which has an arbitration and mediation center and a panel of international neutrals specialising in intellectual property and technology related disputes. See http://www.wipo.int/amc/en/.

A number of arbitral institutions have adopted the UNCITRAL Rules for use in international cases.

The most salient feature of the rules of the ICC is its use of the "terms of reference". The "terms of reference" is a summary of the claims and issues in dispute and the particulars of the procedure, and it is prepared by the tribunal and signed by the parties near the beginning of the proceedings.

In a more recent development, the Swiss Chambers of Commerce of Industry of Basel, Berne, Geneva, Lausanne, Lugano, Neuch tel and Zurich have adopted a new set of Swiss Rules of Commercial Mediation that are designed to integrate fully with the Swiss Rules of International Arbitration that were previously adopted by these chambers to harmonize international arbitration and mediation proceedings across Switzerland. For a recent paper on these two sets of ADR rules and how they may be combined, see http://www.altenburger.ch/uploads/tx_altenburger/jl_2008_Swiss_Rules_Commercial_Mediation.pdf.

Drafting International Arbitration Clauses

Most arbitral institutions have promulgated model clauses for parties to use to authorize the institution to oversee the arbitration. A number of specialized publications regarding the drafting of international arbitration clauses are available.

A number of essential elements should be included in almost all international arbitration agreements. These include the agreement to arbitrate, a definition of the scope of disputes subject to arbitration, means for selecting the arbitrator(s), a choice of the arbitral seat and the adoption of institutional or ad hoc arbitration rules. A number of other provisions can also be included in international arbitration clauses, including the language for the conduct of the arbitration, choice of applicable law, arbitrator qualifications, interim relief, costs, procedural matters and the like.

In order to bridge the gap when parties to an international agreement have difficulty in agreeing upon an arbitral institution, some international arbitration specialists recommend using an arbitration clause that authorizes two arbitral institutions in the same city. Those clauses generally empower the party commencing the arbitration to select the arbitral institution.

Writing in the Business Law Today of the American Bar Association, Eric Sherby (Israel) suggested a mnemonic device "BLINC LLC" designed to enable the draftsman to remember a checklist for quickly drafting an international arbitration clause: Broad, Law, Institutional, Number, Costs, Location Language, and Carve-out.

International Arbitration Institute (IAI)

The International Arbitration Institute, headed by Emmanuel Gaillard, was created in 2001 under the auspices of the Comit Fran ais de l'Arbitrage (CFA) to promote exchanges and transparency in the international commercial arbitration community.

The Association for International Arbitration (AIA)

The Association for International Arbitration is a non-profit organization, founded in Paris in 2001 by Johan Billiet. The Association for International Arbitration has an increasing number of members among arbitrators and mediators of international backgrounds.

The Association was established with the aim of facilitating arbitration, mediation and general forms of dispute resolution internationally. Today, the AIA has developed into an organization dealing in the private international law field to meet the needs of the fast-growing evolution of dispute resolution within the international community. AIA provides information, training and educational activities to expand the promotion of arbitration and ADR globally by means of securing partnerships with various organizations and parties to get involved in the life of the association. The association constantly works to develop partnerships in the international realm and to provide the international community of arbitrators and ADR professionals with continuous exposure to the latest international developments, activities and opportunities in the field. AIA continually encourages the participation and contribution of its members in the pursuit of the association's goals.

International Investment Arbitration

The last few decades have seen the promulgation of numerous Bilateral Investment Treaties (BITs), as well as Multilateral Investment Treaties, which are designed to encourage investment in signatory countries by offering protections to investors from other signatory states. One of the significant features of some BITs is that they provide investors with the ability to resolve disputes with the host states before the International Centre for the Settlement of Investment Disputes (ICSID).

Notes

1. International Commercial Arbitration 国际商事仲裁

本章主要介绍仲裁概念和特点、仲裁协议、仲裁准据法、仲裁机构、仲裁程序、仲裁裁决、国际仲裁裁决的承认与执行及国际商事仲裁等内容。国际商事仲裁主要运用于国际货物买卖合同中的争议、国际货物运输中的争议、国际保险中的争议、国际贸易、支付结算中的争议、国际投资、技术贸易以及合资、合作经营、补偿贸易、来料加工、国际租赁、国际合作开发自然资源、国际工程承包等方面的争议；国际知识产权保护方面的争议；海上碰撞、救助和共同海损中的争议；国际环境污染、涉外侵权行为中的争议等，其特点是以双方当事人的协议为基础；仲裁机构一般是民间性的组织；提交仲裁的当事人有自由选择地点、仲裁机构、仲裁员、仲裁程序和适用的实体法；仲裁裁决是终局的，一旦作出，立即生效。目前，除国际上老牌的国际商事仲裁机构，如国际商会仲裁院、伦敦国际仲裁中心、斯德哥尔摩商会仲裁院、美国仲裁协会外，其他后起的商事仲裁机构，如新加坡国际仲裁中心、中国香港国际仲裁中心、韩国商事仲裁院等，也都在全球范围内积极地拓展其仲裁业务。

中国大陆目前有两个涉外仲裁机构：中国国际经贸仲裁委员会和中国海事仲裁委员会。中国国际经贸仲裁委员会受理中外当事人之间、外国当事人之间的商事纠纷。自1999年以来，中国国际经贸仲裁委员会每年受理案件200件以上，已成为主要国际商事仲裁机构之一。中国海事仲裁委员会是中国唯一受理涉外海事纠纷常设机构。另外，在香港区内设有香港仲裁中心，该中心受理国际商事争议和香港区内的争议案件。中国大陆在1995年制定实施仲裁法。1986年，全国人大常委员会第六届第十八次会议通过决议，中国正式加入1958年联合国主持制定的承认与执行外国仲裁公约，同时作出两项保留，使中国国内仲裁制度和国际仲裁制度有机地结合在一起。中国国际经贸仲裁委员会和中国海事仲裁委员会都有自己的仲裁规则，当事人也可以选择采用联合国国际贸易法仲裁委员会仲裁规则。

2. alternative dispute resolution (ADR)　选择性争端解决方式，诉讼外争端解决方式

ADR机制是一种独立或相对独立于法院诉讼的非诉讼纠纷解决方式。这一概念源于美国，原指本世纪逐步发展起来的各种诉讼外争端解决方式，现已发展为世界各国普遍存在着的、民事诉讼制度以外的非诉讼争端或纠纷解决程序或机制的总称。

3. arbitral tribunal　仲裁庭

仲裁庭是指负责审理和裁决提交仲裁争议案件的临时组织。一般由首席仲裁员（或仲裁长）一人和仲裁员两人组成；如果双方当事人共同选定独任仲裁员一人，则由独任仲裁员单独成立仲裁庭。通常在争议案件审理终结并作出裁决后，仲裁庭即告解散。

4. New York Convention 1958　1958年《纽约公约》

1958年《纽约公约》全称为1958年《联合国承认和执行外国仲裁裁决的公约》(Convention on the Recognition and Enforcement of Foreign Arbitral Awards)。

5. Arbitration Agreement　仲裁协议

仲裁协议是指双方当事人在自愿、协商、平等互利的基础之上将他们之间已经发生或者可能发生的争议提交仲裁解决的书面文件，是申请仲裁的必备材料。

6. UNCITRAL Arbitration Rules　《联合国国际贸易法委员会仲裁规则》

UNCITRAL Arbitration Rules 其英文全称为 United Nations Commission on International Trade Law Arbitration Rules。

7. Arbitral Awards 仲裁裁决

仲裁裁决是指仲裁庭对当事人之间所争议的事项作出的裁决。仲裁实行一裁终局制度，裁决自作出之日起发生法律效力。任何一方当事人不履行仲裁裁决的，另一方当事人可以向人民法院申请强制执行，受申请的人民法院应当执行。根据我国参加的《纽约公约》的规定，我国仲裁机构作出的仲裁裁决，也可以在其他缔约国得到承认和执行，如果被执行人或者其财产不在中国境内的，当事人可以直接向有管辖权的外国法院申请承认和执行。

Study Questions

1. What are the main features and advantages of arbitration?
2. What are the other forms of alternative dispute resolution and their differences?
3. What are the main contents of arbitration agreement?
4. What are the essentials of international commercial arbitration?

Sources of Information and Further Readings

1. Redfern, A. & M. Hunter. *Law and Practice of International Commercial Arbitration*. (4th Edition). Sweet & Maxwell, 2004.
2. http://en.wikipedia.org/wiki/Arbitration
3. http://en.wikipedia.org/wiki/International_arbitration
4. http://www.uncitral.org/uncitral/en/uncitral_texts/arbitration/NYConvention.html
5. China Arbitraiton Online & Arbitration database
6. American Arbitration Association
7. The Association for International Arbitration
8. http://www.pwc.com/arbitrationstudy

Chapter 22

The Dispute Settlement System of WTO[1]

Key Concepts

Appellate Body	conciliation	DSB	arbitration
appellate review	mediation	DSU	

Learning Objectives

1. Understand its vital role of the dispute settlement system in WTO.
2. Understand the main contents of DSU.
3. Understand the functions of DSB.
4. Be familiar with the procedures for the settlement of disputes in WTO.

Dispute settlement is regarded by the World Trade Organization (WTO) as the central pillar of the multilateral trading system, and as the organization's unique contribution to the stability of the global economy. A dispute arises when one member country adopts a trade policy measure or takes some action that one or more fellow members considers to a breach of WTO agreements or to be a failure to live up to obligations. By joining the WTO, member countries have agreed that if they believe fellow members are in violation of trade rules, they will use the multilateral system of settling disputes instead of taking action unilaterally—this entails abiding by agreed procedures (Dispute Settlement Understanding) and respecting judgments, primarily of the Dispute Settlement Body (DSB)[2], the WTO organ responsible for adjudication of disputes. A former WTO Director-General characterized the WTO dispute settlement system as "the most active international adjudicative mechanism in the world today".

Dispute Settlement Understanding

In 1994, the WTO members agreed on the Understanding on Rules and Procedures Governing the Settlement of Disputes or Dispute Settlement Understanding (DSU)[3] (annexed to the "Final Act" signed in Marrakesh in 1994). Pursuant to the rules detailed in the DSU, member states can engage in consultations to resolve trade disputes pertaining to a "covered agreement" or, if unsuccessful, have a WTO panel hear the case. The priority, however, is to settle disputes, through consultations if possible. By January 2008, only about 136 of the nearly 369 cases had reached the full panel process. The operation of the WTO dispute settlement process involves the parties and third parties to a case and may also involve the DSB panels, the Appellate Body, the WTO Secretariat, arbitrators, independent experts, and several specialized institutions. The General Council discharges its responsibilities under the DSU through the Dispute Settlement Body (DSB). Like the General Council, the DSB is composed of representatives of all WTO Members. The DSB is responsible for administering the DSU, i. e., for overseeing the entire dispute settlement process. It also has the authority to establish panels, adopt panel and Appellate Body reports, maintain surveillance of implementation of rulings and recommendations, and authorize the suspension of obligations under the covered agreements. The DSB meets as often as necessary to adhere to the timeframes provided for in the DSU.

From Complaint to Final Report

If a member state considers that a measure adopted by another member state has deprived it of a benefit accruing to it under one of the covered agreements, it may call for consultations with the other member state. If consultations fail to resolve the dispute within 60 days after receipt of the request for consultations, the complainant state may request the establishment of a Panel. It is not possible for the respondent state to prevent or delay the establishment of a Panel, unless the DSB by consensus decides otherwise. The panel, normally consisting of three members appointed *ad hoc* by the Secretariat, sits to receive written and oral submissions of the parties, on the basis of which it is expected to make findings and conclusions for presentation to the DSB. The proceedings are confidential, and even when private parties are directly concerned, they are not permitted to attend or make submissions separate from those of the state in question. Disputes can also arise under non-violation nullification of benefits claims. The final version of the panel's report is distributed first to the parties; two weeks later it is circulated to all the members of the WTO. In sharp contrast with other systems, the report is required to be adopted at a meeting of the DSB within 60 days of its circulation, unless the DSB by consensus decides not to adopt the report or a party to the dispute gives notice of its intention to appeal. A party may appeal a panel report to the standing Appellate Body, but only on issues of law and legal interpretations developed by the panel. Each appeal is heard by three members of the permanent seven-member Appellate Body set up by the Dispute Settlement Body and broadly representing the range of WTO membership. Members of the Appellate Body have four-year terms. They must be individuals with recognized standing in the field of law and international trade, not affiliated with any government. The Appellate Body may uphold, modify or reverse the panel's legal findings and conclusions. Normally appeals should not last more than 60 days, with an absolute maximum of 90 days. The possibility for appeal makes the WTO dispute resolution system unique among the judicial processes of dispute settlement in general public international law.

Members may express their views on the report of the Appellate Body, but they cannot derail it. The DSU states unequivocally that an Appellate Body report shall be adopted by the DSB and unconditionally accepted by the parties, unless the DSB decides by consensus within thirty days of its circulation not to adopt the report. Unless otherwise agreed by the parties to the dispute, the period from establishment of the panel to consideration of the report by the DSB shall as a general rule not exceed nine months if there is no appeal, and twelve months if there is an appeal.

Compliance

The DSU addresses the question of compliance and retaliation. Within thirty days of the adoption of the report, the member concerned is to inform the DSB of its intentions in respect of implementation of the recommendations and rulings. If the member explains that it is impracticable to comply immediately with the recommendations and rulings, it is to have a "reasonable period of time" in which to comply. If no agreement is reached about the reasonable period for compliance, that issue is to be the subject of binding arbitration; the arbitrator is to be appointed by agreement of the parties. If there is a disagreement as to the satisfactory nature of the measures adopted by the respondent state to comply with the report, that disagreement is to be decided by a panel, if possible the same panel that heard the original dispute, but apparently without the possibility of appeal from its decision. The DSU provides that even if the respondent asserts that it has complied with the recommendation in a report, and even if the complainant party or the panel accepts that assertion, the DSB is supposed to keep the implementation of the recommendations under surveillance.

Compensation and Retaliation

If all else fails, two more possibilities are set out in the DSU:

If a member fails within the "reasonable period" to carry out the recommendations and rulings, it may negotiate with the complaining state for a mutually acceptable compensation. Compensation is not defined, but may be expected to consist of the grant of a concession by the respondent state on a product or service of interest to the complainant state.

If no agreement on compensation is reached within twenty days of the expiry of the "reasonable period", the prevailing state may request authorization from the DSB to suspend application to the member concerned of concessions or other obligations under the covered agreements. The DSU makes clear that retaliation is not favored, and sets the criteria for retaliation. In contrast to prior GATT practice, authorization to suspend concessions in this context is semi-automatic, in that the DSB "shall grant the authorization […] within thirty days of the expiry of the reasonable period", unless it decides by consensus to reject the request. Any suspension or concession or other obligation is to be temporary. If the respondent state objects to the level of suspension proposed or to the consistency of the proposed suspension with the DSU principles, still another arbitration is provided for, if possible by the original panel members or by an arbitrator or arbitrators appointed by the Director-General, to be completed within sixty days from expiration of the reasonable period.

While such "retaliatory measures" are a strong mechanism when applied by economically powerful countries like the United States or the European Union, when applied by economically weak countries against stronger ones, they can often be ignored. This has been the case, for example, with the March 2005 Appellate Body ruling in case DS 267, which declared US cotton subsidies illegal. Whether or not the complainant has taken a measure of retaliation, surveillance by the DSB is to continue, to see whether the recommendations of the panel or the Appellate Body have been implemented.

Developing Countries

Like most of the agreements adopted in the Uruguay Round, the DSU contains several provisions directed to developing countries. The Understanding states that members should give "special attention" to the problems and interests of developing country members. Further, if one party to a dispute is a developing country, that party is entitled to have at least one panelist who comes from a developing country. If a complaint is brought against a developing country, the time for consultations (before a panel is convened) may be extended, and if the dispute goes to a panel, the deadlines for the developing country to make its submissions may be relaxed. Also, the Secretariat is authorized to make a qualified legal expert available to any developing country on request. Formal complaints against least developed countries are discouraged, and if consultations fail, the Director-General and the Chairman of the DSB stand ready to offer their good offices before a formal request for a panel is made. As to substance, the DSU provides that the report of panels shall "explicitly indicate" how account has been taken of the "differential and more favorable treatment" provisions of the agreement under which the complaint is brought. Whether or not a developing country is a party to a particular proceeding, "particular attention" is to be paid to the interests of the developing countries in the course of implementing recommendations and rulings of panels. In order to assist developing countries in overcoming their limited expertise in WTO law and assist them in managing complex trade disputes, an Advisory Centre on WTO Law was established in 2001. The aim is to level the playing field for these countries and customs territories in the WTO system by enabling them to have a full understanding of their rights and obligations under the WTO Agreement.

Notes

1. Dispute Settlement System of WTO 世界贸易组织争议解决机制

该机制适用世贸组织成员之间因执行 WTO 协议而产生的争议。因此,争议的主体为该组织的成员,而各缔约方所属的自然人、法人则不能成为该争议解决机制的主体。该机制的主要目标是确保 WTO 各项协议的实施,废除各国与 WTO 协议不一致的有关规定。

2. Dispute Settlement Body (DSB) 争议解决机构

DSB 是 WTO 争议解决机制设立的专门的争议解决机构,DSB 解决的争议不仅包括传统的货物贸易争议(如有关反倾销、补贴与反补贴等方面的争议),而且还包括知识产权保护和服务贸易而引起的争议。

3. Dispute Settlement Understanding (DSU) 关于争议解决规则与程序的谅解书

根据这一谅解书规定,在 WTO 框架下解决争议,主要经历协商(即争议各方必须先自行协商解决)、专家小组设立及对争议事项审查、上诉评审程序、执行程序(如果一方不执行,那么 DSB 授权申诉方中止给对方的减让或对其所承担的其他义务,即所谓的"交叉报复")四个阶段。

Study Questions

1. Under what circumstances may a dispute be submitted to DSB for settlement?
2. Compared with GATT, is there any improvement as regards the dispute settlement system of WTO?
3. What are the requirements for the composition of Panels?
4. What are the procedures for the settlement of disputes in WTO?

Sources of Information and Further Readings

1. http://www.wto.org/
2. http://en.wikipedia.org/wiki/Dispute_settlement_in_the_World_Trade_Organization
3. Lowenfeld, Andreas F. Dispute settlement in the WTO. *International Economic Law.* Oxford University Press, 2002.

Chapter 23

International Center for Settlement of Investment Disputes[1]

Key Concepts

International Bank for Reconstruction and Development

conciliation   arbitration

Learning Objectives

1. Understand the role of the Center.
2. Be familiar with the status of the Center.
3. Understand the methods to be used by the Center for settlement of investment disputes.
4. Understand the methods to be used by China for settlement of investment disputes.

The International Centre for Settlement of Investment Disputes (ICSID), an institution of the World Bank Group based in Washington, D. C., was established in 1966 pursuant to the Convention on the Settlement of Investment Disputes between States and Nationals of Other States (the ICSID Convention or Washington Convention). As of May 2011, 157 countries had signed the ICSID Convention.

Establishment and Organization

The purpose of the establishment of the Center shall be to provide facilities for conciliation and arbitration of investment disputes between Contracting States and nationals of other Contracting States.

The seat of the Center shall be at the principal office of the International Bank for Reconstruction and Development[2] (hereinafter called the Bank). The seat may be moved to another place by decision of the Administrative Council adopted by a majority of two-thirds of its members.

The Center shall have an Administrative Council and a Secretariat and shall maintain a Panel of Conciliators and a Panel of Arbitrators.

The principal functions of the Administrative Council are the election of the Secretary-General and any Deputy Secretary-General, the adoption of the budget of the Center and the adoption of administrative and financial regulations, rules governing the institution of proceedings and rules of procedure for conciliation and arbitration proceedings. Action on all these matters requires a majority of two-thirds of the members of the Council.

The Secretary-General performs a variety of administrative functions as legal representative, registrar and principal officer of the Center. In addition, the Secretary-General is given the power to refuse registration of a request for conciliation proceedings or arbitration proceedings, and thereby to prevent the institution of such proceedings, if on the basis of the information furnished by the applicant he finds that the dispute is manifestly outside the jurisdiction of the Center. The Secretary-General is given this limited power to "screen" requests for conciliation or arbitration proceedings with a view to avoiding the embarrassment to a party (particularly a State) which might result from the institution of proceedings against it in a dispute which it had not consented to submit to the Center, as well as the possibility that the machinery of the Center would be set in motion in cases which for other reasons were obviously outside the jurisdiction of the Center, e.g., because either the applicant or the other party was not eligible to be a party in proceedings under the Convention.

Status, Immunities and Privileges

The Center shall have full international legal personality. The legal capacity of the Center shall include the capacity: (a) to contract; (b) to acquire and dispose of movable and immovable property; (c) to institute legal proceedings.

To enable the Center to fulfill its functions, it shall enjoy in the territories of each Contracting State the immunities and privileges set forth in this Section. The Center, its property and assets shall enjoy immunity from all legal process, except when the Center waives this immunity.

Panels

The Panel of Conciliators and the Panel of Arbitrators shall each consist of qualified persons who are willing to serve thereon. Each Contracting State may designate to each Panel four persons who may but need not be its nationals. The Chairman may designate ten persons to each Panel. The persons so designated to a Panel shall each have a different nationality.

Persons designated to serve on the Panels shall be persons of high moral character and recognized competence in the fields of law, commerce, industry or finance, who may be relied upon to exercise independent judgment. Competence in the field of law shall be of particular importance in the case of persons on the Panel of Arbitrators.

The Chairman, in designating persons to serve on the Panels, shall in addition pay due regard to the importance of assuring representation on the Panels of the principal legal systems of the world and of the main forms of economic activity.

Panel members shall serve for renewable periods of six years. In case of death or resignation of a member of a Panel, the authority which designated the member shall have the right to designate another person to serve for the remainder of that member's term. Panel members shall continue in office until their successors have been designated.

A person may serve on both Panels. If a person shall have been designated to serve on the same Panel by more than one Contracting State, or by one or more Contracting States and the Chairman, he shall be deemed to have been designated by the authority which first designated him or, if one such authority is the State of which he is a national, by that State. All designations shall be notified to the Secretary-General and shall take effect from the date on which the notification is received.

Panel members will possess a high degree of competence and be capable of exercising independent judgment.

Jurisdiction of the Center

The jurisdiction of the Center shall extend to any legal dispute arising directly out of an investment, between a Contracting State (or any constituent subdivision or agency of a Contracting State designated to the Center by that State) and a national of another Contracting State, which the parties to the dispute consent in writing to submit to the Center. When the parties have given their consent, no party may withdraw its consent unilaterally. "National of another Contracting State" means: Any natural person who had the nationality of a Contracting State other than the State party to the dispute, and any juridical person which had the nationality of a Contracting State other than the State party to the dispute.

Any Contracting State may, at the time of ratification, acceptance or approval of this Convention or at any time thereafter, notify the Center of the class or classes of disputes which it would or would not consider submitting to the jurisdiction of the Center. The Secretary-General shall forthwith transmit such notification to all Contracting States.

Consent of the parties to arbitration shall, unless otherwise stated, be deemed consent to such arbitration to the exclusion of any other remedy. A Contracting State may require the exhaustion of local administrative or judicial remedies as a condition of its consent to arbitration.

Conciliation

Any Contracting State or any national of a Contracting State wishing to institute conciliation proceedings shall address a request to that effect in writing to the Secretary-General who shall send a copy of the request to the other party. The request shall contain information concerning the issues in dispute, the identity of the parties and their consent to conciliation in accordance with the rules of procedure for the institution of conciliation and arbitration proceedings. The Secretary-General shall register the request unless he finds, on the basis of the information contained in the request, that the dispute is manifestly outside the jurisdiction of the Center. He shall forthwith notify the parties of registration or refusal to register.

If the parties reach agreement, the Commission shall draw up a report noting the issues in dispute and recording that the parties have reached agreement. If, at any stage of the proceedings, it appears to the Commission that there is no likelihood of agreement between the parties, it shall close the proceedings and shall draw up a report noting the submission of the dispute and recording the failure of the parties to reach agreement. If one party fails to appear or participate in the proceedings, the Commission shall close the proceedings and shall draw up a report noting that party's failure to appear or participate.

Except as the parties to the dispute shall otherwise agree, neither party to a conciliation proceeding shall be entitled in any other proceeding, whether before arbitrators or in a court of law or otherwise, to invoke or rely on any views expressed or statements or admissions or offers of settlement made by the other party in the conciliation proceedings, or the report or any recommendations made by the Commission.

Arbitration

It may be presumed that when a State and an investor agree to have recourse to arbitration, and do not reserve the right to have recourse to other remedies or require the prior exhaustion of other remedies, the intention of the parties is to have recourse to arbitration to the exclusion of any other remedy. Just like the conciliation proceedings, under arbitration, the concerned parties shall also submit a request to that effect.

The Tribunal shall consist of a sole arbitrator or any uneven number of arbitrators appointed as the parties shall agree. Where the parties do not agree upon the number of arbitrators and the method of their appointment, the Tribunal shall consist of three arbitrators, one arbitrator appointed by each party and the third, who shall be the president of the Tribunal, appointed by agreement of the parties.

Except as the parties otherwise agree, the Tribunal may, if it considers that the circumstances so require, recommend any provisional measures which should be taken to preserve the respective rights of either party.

The Tribunal shall decide questions by a majority of the votes of all its members. The award of the Tribunal shall be in writing and shall be signed by the members of the Tribunal who voted for it. The award shall deal with every question submitted to the Tribunal, and shall state the reasons upon which it is based. Any member of the Tribunal may attach his individual opinion to the award, whether he dissents from the majority or not, or a statement of his dissent. The Center shall not publish the award without the consent of the parties. The award shall be binding on the parties and shall not be subject to any appeal or to any other remedy. Each party shall abide by and comply with the terms of the award.

The doctrine of sovereign immunity may prevent the forced execution in a State of judgments obtained against foreign States or against the State in which execution is sought. So Contracting States may equate an award rendered pursuant to the Convention with a final judgment of its own courts. It does not require them to go beyond that and to undertake forced execution of awards rendered pursuant to the Convention in cases in which final judgments could not be executed.

Cost of Proceedings

In the case of conciliation proceedings, the fees and expenses of members of the Commission as well as the charges for the use of the facilities of the Center shall be borne equally by the parties. Each party shall bear any other expenses it incurs in connection with the proceedings.

In the case of arbitration proceedings the Tribunal shall, except as the parties otherwise agree, assess the expenses incurred by the parties in connection with the proceedings, and shall decide how and by whom those expenses, the fees and expenses of the members of the Tribunal and the charges for the use of the facilities of the Center shall be paid. Such decision shall form part of the award.

Notes

1. **International Center for Settlement of Investment Disputes　解决投资额争端国际中心**

　　该中心是根据 1965 年华盛顿《解决国家与他国国民投资争议公约》（简称《华盛顿公约》）而设立的，属于世界银行，总部设在华盛顿。中心的管辖权主要涉及缔约国与另一缔约国国民之间直接因投资而产生的争端。我国于 1993 年加入该公约，但声明只考虑将中国政府与投资人之间因国有化和征收产生的争端交由中心管辖。因我国较好的投资环境，至今尚无此案例。我国政府与外国投资者之间的争议主要通过协商解决、当地救济（即通过我国国内行政管理机构或司法部门解决）、外交谈判及中心国际仲裁进行解决。

2. **International Bank for Reconstruction and Development (IBRD)　国际复兴开发银行**

　　世界银行集团主要包括国际复兴开发银行、国际开发协会（IDA, International

Development Association)、国际金融公司(IFC, International Finance Corporation)、多边投资担保机构(MIGA)及解决投资争端国际中心(ICSID)。IBRD 与 IDA 合称为"世界银行"。根据布雷顿森林会议的决定,IBRD 成立于 1945 年 12 月,其主要任务是向会员国提供长期贷款,以促进战后经济的复兴。IDA 成立于1960 年,其主要任务是向低收入发展中国家的会员国政府提供贷款,比 IBRD 条件优越、期限更长。IFC 成立于 1956 年,主要对发展中国家尤其是欠发达地区的重点生产性企业提供无需政府担保的贷款和投资。

Study Questions

1. What are the generally adopted methods to settle disputes in connection with investment?
2. Under what circumstances may an arbitral award be nullified?
3. What is the jurisdiction of the center?
4. What is the preservation to be made by China in according to this convention?

Sources of Information and Further Readings

1. http://icsid.worldbank.org/ICSID/Index.jsp
2. http://en.wikipedia.org/wiki/International_Centre_for_Settlement_of_Investment_Disputes
3. http://www.worldbank.org/